ABSOLUTE BEGINNER'S GUIDE

TO

Homeschooling

Brad Miser

800 East 96th Street,
Indianapolis, Indiana 46240

Absolute Beginner's Guide to Homeschooling

International Standard Book Number: 0-7897-3277-7

Library of Congress Catalog Card Number: 2004107644

Printed in the United States of America

First Printing: September, 2004

07   06   05   04   4   3   2   1

Trademarks

All terms mentioned in this book that are known to be trademarks or service marks have been appropriately capitalized. Que Publishing cannot attest to the accuracy of this information. Use of a term in this book should not be regarded as affecting the validity of any trademark or service mark.

Warning and Disclaimer

Every effort has been made to make this book as complete and as accurate as possible, but no warranty or fitness is implied. The information provided is on an "as is" basis. The authors and the publisher shall have neither liability nor responsibility to any person or entity with respect to any loss or damages arising from the information contained in this book.

Bulk Sales

Que Publishing offers excellent discounts on this book when ordered in quantity for bulk purchases or special sales. For more information, please contact

U.S. Corporate and Government Sales
1-800-382-3419
corpsales@pearsontechgroup.com

For sales outside of the U.S., please contact

International Sales
international@pearsoned.com

Executive Editor
Candace Hall

Acquisitions Editor
Karen Whitehouse

Development Editor
Karen Whitehouse

Managing Editor
Charlotte Clapp

Project Editor
Matt Purcell

Copy Editor
Karen Whitehouse

Indexer
Ken Johnson

Proofreader
Kathy Bidwell

Publishing Coordinator
Cindy Teeters

Interior Designer
Anne Jones

Cover Designer
Dan Armstrong

Page Layout
Susan Geiselman

Contents at a Glance

Table of Contents

About the Author

Brad Miser has written many books, most of which teach people how to use computers and other technology. The books Brad has written include: *Absolute Beginner's Guide to the iPod and iTunes*; *Special Edition Using Mac OS X, v10.3 Panther*; *Mac OS X and iLife: Using iTunes, iPhoto, iMovie, and iDVD*; *iDVD 3 Fast & Easy*; *Special Edition Using Mac OS X v10.2, Mac OS X and the Digital Lifestyle*; *Special Edition Using Mac OS X*; *The iMac Way*; *The Complete Idiot's Guide to iMovie 2*; *The Complete Idiot's Guide to the iMac*; and *Using Mac OS 8.5*. He has also been an author, development editor, or technical editor on more than 50 other titles. He has been a featured speaker on various topics at Macworld Expo, at user group meetings, and in other venues.

Brad has been involved in homeschooling for more than 10 years. He and his wife homeschool their three children, whose ages range from 9 to 15. Brad has been active in helping with curriculum decisions, testing and evaluating progress, teaching, and other activities. He has also attended homeschool conventions and regularly interacts with many other homeschool families.

Brad is the senior technical communicator for an Indianapolis-based software development company. Brad is responsible for all product documentation, training materials, online help, and other communication materials. He also manages the customer support operations for the company and provides training and account management services to its customers. Previously, he was the lead engineering proposal specialist for an aircraft engine manufacturer, a development editor for a computer book publisher, and a civilian aviation test officer/engineer for the U.S. Army. Brad holds a Bachelor of Science degree in mechanical engineering from California Polytechnic State University at San Luis Obispo (1986) and has received advanced education in maintainability engineering, business, and other topics.

Once a native of California, Brad now lives in Brownsburg, Indiana, with his wife Amy; their three daughters, Jill, Emily, and Grace; and their guinea pig, Buddy.

Brad would love to hear about your experiences with this book (the good, the bad, and the ugly). You can write to him at bradmacosx@mac.com.

Dedication

*We all declare for liberty; but in using the same word we do not all mean the same thing.
With some the word liberty may mean for each man to do as he pleases with himself, and
the product of his labor; while with others, the same word many mean for some men to do
as they please with other men, and the product of other men's labor. Here are two, not only
different, but incompatible things, called by the same name—liberty. And it follows that
each of the things is, by the respective parties, called by two different and incompatible
names—liberty and tyranny.—Abraham Lincoln*

Acknowledgments

To the following people on the *ABG to Homeschooling* project team, my sincere appreciation for your hard work on this book:

Karen Whitehouse, my acquisitions and development editor, who made this project possible and believed that I would be able to write this book. She also provided guidance to me along the way so that the book would be more useful to you. She also copy edited the book to correct my many misspellings, poor grammar, and other problems (obviously, she is a glutton for punishment!). Marta Justak of Justak Literary Services, my agent, for getting me signed up for this project and providing advice and encouragement throughout. Que's production and sales team for printing the book and getting it into your hands.

And now for some people who weren't on the project team, but who are essential to me personally. Amy Miser, my wonderful wife and a dedicated homeschooler, for supporting me while I wrote this book; living with an author under tight deadlines isn't always lots of fun, but Amy does so with grace, understanding, and acceptance of my need to write. She was and is the driving force behind homeschooling in our home and does all the work required and the benefits of which are clear in our three wonderful children; I appreciate her efforts more than I can write. Jill, Emily, and Grace Miser, my delightful daughters who are examples of how well homeschooling can work, for helping me stay focused on what is important in life. (And, a special thanks to Buddy the guinea pig, for his early-morning visits while I was working to cheer me up!)

We Want to Hear from You!

As the reader of this book, *you* are our most important critic and commentator. We value your opinion and want to know what we're doing right, what we could do better, what areas you'd like to see us publish in, and any other words of wisdom you're willing to pass our way.

As an executive editor for Que Publishing, I welcome your comments. You can email or write me directly to let me know what you did or didn't like about this book—as well as what we can do to make our books better.

Please note that I cannot help you with technical problems related to the topic of this book. We do have a User Services group, however, where I will forward specific technical questions related to the book.

When you write, please be sure to include this book's title and author as well as your name, email address, and phone number. I will carefully review your comments and share them with the author and editors who worked on the book.

Email: feedback@quepublishing.com

Mail: Candace Hall
               Executive Editor
               Que Publishing
               800 East 96th Street
               Indianapolis, IN 46240 USA

For more information about this book or another Que Publishing title, visit our Web site at www.quepublishing.com. Type the ISBN (excluding hyphens), or type in the title of a book in the Search field.

Introduction

If you have heard of homeschooling, but aren't sure if it is something you want to pursue…

If you have been thinking about the possibility of homeschooling your children, but haven't yet decided that it is right for your family…

If you've decided that you want to homeschool your children, but you aren't sure where to start…

If you've just started or have been homeschooling your children for a little while, and would like some help…

…You've come to the right place.

About Homeschooling

In some ways, the idea of parents being totally responsible for their children's education—which is the underlying theme of homeschooling—is a new and radical concept. For the past 100 years or so, the emphasis for most education has been through an institution in some form, mostly public schools with a relatively small percentage of families opting for a private school. So, it is only natural when thinking about educating children to focus on the specific schools to which you can or will send your kids. However, over the past couple of decades, many people have observed the continuing decline in both the results achieved by the traditional institutional education system and the moral and cultural climates that kids experience while they are part of that system.

The decline in results being achieved by institutional schools is as undeniable as declining standardized test scores, increasing functional illiteracy rates, alarming comparisons of math and science knowledge in the United States compared to other countries (such as Japan), and in other quantitative results. As the educational system moves further from the fundamentals of good education toward more cultural and sociological experimentation and various non-educational agendas, the academic capabilities of the system continue to degrade.

Along with their increasing academic ineffectiveness, the environments in many institutional schools impact the moral and social development of children negatively. And some schools are downright dangerous places to be.

For these "negative" reasons and even more positive ones, homeschooling continues to increase in popularity as an alternative to institutional, traditional education. Homeschooling offers many benefits for children and their families (which you will learn about in detail in Chapter 1, "What Is Homeschooling All About?"). Over time, homeschooling has proven to be more effective than institutional schools in academic performance. For example, homeschoolers score significantly above national averages on standardized tests. And, many colleges not only recognize the education of homeschoolers as being academically valid, but are starting to actually consider homeschooling to be an advantage. Homeschooling families benefit from greater closeness in their relationships and more flexibility in their schedules. Contrary to the stereotype, homeschooled children are actually better equipped socially than their institutionally educated counterparts.

Today, these benefits inspire many parents to again take responsibility for the education and development of their children—which really isn't such a new idea after all. Prior to the public education boom, most children's educations were directly controlled by their parents. Children were tutored, taught directly by their parents, or attended very small, independent schools. All these activities were directly or closely supervised by parents, which is what homeschooling is all about.

If you've decided that you want to be part of the amazing homeschool experience, this book will be a big help in getting started. If you have just been thinking about homeschooling your kids, you can use the content in this book to help you understand what is required to homeschool effectively; hopefully, this will encourage you to give homeschooling a try. It is my hope that the information in this book will also be helpful to you even after you have been homeschooling for several years.

About the *Absolute Beginner's Guide to Homeschooling*

The *Absolute Beginner's Guide to Homeschooling* provides all the information you need to get started with your own homeschool. From making a decision to homeschool to understanding what you need to do and when you need to do it, this book equips you with the knowledge and understanding you need to educate your children at home effectively and to enjoy doing it.

The book is organized into four major parts:

■ **Part I: Making the Decision to Homeschool**. This part sets the stage for the rest of the book and includes chapters that explain why homeschooling is a large and growing trend, help you understand what is required of you to homeschool your kids, show you how to figure out any legal requirements relating to homeschool in your state, and defend your decision to homeschool when you need to do so.

■ **Part II: Preparing to Homeschool**. In this part, you'll find practical chapters that help you get ready to teach. Topics include how to connect with other homeschool families, what to do to prepare to teach your children, planning the subjects you'll teach and getting the materials you'll use, and creating a homeschool classroom. You'll also learn about the importance of lesson plans and how you can create them. If you have a child who is already in a traditional school, Chapter 10, "Transitioning a Child from Public or Private School to Homeschool," will give you some pointers to help that child make the transition to homeschool.

■ **Part III: Managing a Homeschool**. Part III focuses on topics that will help you run your homeschool effectively. It starts off with chapters on conducting homeschool classes and documenting the results. You'll also find chapters on how you can include field trips, music, sports, other activities, and home projects in your homeschool. From there, you'll learn how, why, and when to use tutors and outside classes. The part ends with chapters on evaluating how your homeschool is working and when, if ever, to transition your children back to a traditional school.

■ **Part IV: Homeschool Resources**. Part IV consists of appendices that contain some resources you will find useful. Appendix A lists contact information for homeschool associations and conventions in every state. Appendix B provides information about a few publishers and retailers who can supply you with teaching materials.

As you read through this book, you will see three special elements: Notes, Tips, and, only rarely, Cautions. Also, each chapter ends with a section titled "The Absolute Minimum." Explanations of each of these special elements are provided for you here.

caution

If there is something you need to be careful or need to be on the look-out for, I will warn you in a Caution. Fortunately, you won't find many of these throughout the book, but when you do see one, you might want to take a closer look at it.

note

Notes look like this. They are designed to provide you with information that is related to the topic at hand but not absolutely essential to it. I hope you will find the Notes interesting, even if you don't find them useful immediately.

tip

Tips help you get something done more quickly and easily, or they tell you how to do a task that is related to what is being described at the moment. You might also find an explanation of an alternate way to get something done.

THE ABSOLUTE MINIMUM

Finally, each chapter ends with "The Absolute Minimum" section. The contents of this section vary a bit from chapter to chapter. Examples of this content include the following:

- A summary of key points of the chapter
- Additional tips related to the chapter's topic
- References to sources of additional information

So, now that you know all you need to about this book, it's time to go to school, homeschool that is....

PART i

Making the Decision to Homeschool

1

WHAT IS HOMESCHOOLING ALL ABOUT?

Because you are reading this (whether you've purchased this book or are just looking at it), you must have some interest in homeschooling. Perhaps you've just heard about homeschooling. Maybe a friend of yours has decided to homeschool her children or maybe you're thinking about homeschooling your own children. Perhaps you have already decided to homeschool your kids. Or, maybe you just don't understand what homeschooling is all about. It doesn't really matter which is true for you at this point. The fact that you have this interest is just where you should be. By the end of this chapter, you'll have added a good fundamental understanding of homeschooling to your interest in the topic.

What Is Homeschool?

At its core, the concept behind homeschooling is really quite simple: Parents accept total responsibility for the education of their children rather than transferring the bulk of this responsibility to an institution (usually a public or private school).

In practical terms, this means that the home becomes the center of a child's education, rather than a school. Parents, who have a deep interest in their children based on love, become the primary educators for their children. Homeschool parents carefully guide their children through their mental, emotional, and physical development. The parents choose an educational path for their children based on each child's personality and gifts. (This is in contrast to an institutional school in which a child's educational path is managed by many different people, none of whom have an overall view of the child's education or even much of a personal interest in the child's well being.) In a homeschool, each child's education is designed specially for that child rather than forcing the child to follow the same path as every other student in an institutional school.

Homeschooling is about academic excellence. Because a child's education is designed just for her, the child's potential can be fully realized. Each child can learn at his own pace. Areas in which a child excels can be maximized and accelerated. Areas in which a child struggles can be focused on until the child really conquers that subject. True learning becomes the primary focus of education.

Homeschooling isn't a practice of isolating children at home, as those who are ignorant of homeschooling sometimes think. Rather, parents include outside classes, tutors, field trips, service work, sports, and other means to add a large variety of learning opportunities and experiences to a child's education. The reality is that homeschoolers enjoy experiences and activities that are simply not possible for children in a public or private school because of the many limitations that are integral to those institutions. These experiences enhance the academic elements of the homeschool to maximize the child's intellectual development.

Homeschooling is about forming close and loving bonds between parents and children and between siblings. This means that parents become the primary influence over their children's development, rather than a group of peers who have the same or less maturity level than the child. Homeschooling is about forming close relationships with people of many ages, rather than only with people in the same grade.

Parents who homeschool recognize that there should be more to a child's education than just intellectual development. As important, or perhaps more so, is the development of a child's moral character and personality. Rather than having this development occur in an unplanned and largely unsupervised setting that is part of an institutional school, parents become the loving and leading influence to help their child become the best person he can be.

Homeschool includes developing a close network of other homeschooling families with whom you can form close and meaningful relationships that last over time. Homeschoolers get together regularly and often to participate in group activities or just to hang out.

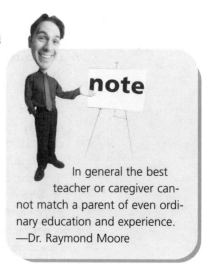

Homeschool is also a way for families to have more freedom and flexibility in how they live. It's about families setting their own schedules and plans rather than dancing to an institutional school's tune.

Finally, homeschooling is about helping children learn how to think and act independently and, therefore, not be driven by group-think and the herd mentality that is such a large part of institutional schools.

note

In general the best teacher or caregiver cannot match a parent of even ordinary education and experience. —Dr. Raymond Moore

Why Do People Homeschool?

There are two general groups of reasons that parents choose to homeschool their children. One group is the many benefits that homeschooling provides: These are the reasons why homeschooling can be such a good way to educate children. The other is the many negative aspects of the modern institutional school system: These are the reasons that sending kids to public schools isn't such a good thing to do.

Great Things About Homeschooling

The many benefits of homeschooling children include

- **Excellent education**. The overriding goal of homeschooling is to educate children. In this, homeschool excels. Because of the many benefits offered by homeschooling, there is simply no better way to educate a child. That homeschooling is a great way to educate a child can be shown in several ways. First, consider the items in this list. Many of these benefits are easy to understand and the positive impact they have on children are obvious. Second, homeschooled children perform better on standardized tests. For example, in a recent comparison of SAT scores, homeschooled children averaged 568 on the verbal test and 525 on the math; the national average was 506 on verbal and 514 on math. While those differences might not seem significant for individuals, as differences in averages for populations of students, they are very significant. Third, homeschoolers are becoming sought-after for higher education. Many colleges and universities have begun to modify their admission practices to not only allow for, but to encourage, homeschoolers to apply for admission.

- **Dedicated teachers with a great teacher-to-student ratio.** One factor that is known to be extremely important to educating a child effectively is the teacher-to-student ratio—that is, the number of students for which a teacher is responsible. Other factors include the degree of connection present between teacher and student and the amount of dedication a teacher has to a specific child. Homeschooling excels in both these areas. Who can be more dedicated to helping a child learn successfully than that child's parent? Parents love their children and dedicate their lives to helping their children successfully grow to maturity. So, no one is more dedicated to a child than the parent. And, homeschooling is done largely on a one-on-one basis; there can't be a better teacher-to-student ratio than that. In these two areas, which are both critical to a child's education, homeschooling is simply the best scenario.

- **Education tailored to a child's capabilities and personality**. Because homeschool is focused on children as individuals, a child's education can be tailored to her capabilities and personality. If a child excels in a specific area, his education in that area can be accelerated. If a child struggles in a particular area, additional resources can be brought to bear to help. Also, the way children are taught can be based on how the child best learns because of the child's personality. For example, if a child is a visual learner, more visual elements can be incorporated into that child's instruction. Instead of the cookie-cutter approach to education that is required in an intuitional setting, homeschool provides the opportunity for a child's education to be designed just for that child.

- **Integrated and consistent education**. Because a homeschooled child's education is managed by the same person over a long period of time, that education can be consistent with a long-term plan in which each topic taught and the experience gained benefits seamlessly with those that have come before. Because the parent is intimately involved with the student over that student's life, the parent understands the child's experiences and background and uses that knowledge to design future educational activities.

- **Better teaching materials**. Homeschoolers have access to the best teaching materials available. And, teaching materials can be selected based on a child's individual needs and capabilities.

- **More efficient use of time**. Homeschools use time more efficiently than do institutional schools. The use of time in homeschools is driven the by the educational and other goals for a child rather than by a rigid schedule. Also, homeschools don't use as much of a child's time in administrative and other nonproductive activities. Homeschoolers can usually accomplish more learning in less time than those being educated in institutional schools.

- **Close family relationships**. Homeschooled families spend lots of time together. This intimate involvement fosters close relationships between parents and children and between siblings. One-on-one teaching, that is a natural part of the homeschool experience, naturally leads teacher and student (parent and child in this case) to have a deep and intimate relationship.

- **More opportunity for children to learn, think, and act independently**. Children who are homeschooled learn to work, act, and think independently. Because they don't live under the social and schedule pressure that is part of an institutional education, homeschoolers naturally become people who evaluate life and make choices based on their own decision making rather than what is expected by a social group or organization. Homeschooled children also learn independently; this training helps integrate learning into the child's life so that they don't see learning as something that is only done in a certain place and at a certain time, but rather is something that is done throughout life.

- **Greater life flexibility and freedom for children and their families**. Homeschool is designed and controlled by parents. This provides enormous flexibility for a family's life. Homeschooled families are not limited to living according to an institution's schedule, but are free to plan and live life as they see fit.

- **More influence by adults, less by peers**. It seems to make sense that children can be best helped toward maturity by those who are already mature. Unlike institutional schools in which children are mostly influenced by other children of the same age and "immaturity" level in largely unsupervised environments, in homeschool, parents and other adults have a much greater influence over a child's maturation process. Peer pressure, which is widely blamed for so many of the problems children experience, is a very minor or non-existent factor in homeschooled children's lives. Instead of peer pressure being a driving force, parent and family influence becomes a primary influence on how children develop; this is a very good thing.

- **More opportunities for experiences**. Homeschooled students can enjoy much greater variety and depth of experiences than can institutionally educated children. Homeschools can include field trips that aren't limited to a specific amount of time and that aren't burdened by the logistical problems of involving large numbers of children in an activity at the same time. These field trips can include those that are tied directly to a student's learning at the time. For example, while studying an historical event, students can visit a related historical site and spend a significant amount of time there (some homeschool families even plan parts of vacations as "field trips"). Other experiences that are very valuable to a child's development also can be included such as service work, part-time jobs, home projects, and others, which become a natural part of the homeschool experience. Homeschoolers learn by doing and experience much more than those being educated in institutional schools. They have more opportunity to apply what they learn to real life and to benefit from the experience that it provides (experience is the best teacher, homeschoolers get more experience).

- **More opportunity for physical activity**. Homeschooled children have the opportunity for lots of physical activity. From exercise to sports to playing outside to performing household chores, homeschooled children can be physically active throughout the day. This is in stark contrast to institutional settings in which children are trained (or forced) to lead largely sedentary lives.

- **Safer emotional, moral, and physical environments**. Because homeschool is family based and takes place to a significant extent in environments that are controlled or influenced by parents, homeschoolers enjoy protection from some of the problems of institutional environments. This protects children when they are most vulnerable and gives them a secure foundation that prepares them to handle the challenges of life as they approach the high school years and when they enter college or begin working.

- **Better integration of all aspects of life including the spiritual, physical, and emotional elements**. Because homeschools are managed by parents and families, important aspects of life can be integrated into a child's development. Being unfettered by government regulations, homeschools can include important spiritual and religious teaching and training along with academic subjects. Additionally, homeschools can incorporate service and volunteer work to help children have a broader perspective of life. In homeschool, all the elements of life can be integrated into a child's development.

Self-education is, I firmly believe, the only kind of education there is.
—Isaac Asimov

Not So Great Things About Public (or Private) School

Institutional schools, such as public schools, have many drawbacks or problems, including those in the following list:

- **Poor academic preparation**. If you pay any attention to news about the performance of public schools, especially in the United States, you can't help hearing about how the academic performance of these institutions has been in a state of decline for more than 30 years. This is shown in many ways. One is the decline in the results of standardized test scores that measure the performance of children compared to objective standards over time. These scores have been in decline for some time. Education in important topics such as math and science have been degrading over the same period; people educated in the public-school system in the United States are routinely shown to be less capable on average than students from countries where the emphasis on more disciplined learning has not diminished as it has in America.

- **Teaching methods that don't work**. The public schools have been laboratories for various teaching methods that were unproven, or at worst have proven to be ineffective. The biggest example was the adoption of "whole-word recognition" reading that "teaches" children to read by recognizing whole words rather than learning to read via phonics. This method, while being shown to be totally inferior to phonics, still continues to be used in some schools.

- **Social and special agendas, instead of an educational, focus**. Over the years, the education children receive in public schools has been diluted by the addition of

> **note**
>
> Public and private schools are both institutional in nature, meaning they are established and governed by an organization. Because public schools are governed through government, they are definitely the most "institutional" of the two types. While private schools can be better, sometimes much better, than public schools, they are still institutionally based, which means that they have many of the same inherent flaws. However, because they are controlled by a smaller and more flexible institution, private schools can be more effective than most public schools.

> Proponents of public education often and regularly explain the problems of the system by claiming that these result from insufficient funding. A quick look at the facts eliminates this claim. The amount of money per student in the public school system has dramatically increased over the past 20 years and the United States continues to spend more per student than some other countries with educational systems that perform better. The problem is that these resources are misapplied; pumping more resources into a bad system won't help as history has clearly shown.

social- and agenda-based indoctrination. Most public schools today spend a fair amount of time teaching non-academic topics relating to social issues. This detracts from the time spent teaching "reading, writing, and arithmetic."

- **"Feel goodism" instead of reality**. Many public school programs are design to "boost a child's self-esteem." Unfortunately, this isn't done by helping children become competent people, but rather by simply trying to make them feel good about themselves just for "being." One example is the replacement and redefining of grades so that children's feelings aren't hurt when they are incapable of doing work (such as eliminating "D" or "F" grades). This inevitably leads to lowered self-esteem when the child doesn't have the skills and capabilities needed to be successful in life.

- **Cooperation at the expense of competition**. History has shown that socioeconomic systems that are based on the principle that competition for resources results in the most benefit to the most people. Unfortunately, competition in many public schools is now discouraged and instead the emphasis is on making everyone "equal." This doesn't prepare children for real life in which they will have to compete.

- **Environments that are damaging to children's moral, emotion, and sometimes physical well-being**. The pervasiveness of drug use, violence, and sexual disease and teenage pregnancy in today's schools is well documented. Placing children in these environments, when they might not be mature enough to make good decisions, puts them at risk for experiences that can be damaging to them for life. At the best, children are exposed to the normal taunting and teasing that seems to be inherent to groups of children who are largely unsupervised. At worst, children are subject to bullying, opportunities for drug and alcohol abuse, and sexual interactions.

- **"One-size fits all" approach**. Because of the enormous number of children that school systems deal with, there is no room for individual differences. All children are taught in the same way and at the same speed, regardless of individual differences. Plus, classes are typically geared toward less capable students so that many students become bored because of a lack of a challenge.

- **Excessive time and resource requirements**. Typical school days are very inefficient. In addition to time wasted commuting back and forth, there are the many nonvalue tasks that are part of school days, such as time spent in administrative tasks. The actual time spent learning in most schools is much less than the amount of time children actually spend at school. Further, with the time and effort parents must use to be involved in the school system, the school becomes the driving force in a family's life.

note

How can we hope to remain economically competitive in a world in which…90% of Dutch high-school students take advanced math courses and 100% of teachers in Germany have double majors, while the best we can say about our "pocket of excellence" is that 75% of [American] students have learned to "critique tactfully?"
—Barbara J. Alexander

Homeschooling Isn't New: A Brief History of Education

It is useful to put homeschool in a somewhat historical perspective. Because of the pervasiveness of public and institutional education over the past 100 years or so, it is easy to think that this way of educating children is the way it has always been done and that it is the best system possible. However, the development of public education into the monolithic system that it has become is a relatively recent turn of events when viewed in an historical context.

In the ancient times, societies in which education was valued, for example in ancient Greece, most education was done through tutoring and other very focused avenues. As time passed and institutions starting providing education, these institutions tended be religiously based and were largely independent of any large organization. This was mostly the situation in the earliest American communities; most colleges that were started in that period were actually founded for religious purposes.

In the 1700s through the 1880s, schools were often established by and for local communities. These schools were funded and controlled by the local communities and usually consisted of a single teacher and a single schoolroom. The amount of time children spent in school was fairly limited in both the number of days they attended and the hours of instruction per day that they received. Because these schools were based in and controlled by people in the local community, they answered directly to the people whose children were being taught. In the times when children weren't attending school, parents often taught them at home or they learned independently.

Eventually, the system of locally operated and controlled schools evolved into larger and larger networks of schools forming school districts and corporations. State governments began to take more control of the school systems and the federal government began to get involved. As school systems increased in size, including the inherent growth in state and federal bureaucracy, the ability of parents to have a significant influence over how their children are taught diminished.

By the 1970s, governments and other large bureaucratic organizations, including the teachers' union, had mostly taken control over schools and local participants actually had very little say over what occurred in those schools. This "evolution" (or devolution depending on your point of view) continues today. The policies and practices of school systems today are largely determined by state and federal policies and programs. Parents have little say in how schools are actually run. Their primary influence over school systems is indirect through school board elections, but even these school boards are typically limited in their authority to manage the schools.

note

It's interesting to think about some of the amazing people who have achieved remarkable things without what we usually consider to be a formal education. For example, Abraham Lincoln was largely educated at home and had very little formal schooling. There are many other examples of people like this. It is only relatively recently that society has equated a formal, institutional education with the potential for success.

The truth is that schools don't really teach anything except how to obey orders.—John Taylor Gatto (New York City and State Teacher of the Year)

The decline in what many consider to be the general levels of societal accountability and responsibility has fed the decline in the educational system and vice-versa. Because the education system doesn't prepare children adequately, on many levels, society in general experiences a decline.

Actually, the homeschool movement drives the responsibility for education back to the parents, those with whom it originally belonged. As more people embrace the opportunity to provide the best possible education for their children, the number of homeschooling families will continue to increase.

How Many Homeschoolers Are There?

Given all its benefits, you might wonder how many people homeschool. That is actually an interesting question and one that is quite difficult to answer. The number of homeschooled children is difficult to determine for two main reasons:

- **Many homeschoolers aren't counted in anyway**. As you will learn in Chapter 3, "Determining the Legal Requirements for Homeschool in Your Area," many states don't require homeschoolers to register in any way. In these states, it is virtually impossible to calculate the number of children who homeschool. And, because many homeschoolers want to avoid government interference in their schools, they don't typically volunteer for any sort of registration process.

- **Political and social agendas bias studies**. Many studies of this question are biased either by anti- or pro-homeschooling biases. For example, it is incumbent in the agendas of organizations such as teacher's unions to minimize the number of homeschoolers for political reasons. School systems don't want the number of homeschoolers to be known accurately in the event that these numbers would detract from the funding made available to their schools, which is often based on the total size of the populations they serve. School systems can see homeschoolers as a threat to their funding sources.

However, there is considerable quantitative and qualitative evidence that the number of homeschoolers is significant and continues to increase at a dramatic and increasing rate.

There have many attempts to calculate the number of homeschooled students in the United States. For the reasons mentioned previously, the results of these studies vary widely. The U.S. Census Bureau (*Home Schooling in the United States: Trends and Characteristics* by Kurt J. Bauman) estimated that 791,000 children were homeschooled in 1999. Today, as a general idea, most agree that the number of homeschooled children in the United States is somewhere between 900,000 and 2,000,000. Those with a pro-homeschool view would like to lean toward the higher end of the range while those with an anti-homeschool bias would tend to lend credence toward the lower end of the range.

Regardless of the estimated total homeschool population, most experts (pro- or anti-homeschool) agree that homeschooling is increasing in popularity at an extremely high rate; many estimates place the growth rate between 7% and 15% per year (*Reaching the Homeschool Market* by Mark Lardas in Tdmonthly magazine, October 2003).

In addition to the quantifiable evidence of the growth of homeschooling, there is significant anecdotal evidence that the homeschool movement is large and continuing to increase in influence. For example, the number of publishers and retailers whose business is related to homeschool continues to increase. Businesses that provide discounts and other incentives to students are more frequently including homeschoolers in their definition of student (examples include Apple Computer and Microsoft). The number of homeschool associations, Web sites, and other resources for homeschoolers continues to increase dramatically. And, while not so long ago it was unusual to hear about homeschooling either personally or via the media, it is a topic that seems to pop up regularly now.

note

I have never let my schooling interfere with my education.—Mark Twain

Although the exact number of homeschoolers isn't clear, what is clear is that the number of homeschoolers is significant and continues to grow at a brisk pace. As more people discover its benefits, we can expect this trend to continue.

THE ABSOLUTE MINIMUM

Homeschool is parents taking full responsibility of their children's education rather than largely turning that responsibility over to an institution. Homeschooling provides the opportunity for parents to take control over their children's education and growth, and who is better qualified to do so?

- Homeschooling offers many benefits, and these positive reasons are why many people choose to homeschool their children.

- There are also many good reasons to homeschool as a means of keeping children out institutional schools, such as public schools.

- The concept of education not being controlled by large bureaucratic organizations isn't really new. This dynamic is relatively recent from a historical perspective.

- The exact number of children who are homeschooled isn't known. Reasonable estimates range from 900,000 to 2,000,000. In any event, it is clear that homeschooling is a large and rapidly growing movement.

2

DECIDING TO HOMESCHOOL—OR NOT

As you learned in the previous chapter, homeschooling offers many benefits to your kids and to your family, which is why so many people are choosing this option. When compared to other education options, homeschool tops the list (in my opinion anyway!) and can be an excellent choice for your family. However, deciding to educate your children at home is a major commitment for your family and has ramifications for your children's future. It is not something that should be taken lightly nor should the decision to homeschool be one made quickly or without a lot of thought. (Of course, since you are reading this book, you are already demonstrating that you take this choice seriously.) In this chapter, we'll take a look at how you might make the decision to homeschool, and just what will be required of you and your family to homeschool successfully.

Making the Choice: Is Homeschool Right for Your Family?

You've obviously either decided to homeschool your children or you have been considering the option to homeschool your children—or you wouldn't be reading this right now. In any case, making the decision to homeschool your children isn't something that can be done without serious consideration of the pros and the cons of doing so. Obviously, your children's education has a major impact on the rest of their lives. However, the decision to homeschool also has major implications for your entire family.

Making a decision to homeschool requires that you understand both the benefits of this option (if you read Chapter 1, "What Is Homeschooling All About?" you have a good idea about these) and the requirements to do so (which is what this chapter is all about). After you have a firm grasp on these factors, you can make a good decision about whether homeschool is a good option for your family.

What Is Needed from You to Homeschool Successfully?

If you are going to be your homeschool's primary teacher, principal, janitor, and so on, homeschooling your children is a major commitment on your part. In terms of time alone, you can expect that running a homeschool will require at least as much time and effort, and probably more, as a full-time job because running a homeschool successfully is in reality a full-time job. The following is a list of some of what will be required from you to homeschool successfully:

- **Willingness/eagerness to learn**. It has been said that to teach is to learn twice (Joseph Joubert), and that is definitely true when you homeschool. As you teach your children, you will find that you are learning as much as they are—and even more because you are learning about the topics you are teaching, plus learning about teaching itself. Along the way, you'll also learn a lot about your children and yourself. Homeschooling is a great learning experience for you and your entire family. To homeschool effectively requires that you be willing, able, and eager to learn.

- **Effort (aka Hard Work)**. Anything significant in life requires effort; the effort required is often in proportion to the benefits of the results of that effort. This is definitely true for homeschooling. While you will need to work very hard to homeschool, you will find that the results you achieve make your hard work more than worthwhile.

- **Discipline**. When you homeschool, you will be calling the shots. With this authority comes responsibility. You will need to be disciplined about your homeschool so that you apply consistent effort over a long period of time. You'll need self-discipline to do the work required to homeschool, and you'll need to be able to help your kids develop their own self-discipline to be able to learn.

- **Time**. As I mentioned previously, running a homeschool requires that you dedicate lots of time to it. In most cases, especially once you get past the first or second grade or if you have more than one child, running a homeschool will require as much time as or more time than a full-time job. To be successful, you need to have this time available. For this reason, I don't recommend that you attempt to homeschool if you also have a full-time or close-to full-time job already. In that case, there simply won't be enough time for you to homeschool effectively.

- **Flexibility**. This one is as much a benefit as it is a requirement. Homeschooling both offers and requires flexibility. Because you won't be operating under a structured organization, such as a traditional school, you need to be flexible in your approach. And, unless your kids are clones, it is likely that you will need to be flexible with each child's learning style (you'll learn more about this later).

- **Patience**. When it comes to homeschooling, patience is more than a virtue, it is a requirement. Teaching children requires patience as anyone who works with, or even knows, children understands. Because you will have the bulk of the responsibility for your children's education, you'll need to have a good chunk of patience to go along with it.

note

Although I don't recommend that you attempt to homeschool if you have a full-time job outside of your home, that doesn't mean that you can't earn income while you homeschool. There are many ways to homeschool and earn income at the same time. For example, you can have a part-time home business. You can even incorporate a business into your homeschool, especially when you are working with older students because you might be able to have them participate in the business as part of their learning. Later in this book, we'll take a look at some ways of incorporating such real-life activities into your homeschool.

■ **Dedication**. To be a successful homeschooler, you need to be dedicated to the pursuit. Although it is fine (and expected) that you'll occasionally have "off" days, you will need to be very dedicated to making your homeschool work. Homeschooling effectively will require that you work at it throughout the school year and that it be your number one priority.

■ **An adventurous spirit**. Homeschooling is a great adventure with all the requisite planning, unexpected events, hard work, rewarding accomplishments, and occasional moments of terror that an adventure entails. To be a homeschooler is to embark on a great life adventure. You need to be seeking an adventure if you want to homeschool.

Now that you have a good idea of what is required, take a look at some things that you might think are required, but aren't:

■ **A college education**. Although a college education is always valuable, you don't need a degree to run a successful homeschool. As long as you can learn yourself, you can homeschool effectively.

■ **All the answers**. Although you will be primarily responsible for your children's education, that doesn't mean that you must have all the answers to every issue or question you'll face. There are many people and resources that you can draw on for help. And, running a homeschool successfully is best done with lots of input from and interaction with other people. You just need to understand how to connect to these people and resources, which is a major part of what you will learn in this book.

> **note**
>
> In some areas, you might be required to have some sort of certification from the state or local government to be able to homeschool your children. (Fortunately, in most areas, this is either not required or is easy to obtain.) Check Chapter 3, "Determining the Legal Requirements for Homeschool in Your Area," to learn how to find out if this certification is required in your state.
>
> The roots of education are bitter, but the fruit is sweet.—Aristotle

■ **Perfection**. Contrary to what people sometimes think, you don't have to be perfect to homeschool effectively. With strong dedication, a little perseverance, and effective homeschooling strategies, you'll be amazed at how successful you can be.

What Is Needed from Your Spouse to Homeschool Successfully?

A homeschool works best when one parent can be dedicated to the effort while the other fills the essential support roles. Because homeschooling requires such a major time commitment, the person who doesn't have a full-time career outside of the home is typically the person who carries the bulk of the load in terms of planning and running the homeschool. However, a homeschool will benefit significantly from the enthusiastic participation of a spouse.

To be the supporting part of the homeschool team, the spouse can do the following:

- **Encourage**. If there is one thing that every homeschool manager needs, it is encouragement. When you are slogging through what can sometimes be a daily grind of homeschooling, it is important to have someone to encourage you along the way. When enmeshed in the details, it can sometimes be difficult to see the progress that is being made. A spouse can encourage the homeschool manager by recognizing this progress and being the homeschool manager's cheerleader to help get through the inevitable rough spots that occur for every homeschooler.

- **Support**. In the best scenario, the spouse of a homeschool manager will provide the financial resources needed to run the homeschool. Support, however, doesn't stop there. The spouse can also support the homeschool by helping make some of the many decisions that are required to run a homeschool. The spouse can also support by just listening when the homeschool manager needs to share frustrations or joy

note

In today's world, statistics show that many kids are being raised in single-parent homes. Unless a single parent has a means of support other than a full-time career, it is unlikely they will have the time available to homeschool effectively. For that reason, I usually don't recommend that a single parent homeschool children. Where there is a will, there is a way is a true expression, so I am sure there are lots of examples of single parents homeschooling their kids effectively; but in general, the demands of financially supporting a family and homeschooling children are simply too much for one person. Of course, there are other less common situations in which a single parent family can still benefit from homeschool. For example, a grandparent or other relative might take responsibility for a homeschool while the parent plays the supporting role usually taken on by a spouse.

about what is happening. And because everyone needs a day off now and again, the spouse can also take over the homeschool once in a while to give the manager a break.

- **Be involved**. A homeschool will work best when the spouse who isn't managing the homeschool is still involved with it in a significant way. There are many ways a spouse can be involved even if they aren't the primary teacher or manager. For example, the spouse can help make curriculum decisions. Or, the spouse can teach topics outside of the "normal" school time. Of course, just as with a traditional school education, students need help with their work from time to time—a spouse can be really helpful by being available to assist students with their work.

- **Do special projects**. The best homeschools include a variety of activities, such as field trips, projects, and so on. A supportive spouse can be helpful by taking on some of these short-term activities. For example, a spouse can arrange and lead a field trip. Or, a spouse can plan a home project with the idea of incorporating it into school activities.

What Is Needed from Your Kids to Homeschool Successfully?

Obviously, homeschool is all about preparing your kids for life so they have a major participating role in the process. The requirements from kids to be homeschooled successfully aren't really that much different from those involved in a traditional school situation. They need to be able and willing to learn, be disciplined to do the work that is required of them, and so on.

One thing that will be required is for them to accept that their lives are different from many other kids who are involved in a traditional school that they will encounter along the way. Some kids accept this difference more easily than others do. Mostly, the acceptance of homeschooling by your children will depend on the attitudes that you convey.

Accepting this difference isn't usually a problem for homeschoolers who have been in homeschool their entire school lives. In such cases, homeschool is all the children have known so it doesn't seem different to them. Sure, they know that most kids go to a traditional school, but because they can't relate to that experience, not doing so isn't a problem for them.

And, most homeschooled children, whether they have been so their entire school lives or not, understand the benefits being homeschooled offers to them—such as shorter, more efficient school days, more variety in what they do from day to day, avoiding some of the nastiness that is involved with institutional education, and so on.

note

However, for some children who have been in institutional education for a significant period of time, acceptance of being homeschooled can be a challenge, especially if a child derives most of his or her value from being involved with peers (which might be part of the reason you decided to homeschool them to begin with!). If they are to be successful in a homeschool, you will need to help these

If you consider what are called the virtues in mankind, you will find their growth is assisted by education and cultivation.—Xenophon

kids make and accept the transition to homeschool. Because this can be an important issue to deal with, Chapter 10, "Transitioning a Child from Public or Private School to Homeschool," goes into this topic in some detail.

In any case, a big part of making kids feel comfortable about being homeschoolers is being involved with other homeschooled kids. For this and other reasons, having close relationships with other homeschoolers is a must to have a successful homeschool. You'll learn about this in Chapter 5, "Locating and Networking with Other Homeschoolers."

What Is Needed from Your Family to Homeschool Successfully?

One of the great things about a homeschool is that it involves your whole family. It is definitely a family effort and requires that everyone in your family is involved and in close relationships with one another. Along with being a requirement, this is also one of the major benefits of a homeschool (as you read in Chapter 1). Homeschooling is a family project and your ability to homeschool effectively will require that your family works together.

Making a Decision to Homeschool

Now that you have read Chapter 1 and most of this chapter, you should be in a position to make a good decision about homeschooling your children. You understand the many benefits that homeschooling provides and you also know that it is a serious undertaking that requires lots from you, your spouse, and your kids.

Deciding to homeschool is an important decision so take your time making it. Get all the information you can. Talk to as many homeschoolers as you can. Read some or all of this book and others that cover this topic. Explore your options for public and private schools.

As you gather all the information you can, let me warn you that it is unlikely that the result of your efforts will be a clear, unequivocal decision to homeschool or not. It is likely that even when all signs point to homeschooling as your best option, you will still have doubts, most likely you will have some doubts as to your ability to handle this responsibility for your kids. This is natural and every homeschooler faces these same doubts. You just need to get enough information so that you can feel as confident as possible in your decision.

In the end, only you can make this choice for your family.

You've Decided to Homeschool, Now What?

Up to this point in the book, I have assumed that you are not yet a committed homeschooler. That assumption ends here. From this point forward, I assume you have decided to homeschool. So the rest of the book is dedicated to helping you homeschool as effectively as possible. (If you have

note

One of the most important things you can do to help you decide if you want to homeschool your children is to talk to people you know and respect who are homeschoolers. Ask questions of these people, such as why they homeschool, what the challenges are, what the benefits are, and so on. If you don't have any homeschoolers in your immediate circle, check out Chapter 5 for information about making contact with homeschoolers.

Deciding to homeschool doesn't mean that you are locked into that decision for life. Many people decide to homeschool on an annual basis. The first year may be to try it out to see if you can make it work. The decision to homeschool for subsequent years might involve testing and assessing a student's progress, considering your own capabilities and desires, and so on. Typically, this decision is easier when children are young and it gets more difficult as they move toward college.

decided not to homeschool, that decision doesn't have to be permanent. You should also reconsider this decision as you move through life. When you do, you can always come back to this book for help.)

After you have decided that you want to homeschool, it's time to get to work and make it happen. The following chapters will guide you through this process.

As you get started, let me encourage you about several areas of struggle that you are likely to face immediately.

Don't be surprised if you feel overwhelmed at times with all the responsibility you have assumed. And, there are many, many decisions you will need to make, such as topics, curricula, activities, and so on. All homeschoolers have these feelings now and again. To help deal with these emotions, have a good plan and concentrate on what you need to do next. Action is the best antidote for feeling overwhelmed. Being able to share and be encouraged by other homeschoolers is also very important to overcoming this feeling.

Another area in which you are likely to struggle with your decision is your own confidence. Being responsible for your children's education is a big load to carry and we all question whether we are really able to do this well or not. First, realize that you care for your children more than anyone else does and you have their best interests at heart. This will lead you to do everything you can to ensure that your homeschool prepares your children for life very effectively. Second, don't compare your homeschool to some ideal of the perfect education. It should be obvious to you that institutional education is far from perfect. Having a realistic view of what the education options really are will help you realize that you are probably in a much better position to help your children be successful than those who are involved in institutional education.

Be aware that some people, perhaps even some who are close to you, may not understand your decision and might even challenge you about it. Even though millions of children have been educated successfully in the home, it is still outside the mainstream and so it could be feared or misunderstood by some people. Some people will be genuinely concerned for your kids. Others might have an agenda against homeschooling or think that it is "weird." In either case, it is likely that at some point, you will encounter people who question your decision. This won't be a problem for you for a couple of reasons. One is that you will have taken the time to consider most of these objections already during your decision-making process. The other is that in Chapter 4, "Defending Your Decision to Homeschool," you'll learn what the most common of these objections are and how you can respond to them without being defensive.

THE ABSOLUTE MINIMUM

Deciding to homeschool isn't a simple or easy choice to make. But, it is an important one and deciding to homeschool might just be the best decision you ever make for your family. In this chapter, you learned some of the important factors you need to keep in mind while you make this decision.

- When you think about homeschooling, you need to weigh the benefits (Chapter 1) versus the requirements (this chapter).

- Although homeschooling doesn't require that you be the world's best teacher, it does require that you be dedicated and have the time available that is needed to do it well.

- Ideally, one spouse will be dedicated to managing a homeschool, while the other plays the very important support role.

- Although it usually isn't an issue, some children might have a hard time accepting being "different" by being homeschooled. You'll learn how to help such kids later in this book.

- Homeschooling involves the entire family, which is a requirement for doing so, and a benefit of doing it at the same time.

- Just like other important decisions you make in your life, making a decision to homeschool requires you to do your own homework.

- After you have decided to homeschool, it is likely that you will face several challenges that are common to most, if not all, homeschoolers. Fortunately, these are relatively easy to deal with.

IN THIS CHAPTER

- Understand why legal requirements are important to your homeschool

- Determine the legal requirements for homeschool in your state

- Find out what interaction will be required with local school officials, if any

- Notify your state that you are homeschooling, if required

- Document all the legal activity specifically related to your homeschool

- Be aware of legislative and legal activity occurring that might have an impact on your homeschool

3

DETERMINING THE LEGAL REQUIREMENTS FOR HOMESCHOOL IN YOUR AREA

For sometimes better and oftentimes worse, government is involved in many of the activities we choose to undertake. Homeschooling is no exception to this statement. One of the first tasks you need to do after you have decided to homeschool your children is to find out to what extent your state and local governments are going to be involved in the operation of your homeschool. The level of involvement of these governments is determined by the regulations they have established regarding education, and more specifically, regulations related to the alternatives to public schools.

What Has Your State Government or Local School System Got to Do with Homeschool?

Although the general requirements regarding education are laid out at the federal level, public education is mostly the responsibility of state and local governments. Because of this, federal education regulations won't have any impact on your homeschool.

However, any state or local government regulations that govern the area in which you live definitely do have an impact on your homeschool. Failure to comply with such regulations can result in less severe consequences to you, such as warnings or fines, to extremely severe consequences, such as you being unable to homeschool your kids or having child protection agencies investigate or interfere with your family. You should carefully consider and comply with regulations that govern your homeschool.

There are two areas of regulation that you need to consider: state and local guidelines.

Your state certainly has regulations that govern the operation of its public education system. It probably also has regulations that relate to "alternative" or "alternate" schools. These regulations are generally related to private schools, such as schools run by religious organizations. In most cases, these "alternate" regulations are the ones that govern homeschools. No matter which state you live in, you need to understand your state's education regulations that impact your homeschool. The good news is that it is relatively easy to determine your state's regulations. You'll learn how to do this in the next section.

Public schools are actually run by local governments at the city or county level. In some cases,

caution

Public education policies are drastically different in different countries. Because I live in the United States, the information in this chapter is directed toward its education regulatory system. If you live in a different country, you will need to investigate the regulations and policies that your country enforces. This chapter will provide some general guidelines for you, but you will have to find specific information for your country and region.

note

Strange as it seems, no amount of learning can cure stupidity, and formal education positively fortifies it.—Stephen Vizinczey

As homeschooling continues to explode in popularity, it will be interesting to see if states will start creating more regulations about homeschools. Hopefully not, because more regulation can only make homeschooling more difficult, but that remains to be seen.

these local governments also will have regulations about alternate schools, again with most of this regulation being directed toward private schools. In many cases, as long as you meet your state's regulations, you will also meet your local government's requirements. In reality, many of the specific regulations that are part of a state's education requirements are administered at the local school level. For example, some state governments require that the public school system have oversight over homeschoolers in their jurisdiction, such as submitting the results of standardized tests to the local school authorities. In the worst case, the local school overseers might attempt to dictate the curricula your homeschool uses, but that is very unlikely. In other cases, you might have to submit to some sort of supervision of your homeschool. Even in these more difficult circumstances, it is still possible to have a good homeschool experience. Dealing with your local school officials is explored in detail a bit later in this chapter.

VOUCHERS OR TAX CREDITS FOR HOMESCHOOLERS

One area in which government could be a great help to homeschoolers is by the creation of vouchers or tax credits for homeschoolers. As a homeschooler, you are responsible for all the costs associated with educating your children. And, assuming you pay the taxes that support public education in your area, you also "pay" for public education services that you don't use.

Over the past several years, the concept of vouchers has been attempted in several areas. Basically, the idea of a voucher is that parents can choose to use the voucher to pay for a private education for their children instead of sending them to public school. The basic concept is to promote the improvement of public education by increasing the level of competition with private schools. (The idea is to provide vouchers to people who normally can't afford to both pay both taxes and to send their kids to private schools. These vouchers can be used to pay tuition—the schools to which the vouchers are submitted get reimbursed by the government.) Vouchers tend to be very controversial because they threaten the public education system's monopoly and all that that monopoly engenders.

Although vouchers aren't currently being contemplated for homeschoolers, they are still an important topic for us as well. That's because any effort to loosen the grip that government has over the mandatory direction of tax dollars to public education services that we don't use will eventually be beneficial to us as well. For example, it is conceivable that someday, should vouchers become an accepted tool, we might get vouchers for materials we use in our homeschools (we could transfer some of the tax dollars we spend on public education toward the costs of educating our kids at home).

A more realistic goal is to obtain tax credits for homeschooling. This idea has some precedent already in the childcare tax credit system that is currently in place. If you pay for childcare outside of your home, you can get tax credits for doing so. It doesn't seem unreasonable to me that those of us who take the responsibility of our children's education should somehow be able to recover some portion of our taxes that we pay to support public education. A tax credit system would enable us to do so. As a homeschooler, you need to be aware of such issues in your area and support those that would benefit you.

Determining the Legal Requirements in Your State

As a homeschooler, you must understand your state's education regulations that impact your homeschool. Then, you must make sure that your homeschool complies with these regulations and that you can document that it does so.

HOMESCHOOLING AND THE HOME SCHOOL LEGAL DEFENSE ASSOCIATION

The Home School Legal Defense Association (HSLDA) is a national, non-profit organization established to "defend and advance the constitutional right of parents to direct the education of their children and to protect family freedoms."

The HSLDA is an outstanding source of information about the legal implications of homeschooling across the United States. Much of the specific information included in this chapter is based on information compiled by the HSLDA. In addition to providing information to homeschoolers, the HSLDA also represents homeschooling families in court cases and advocates for homeschoolers in legislation, the media, and in other venues.

You can contact the HSLDA by visiting its Web site at www.hslda.org or by calling 640-338-5600.

> **note**
>
> Even in the most regulated state, homeschooling is still permitted. In no case can you be prevented from homeschooling your child, given you meet the basic requirements. In fact, most of the states' requirements are quite reasonable and are likely to be things you would do even if they weren't required.

Types of State Regulations Related to Homeschool

There are four basic levels of state regulation regarding homeschooling, as summarized in the following list:

- **Least**. In these states, such as Indiana, Texas, Illinois, and Idaho, parents aren't required to provide any information about their homeschool to the state. Although there are regulations that provide general guidelines about how children should be educated, parents are under no obligation to inform the state about how they educate their children.

■ **Minimal**. In these states, such as California, New Mexico, Alabama, and Kansas, you only need to inform the state that you are homeschooling your children. After that, the state assumes you are meeting its general guidelines and doesn't attempt to oversee your homeschool.

■ **Moderate**. States with moderate regulation, such as Colorado, Iowa, Arkansas, and Florida, require that you formally notify the state about your homeschool. You must also submit some sort of progress report to the state, such as test scores or professional evaluation of your students' progress.

■ **Significant**. These states, including Washington, Minnesota, New York, and Maine, are the most difficult in which to homeschool. In addition to notification and progress evaluation, you also may be required to use approved curricula, have a teaching credential, or submit to home visits by state officials.

caution

Even if you live in a state that has the least or minimal levels of regulation regarding homeschooling, you still need to be aware of and document your compliance with these general requirements. Should your homeschool be challenged legally, you must be able to demonstrate that you do meet whatever regulations have been established—even if you aren't required to do so formally under normal conditions.

How to Determine Your State's Regulations

There are several ways to determine which general type of regulation your state has, and then to determine what the specific regulations are.

One way to do this is to contact your state's department of education and request copies of the relevant regulations. You should be able to find a phone number for this department in a telephone book. You probably can get this information from your local public library as well. You can locate your state's education department's Web site, which also will provide the information you need.

However, a better way to find this information is to use the Web to visit the HSLDA Web site. On this

note

If you don't have a computer with Web access, you should strongly consider adding one to your homeschool. The Web provides limitless resources that you can use for your homeschool in various ways. This topic is addressed more fully in Chapter 8, "Preparing a Classroom in Your Home."

Web site, you will find excellent summaries of the legal requirements for each state. To do so, use the following steps:

1. Use Web browser to visit **http://www.hslda.org**, which is the home page of the HSLDA.

2. From the site's **Homeschooling** menu, choose **Homeschool Laws**. On the resulting screen, you will see a diagram of the United States. Each state is color-coded to indicate its relative level of regulation (see Figure 3.1).

FIGURE 3.1

This map on the HSLDA Web site shows the relative regulation of each state in the United States.

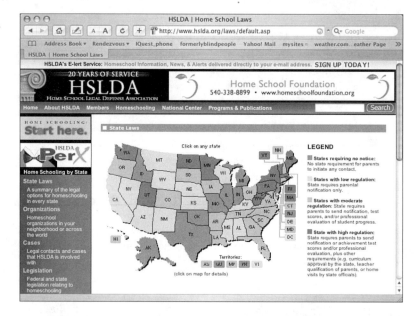

3. Click your **state's icon** on the map. The screen will be refreshed to show specific information about your state (see Figure 3.2).

4. Read the **information** related to homeschool regulations for your state. Note that for some states, there are multiple sets of regulations, called "options," which could impact your homeschool. Make sure you explore each option.

tip

I recommend that you add your state's information as a bookmark or favorite in your Web browser. You will likely want to come back to this page frequently.

FIGURE 3.2

Here you can see the regulation information for my home state Indiana.

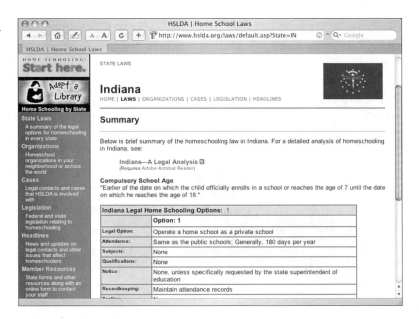

The tables presented on the screens for your state will tell you about the specific regulations with which you will have to comply. The tables generally cover the following information:

- **Legal options**. A description of the various options under which homeschools can be operated.

- **Attendance**. Information about attendance requirements, such as the number of instruction days that must be provided per year.

- **Subjects**. Curriculum requirements for the state are defined here.

- **Qualifications**. This information will tell you if your state requires that you have some sort of teaching certification to operate a homeschool in your state.

- **Notice**. If you are obligated to notify the state that you are operating a homeschool, information here will let you know.

- **Recordkeeping**. Information here tells you the kind of documentation you are required to maintain, such as attendance records, test scores, and so on. You should consider this as only the absolute minimum. You will want to keep lots of documentation for your homeschool (you'll learn about that throughout the rest of this book).

- **Testing**. Testing requirements your state might have, such as for standardized tests your students might be required to take, are outlined here.

The following sections provide an example of a state in each category to help you interpret the requirements for your state.

Indiana: An Example of a State with Least Regulation

If you are fortunate as I am, you live in a state with little regulation, such as Indiana. Such a state provides you with the most freedom and requires the least amount of work dedicated to meet or document regulations (which means you can spend more time on your homeschool).

Indiana's legal requirements are summarized in the table shown in Figure 3.3.

note

HSLDA is supported by member contributions. If you use any of its resources, I strongly encourage you to support this amazing organization by becoming an official member.

FIGURE 3.3

Indiana has very few legal requirements as you can see in this table (lucky me!).

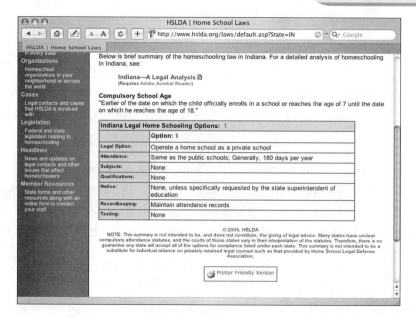

As shown in the figure, you can see that there is one option for homeschoolers in Indiana, which is to operate as a homeschool. In Indiana and similar states, the only requirement is that school is held at the same time as the public schools, which requires 180 days of instruction. The only records Indiana homeschoolers are required to maintain are attendance records—an Indiana homeschooler has to be able to show that the 180-day requirement was met. What all this means is that homeschoolers in Indiana (and similar states) aren't really impacted by state regulation in any significant way.

California: An Example of a State with Minimal Regulation

Next up on the regulation category list are states with minimal regulation, an example of which is California (see Figure 3.4). California has four options. One is to qualify as a private school, which means that as a homeschooler you have to meet the same requirements as a private school. Another is to use a private tutor. The third and fourth options are to use an independent study program administered by a private school (option 3) or administered by a public school (option 4).

> **tip**
>
> Each state's page includes a legal analysis document that is prepared by the HSLDA. This provides more detail than the summary presented in the table, and includes significant court cases related to homeschooling in the state. You should download and read this document for your state.

FIGURE 3.4

States with a minimal level of regulation, such as California, aren't much more difficult to homeschool than those with the least level of regulation.

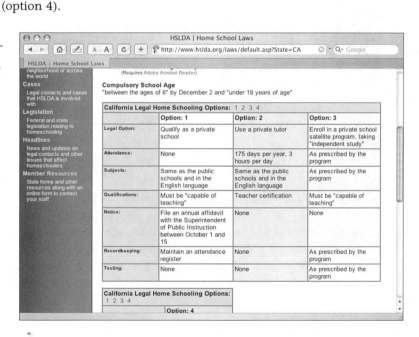

As you can see in the figure, the requirements for each of these options vary slightly. The one that is most relevant for homeschoolers is to qualify as a private school. To do so, you are required to teach the same subjects as the public schools and teach in English. You must provide a formal notification that you are homeschooling with the Superintendent of Public Education. The only required documentation is an attendance log. No testing is required. As you can see, homeschoolers in states like California won't have to spend a lot of time dealing with government regulations, which is a good thing.

Iowa: An Example of a State with Moderate Regulation

As we move up in complexity, we get to states with moderate regulations, such as Iowa (see Figure 3.5). Iowa has two options. One is to operate a homeschool. The other is to operate a homeschool that is supervised by a licensed teacher.

FIGURE 3.5

Rated as moderate in regulation, Iowa's most significant requirement is that students demonstrate progress by submitting standardized test results or a portfolio to the local school district.

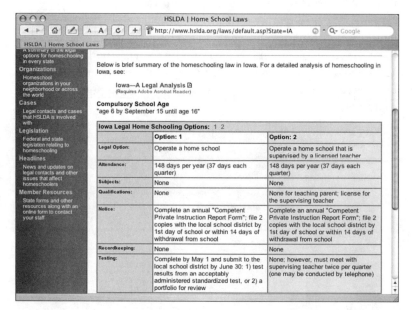

To operate a homeschool without supervision, you must have at least 148 days of instruction. A formal notification must be submitted to the local school district. No records are required, but standardized test results or a portfolio must be presented to the local school district each year to demonstrate progress.

The requirements to operate a homeschool with supervision are the same except that the supervising teacher must have a license, and the testing requirement is that the parent must meet with the supervisor twice per quarter.

New York: An Example of a State with Significant Regulation

Even states with significant regulation, such as New York, still make it possible to homeschool without huge amounts of effort to demonstrate that you meet all requirements (see Figure 3.6). New York offers one option, which is to operate a homeschool. It has an attendance requirement of 180 days that is further defined with hours of instruction for specific grade ranges. Specific sub-jects must be taught at each grade level. While first appearing to be limiting, a closer look reveals that most of these topics are likely to be taught whether they are required by the state or not. A specific teaching certification is not required. A formal notice is required as are attendance records along with quarterly documentation regarding the specific instruction that has occurred. Standardized testing or written evaluations are also required.

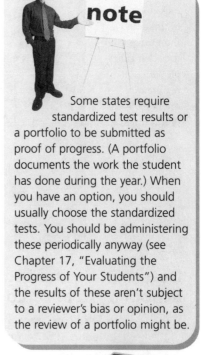

note

Some states require standardized test results or a portfolio to be submitted as proof of progress. (A portfolio documents the work the student has done during the year.) When you have an option, you should usually choose the standardized tests. You should be administering these periodically anyway (see Chapter 17, "Evaluating the Progress of Your Students") and the results of these aren't subject to a reviewer's bias or opinion, as the review of a portfolio might be.

Determining the Legal Requirements for Your School System or Local Government

If you live in a state that requires some type of oversight of your homeschool by the local school system, you will need to figure out exactly what that means for your homeschool. (If you live in a state that doesn't require you to interact with a local school system, consider yourself fortunate and skip the rest of this section.)

caution

As is clear on the HSLDA Web site, its summaries of state law are only summaries of the laws and not the laws themselves. If you want to be absolutely certain of the exact requirements of your state, you can locate and review the actual laws that govern homeschool. That assumes they are written in such a way that they will be understandable to regular people of course, which isn't always (or often) the case.

FIGURE 3.6

Although New York's table looks more intimidating than those from the other example states, its regulations aren't really all that restrictive.

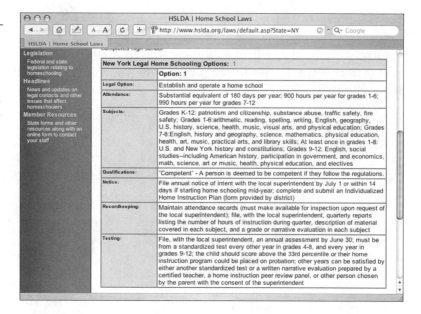

Determining the Legal Requirements for Your School System or Local Government

There are several basic ways in which you might be required to be under the auspices of a local school system:

- **Provide standardized tests**. In some states, you must file standardized test scores with the local school system (usually with the superintendent's office). Some states allow you to administer these tests yourself while others require that these tests be conducted by a licensed teacher. Certain states only require that you have students take these tests at specific points in the education process and that you maintain the results as part of your documentation. This isn't much of a burden because you should include standardized tests in your homeschool regardless of whether they are required by your state or not.

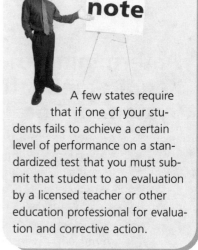

note

A few states require that if one of your students fails to achieve a certain level of performance on a standardized test that you must submit that student to an evaluation by a licensed teacher or other education professional for evaluation and corrective action.

- **Submit a portfolio**. As a means of measuring progress, some states require that you submit a portfolio that documents the results of your homeschool, usually on an annual basis. The local school officials evaluate your portfolio to ensure that your homeschool is providing a proper education to your children. You'll learn about preparing a portfolio, which you should do as part of your normal homeschool documentation even if it isn't required by the state, in Chapter 12, "Documenting Your Homeschool."

- **Report to a school representative**. Some states require that you be "supervised" by a local school representative such as a teacher or administrator. Typically, you are supposed to report to your supervisor on a quarterly basis. The idea is that the supervisor will attempt to evaluate your homeschool to ensure your kids are being educated properly. In reality, what actually happens varies dramatically from school district to school district and even among individual supervisors. Supervisors who support homeschooling are likely to be less intrusive than those who "have an axe to grind."

- **Provide periodic progress reports**. Some states require that you provide periodic progress reports whether through a local school supervisor or independently. The formats of these reports vary based on the school district under the jurisdiction you fall.

When you determine that your state's legal requirements involve some level of interaction with a local school system, you will need to contact the responsible officials in the school system (typically the superintendent's office) to identify what exactly you need to do to comply with the requirements.

I recommend that you meet with the person that is responsible for overseeing your homeschool as soon as you realize that your homeschool will have some level of oversight requirements. This helps you get the information from the source and starts to establish the required relationship with the proper officials.

To prepare for this meeting, make sure that you review and understand the specific requirements for your state. Identify each requirement individually so you will be prepared to address each with the school officials.

When you meet with the officials, get all requirements in writing so that you have a clear and definitive record of the requirements from the responsible officials. Make sure the specific people you have to deal with are also noted in the requirements. Also make sure that you understand exactly what is expected of you, with whom you need to deal, and when you need to deal with them. If a requirement is presented to you that is not in accordance with your understanding of the state regulations, make sure you get it clarified and that the school officials can prove that the requirement is actually part of state law.

Managing Your Relationship with Local School Officials (if Necessary)

When you interact with local school officials, your attitude will have a large impact on how your relationship goes. While you shouldn't be intimidated by these officials, neither should you be challenging to them. In most cases, overseeing your homeschool is a task that these officials will see as just another task piled on top of too many others. The easier you make it for these officials to satisfy their obligations, the less trouble and interference you are likely to have from them. Be as cooperative as you can and, of course, treat them as you would like to be treated.

Most school officials sincerely believe they are trying to do the best they can to ensure that children, including yours, are being educated properly. So if you can reassure them that yours are, you will be go a long way toward preventing any problems. As the expression implies, the squeaky wheel gets the attention—your goal should be to be as "unsqueaky" as possible so that you limit the attention your homeschool receives. (Not for the reason that you are trying to hide something, but rather that the less time you have to spend legitimizing your school, the more time you have to devote to educating your kids.)

Rarely, you will encounter a school official who is subtly or blatantly hostile toward homeschool. In that case, you are likely to have problems with them. The best way to combat this is to conduct yourself in strict accordance with the legal requirements so that you don't open yourself for attack. Always get things in written form—this will ensure that such officials are more careful about adding to the actual requirements. Make sure you understand all the legal requirements so that you can conduct yourself accordingly. If local school officials get out of hand and start to challenge or impede your ability to homeschool your children, you might need to take legal action against them. This is covered in Chapter 4, "Defending Your Decision to Homeschool." Fortunately, this scenario is unlikely—in most cases, as long as you are reasonable and cooperative, you won't have any trouble with local school officials.

tip

When you have an option in oversight from local school officials, such as being able to provide standardized test scores or a portfolio, always choose the option that is more objective than subjective. Standardized tests are usually the best choice because they are not subjectively evaluated. The results of these tests are quantitative and so they can't be interpreted with a bias. This removes the potential for your homeschool to be undermined because an overseer has a bias against homeschool.

In any case, you should document every meeting you have with a school official. Take notes during the meeting and prepare a formal minutes document of your meeting after it concludes. Generally, you should provide a copy of these documents to the people you met with; should there ever be a question about what actually occurred, your case will be much stronger if you have a trail of documentation backing up your side.

tip

In addition to documenting any meetings you have with school officials, you should also keep a log of any phone conversations you have with them.

Notifying the State About Your Homeschool

All states except those in the "Least Regulation" category require that you provide some sort of notification that you are homeschooling your children. Make sure that you understand the type of notification you are required to provide. Some states have specific forms you must complete, while others just require "notification." This notification is typically due well before the school year starts or soon thereafter. Your state's regulations will tell you where, how, and when this notification is required. After you file your notification, make sure you keep a copy and can prove when and to whom you submitted it.

Documenting Legal Requirements for Your Homeschool

After you have determined the state requirements for your homeschool and understand any involvement with the local school system that is required, you should create a file with all the relevant legal documentation in it. This file should include the following documents:

- The HSLDA analysis of your state's requirements. You can print this out from the HSLDA Web site.

- A copy of your state's actual legal requirements for homeschool. While you are likely to use the HSLDA analysis to understand your state's requirements, your documentation package should include the actual legal text. You should be able to get this from your state's education office or from a local library.

- Written requirements presented to you by local school officials who will have oversight of your homeschool, if required. This should include what specifically you are required to do, who your contacts are, and when specific actions are due.

- Minutes of any meetings or records of phone calls you have with local school officials.

- Copies of any documents you submit regarding your homeschool, such as your notification to the state, along with documentation of how and when you submitted those documents.

Education makes a people easy to lead, but difficult to drive; easy to govern but impossible to enslave.
—Baron Henry Peter Brougham

Monitoring Legal Activity Regarding Homeschooling

It is a fact of life that education legislation changes frequently, and this can impact homeschooling. At any point in time, there is usually various legislative and legal activity occurring in several states that impact homeschooling in those states with the possibility of impacting it in other states as well.

Although you don't have to become a political activist when you homeschool, you should keep an eye on current activity in your state along with others to make sure that you are aware of any changes that might impact your homeschool. Homeschooling, like other rights, needs to be protected from the ever-increasing levels of government regulation and bureaucracy. To help with this, you need to be aware of what is happening.

The easiest and best way to keep informed is to participate in the HSLDA. In addition to providing information about state requirements, the HSLDA maintains a close watch on the legal activity regarding homeschooling in every state. You can get this information by visiting the HSLDA Web site (see Figure 3.7). The Legislation Watch area provides you with a summary of current legislative activity at the federal level and in each state with an assessment of how that legislation will impact homeschool (make it better, neutral, or worse).

The HSLDA is involved in many of the court cases that involve homeschooling. These cases can have significant ramifications for all homeschoolers so it is good to be aware of them. Again, you can use the HSLDA Web page and other resources to know what is happening in this area.

FIGURE 3.7

You can use the Legislation Watch section of the HSLDA Web site to keep tabs on legislative activity at the federal and state levels that might impact your homeschool.

THE ABSOLUTE MINIMUM

The good news about the legal requirements for homeschooling is that most states are quite reasonable and you can usually comply with requirements with little additional activity. When thinking about homeschooling in your state, remember the following points:

- All states have various regulations that govern education in those states, including homeschool education.

- The types of regulations you will have to deal with vary widely among the different states. At the "low" end are states that don't require you to even provide notification about your homeschool. At the "high" end are states that require you to submit to some form of oversight. In all states, homeschooling is legal and you cannot be prevented from teaching your kids at home as long as you comply with the state requirements. Using the HSLDA Web site, it is easy to determine the regulations in your state.

- In states that require some form of oversight by local school officials, you need to determine exactly what is required of you. You can do this directly with the officials who will have oversight of your homeschool. Most of these officials will be reasonable as long as you are cooperative with them.

continues

- If you live in a state that requires notification of your homeschool, make sure you file the proper paperwork by the deadline.

- Keep a legal documentation file for your homeschool that includes copies of any and all documents relating to your compliance with government regulations. In addition to helping you understand exactly what you need to do, this file will be very helpful should there ever be some sort of legal challenge to your homeschool.

- You should keep any eye on significant legislative and legal activity that might impact your homeschool. Again, the HSLDA is a great source for this information.

4

DEFENDING YOUR DECISION TO HOMESCHOOL

Homeschooling is different than the "norm" (that is, kids go to an institution to be educated), so you can expect to be challenged in various ways. The good news is that homeschooling is legal in every state of the United States and in many other places in the world. If you live in the United States. or other country where homeschooling is legal, it is highly unlikely that you will ever face a serious legal challenge to your homeschool. However, you can expect to be challenged on an informal basis about your decision to homeschool both by people who mean well and by some who don't. The purpose of this chapter is to help you understand both kinds of challenges so that you are equipped to respond to either type effectively.

Responding to Other People's Concerns About Your Decision to Homeschool

Although homeschooling has increased dramatically over the years, it is still relatively uncommon. It is human nature to at least question, and sometimes fear, the unusual, so you can expect that some people will have concerns about your decision to homeschool your children. Some of these people will voice their concerns directly to you.

There are two general types of people who might question you about your decision to homeschool your kids.

Some people will have genuine concern for your kids and might just be ignorant of the benefits of homeschooling. These people often include family and friends. Usually, you should be prepared to respond to their questions in an informative and nondefensive way. Of course you have your kids' best interests at heart and if these people have the same concern, there is common ground for discussion. In many cases, you can respond to their questions in a meaningful way to reassure their concerns and make them feel comfortable and even sanguine about homeschool. And, you can often learn things from these discussions that will help you better prepare your kids for life.

> **note**
>
> My wife and I have been homeschooling our children for almost 10 years now. It is interesting to me the difference in reaction I get when I tell people we homeschool now versus when we first started. At that time, I was more likely to receive a puzzled or pained expression and mild curiosity or hostility. Now, I usually get either a positive response or I am told that the person knows someone else who homeschools.

Others have a political or social agenda that they feel is challenged by homeschooling; these people aren't really interested in the reasons you feel homeschooling is the best option for your kids, but are more interested in defending their agendas. People in this category are usually easy to identify as they will quickly become hostile when you respond to their challenges. When you sense someone in this camp is questioning your position, you should decide if the conversation has any potential for benefit. Often, you might decide that such a person isn't really interested in a discussion and simply wants to propagandize, in which case further discussion is a waste of time. However, sometimes even people with an agenda are willing to listen to reasonable arguments, in which case you might be able to help educate them about homeschooling.

In the remainder of this section, you will see some common questions or objections you are likely to receive from either type of person. For each objection, possible responses are provided to help you better inform others about homeschooling. The objections are grouped into six general categories.

Socialization

This is definitely the most commonly expressed concern and is stated in a number of ways, such as the following:

- What about spending time with kids their own age?

- What about friends?

- How will they learn to deal with other people?

- How will they learn to deal with the real world?

- Some of my best memories are from my school days, aren't you depriving your kids of this opportunity?

- Won't your kids be too sheltered?

Although this list contains some of the more common ways this concern is expressed, it is by no means exhaustive. This class of concerns is far and away the most common you are likely to hear when people find out you are homeschooling. The ironic thing is that homeschoolers actually have better socialization opportunities than do their institutionally educated counterparts (as you'll find out in the list below).

Following are some points that you might use to respond to socialization questions:

- Kids being primarily influenced by their peer group (by spending all day with other kids their own age) isn't a good thing, actually. It amazes me that the most common cause cited for problems such as drug abuse, unwanted pregnancies, and other such issues is peer pressure.

note

When you are defending your decision to homeschool, try not to be defensive about it. The fact is that homeschooling stacks up well to all the other educational options and soundly "beats" them in my opinion. In the end, you decide that homeschooling is best for your kids. Be comfortable and confident in that decision and you will be better equipped to educate others about homeschooling. Because dealing with our kids can quickly get emotional, especially when someone challenges our decisions about our own kids, such discussions can get out of hand, especially if you aren't confident in your choice. You don't need to worry about convincing anyone that homeschooling is the best choice for you; all you should try to do is to present some of the reasons you have chosen to do so. It is up to the other person to evaluate these reasons for themselves.

And yet, many people still think that kids spending most of their time being influenced by other kids in an institutional setting is a good thing. It seems clear that less peer pressure and more "parental pressure" on kids can only be good for them. It is much better that kids be primarily influenced by their parents and families than by other kids who lack the maturity and wisdom needed to guide their development.

■ Homeschooled kids have more and more varied opportunities to interact with other people than "regular" school kids do. If you look at how typical school kids spend their days, they are basically "locked" in a situation in which the vast majority of their interaction is with kids their own age, with some of that time being unsupervised or inadequately supervised. Homeschoolers, on the other hand, have a more varied social life and spend lots of time with their parents and families, other homeschooled kids (typically of a wider age range than they deal with in regular schools), as well as adults during activities such as field trips, special projects, and so on.

■ Contrary to what many people think, homeschoolers are not isolationists. In fact, the reality is just the opposite. Effective homeschoolers spend lots of time with other people, such as with homeschool groups (Chapter 5, "Locating and Networking with Other Homeschoolers"), field trips (Chapter 13, "Planning and Taking Field Trips"), music and other activities (Chapter 14, "Incorporating Music Lessons, Sports, Service Work, and Other Experiences into Your Homeschool"), and so on.

■ The "nostalgia" objection is also false. Most people tend to remember only the "good" times at school and seem to forget all the abuse that goes on in typical school environments (teasing, taunting, bullying, cliques, and so on) even for kids who mostly fit in. Heaven help the kids who don't fit in! Homeschoolers generate plenty of their own good memories, without many of the painful and unproductive experiences of institutional school environments.

■ Because homeschoolers tend to spend more time with a variety of people (rather than mostly with kids their own age), they tend to develop better social skills than do traditionally educated kids. Most homeschoolers are more comfortable interacting with adults, older kids, and younger kids than their institutionally schooled counterparts.

■ Homeschoolers spend lots of time with their parents, especially with the parent who manages the homeschool. This is a good thing because the parent is able to help the child develop in a positive and purposeful intellectual and moral climate.

Effectiveness of Education/Qualifications to Teach

The concerns in this group are related to the effectiveness of homeschooling and generally come from two assumptions. One is that someone who doesn't have a teaching credential or education can't teach effectively. The other is that someone who does have a teaching credential or education can teach effectively. Both assumptions are not based on reality.

Let's address the first assumption by considering the following points:

- Homeschoolers outperform their counterparts on standardized tests. On average, homeschooling simply works better than institutional education does.

- Homeschoolers can learn more efficiently than institutional school kids, which results in more learning in the same or less time. Actual instruction time in most school situations can be boiled down to 2-4 hours per day when you take away all the wasted time, such as commuting, various breaks, waiting for administrative activities, and so on. Plus, homeschool's pace can be set for each student, unlike the typical classroom in which the pace is usually based on the lower end of the performance spectrum, often leaving high-performing students bored and unchallenged.

- Two of the factors most cited as being critical to successful education are the level of commitment (involvement) of the teachers to their students and the ratio of students to teachers. Homeschooling comes out way ahead on both of these counts. No one cares more about your children than you do, so you are highly motivated to ensure that they are educated well. And, your student-to-teacher ratio will be far better than any institutional situation. If you have a large family with 5 kids, your ratio is still only 5:1 while a typical public school class might have a 25:1 ratio.

- Although you are the primary teacher in your school, you aren't the source of all the information provided to your students. You use the same or better textbooks than institutional schools use. Plus, you have much better access to other resources and can take advantage of these resources more easily than traditional schools (see Chapter 7, "Planning Subjects and Obtaining Teaching Materials for a School Year").

- You can, and should, take advantage of tutors and outside classes to supplement areas in which you might not be able to teach effectively or just to broaden your children's experience (see Chapter 16).

- Homeschoolers learn to think independently. Because they aren't part of a "pack," homeschoolers tend to develop more independent thinking skills than do their school counterparts. This better prepares them to succeed in college and careers.

■ You know your students much better than any formal teacher would. This enables you to tailor your instruction more closely to each student's personality and needs better than that which might happen in a public or even private school.

The fact that someone has a teaching credential by no means guarantees that they are an effective teacher. I am sure anyone who was educated in an institutional school (as I was) can confirm this. Plus, teachers are often overloaded and don't have the time to spend making sure students are learning to their potentials, especially if a student doesn't learn well using traditional techniques.

College

The ability of kids who have been homeschooled to get into college is of concern to many. This might have been a challenge at one point, but the situation now is that many colleges allow, or actively support, homeschoolers into their programs. This is because several studies have shown that homeschoolers tend to perform well above the average in college. And, many colleges recognize that homeschoolers tend to be more mature and have less potential for "getting into trouble."

For colleges that base acceptance primarily on standardized tests, such as the SAT, homeschooling is not a problem because homeschoolers can take such tests as easily as institutionally educated kids can. And, homeschoolers tend to perform better on these exams than the average.

Most colleges that also consider high-school performance, activities, and other elements of an institutional education, allow homeschoolers to present portfolios for consideration in the application process. This gives homeschoolers as much opportunity to be accepted as any other students.

Preparing a homeschooler for college is addressed in more detail in Chapter 18, "Deciding If and When to Transition Students to Public or Private School."

Sports and Activities

This group of concerns is focused on the opportunities for kids to participate in sports and other "extracurricular" activities. The bottom line is that homeschooling actually allows kids more opportunities to participate in sports and other activities.

Most activities that are available to kids in school are also available to homeschoolers. For example, any activities that aren't tied to a specific school, such as traveling sports leagues, are available to homeschoolers. There are also many sports that are available specifically to homeschoolers, for example, basketball leagues. These leagues offer the same opportunities as school-based sports, with cheerleaders, tournaments, and all that goes with school sports.

Because homeschoolers have more flexible schedules than institutionally educated kids, they actually have more opportunities to participate in activities. For example, homeschoolers can participate in activities that occur during school hours, such as arts programs, service opportunities, and so on.

And, homeschools usually involve more activities than do institutional schools such as field trips, projects, and so on.

The only activities that might be unavailable are those that are directly tied to a specific school, such as football or baseball teams. I wrote "might be" because some schools allow homeschoolers to participate in their team sports.

Information about how you can take advantage of sports and other activities as part of your homeschool is provided in Chapters 13, 14, and 15.

Legal Concerns

Some people wonder if homeschooling is legal. The fact is that it is legal in every state in the United States as well as many other countries. Because Chapter 3 is dedicated to this topic, I won't go into any detail here. Suffice it to say that if you are familiar with the legal requirements for homeschooling in your state, this should be a very easy concern for you to address.

Public Schools

Frankly, this is one of the silliest objections to homeschooling there is. The basic concern is that people are worried about the welfare of the public school system if too many kids take advantage of alternative options. Personally, I wouldn't even dignify this concern with a response, but there are several possible responses as you can see in the following list:

- Removing kids from public schools doesn't directly affect the funding those schools receive; homeschoolers pay the same taxes that support public schools that everyone else does. In fact, removing kids from public schools improves the funding per student ratio because the same amount of funds educates fewer children. Because the effectiveness of public education is largely believed to be a result of the amount of funding provided to it (which isn't true by the way), people who have this concern should actually be glad you have removed your children from the public schools.

- Many public schools are failing to educate kids effectively. There are numerous studies that show that the effectiveness of public schools continues to decline. Why would I want my child to be part of a failing system just to support that failing system?

- Decreasing enrollment in public schools, through private schools, home-schooling, and other options, should increase the pressure of competition on those schools. Competition will have a positive impact on the public schools and should result in improvements in the public school system.

Defending Against Formal Attacks to Your Homeschool

Fortunately, it is highly unlikely that you will ever need to use the information in this section (which is why most of the chapter is devoted to defending your homeschooling decision when challenged informally). Because homeschooling is a legal and well-recognized right in all the states in the United States as well in many other countries, the odds are that you will never be in a situation where legal authorities are involved in your homeschool. This is especially true if you do your best to comply with your state's regula-tions governing homeschooling (see Chapter 3, "Determining the Legal Requirements for Homeschool in Your Area").

In rare situations, there might be some attempt at legal interference with your homeschool. Any legal challenges are most likely to come from your local public school district offi-cials. If your homeschool should be legally challenged in some way, don't attempt to resolve the case yourself. Seek legal help immediately.

tip

Besides making sure you comply with your state's requirements, documenta-tion can be your best defense in any legal situation. Always keep your homeschool well documented and maintain your documentation in an organ-ized way so that you can use it effectively should you ever need to present it.

The best source of this help will be an attorney who has experience in homeschool-ing issues. An excellent source of such help is the Home School Legal Defense Association. You can contact the HSLDA via its Web site (www.hslda.org) or by tele-phone (504-338-5600).

THE ABSOLUTE MINIMUM

You will occasionally need to defend your decision to homeschool. Most of the time, this involves answering people's questions. In very rare situations, this might involve legal action. When you defend your homeschool, keep the following points in mind:

- There are two types of "personal" challenges with which you might have to deal. One involves questions from people who are genuinely concerned about your kids; this is a good thing and you should try to help such people understand why you decided to homeschool. The other involves people who are motivated by a political or other agenda; don't feel you need to "do battle" with such people, although you might do so in order to try to educate them.

- The most commonly cited objection to homeschooling is the "socialization" issue. This issue is easily addressed with a few key points as mentioned earlier in the chapter.

- Next to socialization, the quality of the homeschool education is the most popular objection. However, homeschooling actually results in a better education than institutional schools as shown quantitatively by test results and qualitatively in other ways.

- Other concerns people might have range from legitimate (such as "what about college?") to the silly (homeschooling is bad for the public school system).

- If you should ever need help defending your homeschool from a legal challenge (which isn't likely at all), your first response should be to get legal help—contact the HSLDA immediately.

PART  II

PREPARING TO HOMESCHOOL

IN THIS CHAPTER

- Understand why networking with other homeschoolers is critical

- Connect to homeschoolers you know already

- Find a homeschool mentor

- Join formal or informal homeschool groups

- Become part of a homeschool association

- Participate in homeschool conventions, conferences, and seminars

5

LOCATING AND NETWORKING WITH OTHER HOMESCHOOLERS

While as a homeschooler, you are primarily responsible for the education of your kids, there is no reason you need to go it alone. In fact, for best results you definitely should not go it alone. Having close relationships with other homeschooling families, having an active homeschooling network, and taking advantage of homeschool associations and conventions is essential to homeschooling effectively and enjoying the process along the way.

Understanding Why a Homeschool Network Is So Important

There are many reasons you should build a network of homeschool people with whom you interact regularly:

- **Encouragement and support**. There's nothing like being able to share the joys and frustrations of homeschooling with other people who have similar experiences and who can help you deal with them.

- **Advice**. A homeschool network provides people who probably have done what you are trying to do already and who are willing to share their experiences. You can also talk over ideas you have to get the opinions and suggestions of others. When you are struggling with a decision, such as trying to find a specific book for a topic, having other people to ask can be invaluable.

- **Help with field trips, sports, and other activities**. Knowing other homeschoolers gets you in touch with various activities in which you might want to participate such as field trips, sports leagues, dance classes, orchestras, and so on. For example, you can take turns with other homeschoolers planning field trips—it isn't much harder to plan a field trip for several families than it is to plan it for one family. Having a group of homeschoolers often provides access to experiences that aren't available to just a single family. For example, many local theaters have matinee programs for schools. You can often take advantage of these programs as a homeschool group. However, because homeschool groups are typically smaller and have a more flexible schedule than do school groups, you might gain access to backstage tours and other opportunities.

- **Help finding resources you need**. Other homeschoolers can also provide advice to you about curricula, books, videos, tutors, and other resources you will need. It isn't unusual that another homeschool family is already using a resource that you are considering. You can get a recommendation about that resource and check it out for yourself before you buy it.

- **Social interaction for you and your kids—AKA fun!** Homeschoolers need friends just like other kids, and other homeschoolers are the most likely source. Having a group of homeschoolers with whom you

note

An education isn't how much you have committed to memory, or even how much you know. It's being able to differentiate between what you do know and what you don't. —Anatole France (1844–1924) interact regularly provides a pool of potential friends for your kids for home-school experiences or just for hanging out and having fun. Plus, you might want some new friends for yourself as well! Homeschoolers tend to have similar values and interests so the odds of finding friends among other home-schoolers are better than in other circles.

Connecting with Other Homeschoolers (You Probably Know Some Already)

Connecting with other homeschoolers probably won't be as hard as you imagine—it is likely that you already know several homeschoolers even if you don't know that you do. Just keep your ears and eyes open as you live your daily life and you are bound to come across homeschoolers with whom you can build relation-ships. Here are some sources from which you are likely to find other homeschoolers:

- Public libraries, especially during regular school hours
- Churches
- Your friends and family
- Places where your kids participate in activi-ties, such as dance lessons, music lessons, or sports programs
- Co-workers and other acquaintances or their spouses
- Formal homeschool groups in your area
- Homeschool conventions
- Internet Web sites connected to your state, city, or town
- Tutors (they might have some homeschool-ers as clients)

note

It's better to give than to receive and as you link up with other homeschoolers, you should do plenty of both. Remember to look for opportuni-ties to help other homeschoolers, just like others are helping you. Be sensitive when you ask for help—remember that others have their own homeschools to manage!

Finding Homeschooling Mentors

One of the best relationships that you can cultivate is with one or more homeschool mentors—a mentor is simply someone who has more experience with homeschool-ing than you do (hopefully quite a bit more), who is willing to share their experience with you. A homeschool mentor is especially important when you are just getting started. While it is my hope that this book and the resources it connects you with provide lots of information you can use to get started with your homeschool, there is no substitute for a real person as a mentor. A mentor can provide specific advice to you and can encourage you with both words and by the results they have achieved with their own children.

Ideally, your homeschool mentor will be someone with whom you already have a close personal relationship. It is possible, though, to develop a mentor relationship with someone whom you don't know well, too.

In addition to advising you, a mentor can also help you in the following ways:

- Help you connect to other homeschoolers.
- Make you aware of activities in your area that might be beneficial for your homeschool.
- Let you observe or participate in their own homeschool to see what they do; this can be especially helpful before you start your own homeschool.
- Help you get the most out of homeschool conventions in your area.
- Help you deal with local school officials if needed (assuming that your mentor deals with the same officials, of course).

When you look for a mentor, there are several characteristics you should seek.

First, look for someone who has homeschooled their own children successfully. The best way to assess this is to know the students they have taught. Look for someone whose kids you admire for their personal characteristics, academic achievements, and so on. (If someone who is homeschooling has kids that you don't admire, that person probably is not a good candidate for your mentor!)

Second, consider the person's experience. A mentor should have substantially more experience than you do, preferably they should have taught at least one child who is 3 or more years ahead of your first student. This enables them to draw from more experience when advising you.

Third, make sure the person is willing to take on this role. Being a mentor is a significant undertaking—as you will no doubt have many questions and will consume lots of his or her time. I recommend that before you start acting as if someone is your mentor, you have a specific discussion with her to determine if she is interested in having such a relationship.

Fourth, assess whether a prospective mentor is able to offer advice effectively. Just because someone has homeschooled their own kids successfully, don't assume they have the personality and abilities to be a good mentor. For example, some people can teach children very well, but can't do the same with adults.

When you locate a mentor, let me offer you some free (well, it's free because you already paid for this book) advice. Be very considerate of your mentor's time. As you well know, homeschooling requires lots of time and effort. If your mentor is currently homeschooling, they have plenty to keep busy! You need to be mindful of how much time you are consuming. For example, make sure you do your own homework before you ask questions so that you use your mentor's time efficiently. Although a mentor will be willing to help you, you shouldn't rely on that mentor completely. Your homeschool is still your responsibility; benefiting from a mentor should be only one of the sources of help from which you draw.

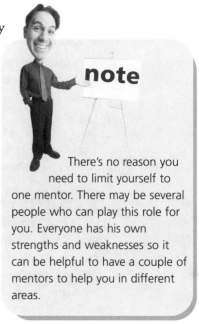

note

There's no reason you need to limit yourself to one mentor. There may be several people who can play this role for you. Everyone has his own strengths and weaknesses so it can be helpful to have a couple of mentors to help you in different areas.

Understanding and Finding Local Homeschool Groups

Connecting to or building a local homeschool group is an important aspect of homeschooling effectively. Let's take a look at what a homeschool group is and how you might participate in one.

What Are Homeschool Groups?

There are two basic kinds of homeschool groups in which you might want to participate: informal or formal.

Informal Homeschool Groups

An informal homeschool group is usually just a group of friends or acquaintances who share advice and resources without having a formal structure in place. The functions of such a group ebb and flow with times and the people currently involved. Tasks such as planning a field trip are usually shared, but there isn't a requirement that each person perform some role. Usually, one person will just take the lead for an activity and will make it available to others. The usually unsaid and unenforced expectation is that others will return the favor at some point.

Informal homeschool groups have several benefits. The biggest is that such groups are usually composed of people who are already friends so relationships among the group members are already established. And because of these friendships, group interactions are pleasant and comfortable. Again, because the relationships of the participants are already established, it is likely that they have lots in common so that activities planned for the group will likely have broad appeal. Participating in an informal group provides lots of flexibility because you won't have formal commitments over a long period of time.

This kind of group does have some disadvantages as well. Because there aren't any formal requirements for everyone to contribute, it is possible that the load won't be evenly shared. If the group consists of some people who tend not to want to take responsibility for projects, it is likely that those who are willing will take on a larger share of the work. An informal group, by its nature, isn't committed to providing you with anything in particular so you can't really count on specific things from the group. And the group's benefits to and requirements of you can vary over time. Also, because these groups tend to be formed by people who are already connected, the experiences, interests, contacts, and capabilities of those in the group will tend to be similar as well, which can be limiting.

Formal Homeschool Groups

A formal homeschool group is one that has a defined structure and organization, such as requiring membership and having officers. Participating in these groups is usually much more of a commitment because the responsibilities for specific tasks are assigned to people and members are required to perform a certain amount of work to continue as members of the group. In other words, sharing the workload is enforced. There are also more structured activities, such as meetings. Dues are usually required to cover the group's expenses.

The benefits of a formal homeschool group include the following:

- **You know what to expect**. Because the responsibilities and obligations of group members are formalized, you will know what is expected of you and what you can expect from other members.

- **Broad range of experience, skills, contacts, and so on**. Because formal groups can be composed of people who aren't necessarily from the same social sphere as you, formal groups tend to have a broader range of people involved. You will likely have a broader and more diverse homeschool network if you participate in a formal group.

- **More resources and opportunities**. Formal groups tend to provide more resources and opportunities for you. Members are required to contribute to the group, for example, being required to plan one field trip per quarter or to teach a class. This means that everyone provides something for the group so you will have more opportunities.

- **Access to classes and tutors**. Formal homeschool groups are a great way to locate and participate in classes or to find tutors for specific subjects.

- **Facilities**. Well-financed homeschool groups have a facility at which classes can be held, resources are provided, and so on. In effect, these facilities are a homeschool school building.

There are several downsides to formal homeschools group as well. First, they are formal, structured organizations with all that such entities entail. There are the usual bureaucratic obligations, such as the tasks required to keep the organization running—that is, having elections, attending meetings, administering memberships, managing money, maintaining a facility, and so on. Second, participating in a formal homeschool group requires a commitment on your part. This reduces some of the flexibility that you enjoy as a homeschooler. You'll be required to perform certain duties as a requisite to enjoying the benefits of the group.

What Kind of Homeschool Groups Do I Want to Participate In?

Every homeschooler should be part of an informal homeschool group so finding and participating in such a group really isn't an option. You will need the support, encouragement, contacts, resources, and other benefits, which you learned about earlier in this chapter, provided by such a group to homeschool effectively.

Whether you also want to participate in a formal homeschool group depends on several factors.

■ Is a formal group available to you? Although you can find or create an informal homeschool group in any area, not all areas have formal local homeschool groups. If not, you won't have that as an option.

■ What is your personality regarding formal organizations? Some people get benefits and enjoyment from participating in formal organizations while others just get annoyed.

■ What are the goals for your homeschool and what additional resources do you need to achieve those goals? If you need a lot of outside support, such as more classes taught by someone else, a formal group might be very helpful to you. If you are mostly self-sufficient, an informal group might meet all of your needs.

■ Do you know at least several homeschooling families already? If you don't have relationships with at least several other homeschoolers, you should definitely attempt to find and join a formal group to get a start building your homeschool network. As you participate in a group, you will naturally gravitate to others who have similar interests and compatible personalities; this can be a good start toward creating informal homeschool groups.

■ Where are you in your homeschooling career? Formal groups can be most helpful when you are just getting started, especially if don't already have relationships with other homeschoolers, or you are near the end of the process when you might need more outside classes and tutoring support.

Finding a Homeschool Group

How you find homeschool groups depends on the kind of groups in which you want to participate.

Finding an Informal Homeschool Group

As you identify people you know who homeschool, you will naturally become aware of the informal groups in which people you know participate. It is common that when a homeschooler finds out you are getting started, that person will invite you to various activities the group is doing. This is an excellent, and the most likely, introduction into an informal group and is the way most people get involved. Once you become involved in one group, the connections you make in that group will inevitably lead you to become aware of and connect with other groups.

If you don't get invited to other people's groups, you should "start" one on you own. It is easy enough to do so, just plan an activity for homeschoolers you know to participate in. It might be as simple as a group project or you might want to set up a field trip. Make it known that you desire to be part of an informal group and ask others if they are interested in the same. The vast majority of homeschoolers are involved in these groups so this isn't something out of the ordinary. Inviting other homeschoolers to your activities will invariably lead to you being invited to their activities.

If you don't know anyone else who homeschools (which means you probably aren't looking very hard!), you should try to find a formal group. Participating in a formal group will also lead you to finding or creating an informal group.

Finding a Formal Homeschool Group

The first place to look for a formal homeschool group is your own homeschool network, such as people you know who homeschool, your mentors, your informal group, and so on. Ask these people if they are members of a group or know of anyone who is. It is likely that someone in these circles either participates in a group or knows of one in your area.

As with most other information for which you search, the Web can be a great place to start in your search for a formal homeschool group. You can use any of the standard search pages to help you find groups that might be useful to you. As you can see in the following example, finding groups in your area can be done quickly and easily.

Suppose I live Indiana (which I do) and am looking for a homeschool group. Here is how I would go about finding one using the Web:

1. Open a **Web browser** and move to **www.google.com** or other Web search page.

2. Enter search text; try "**homeschool groups *yourstate***" where *yourstate* is the name of the state in which you live (see Figure 5.1).

FIGURE 5.1

Here, I have searched for homeschool groups in Indiana.

3. Follow the **links** on the search results page that look promising (see Figure 5.2). You will quickly find information about groups in your state, including their location, Web site addresses, email addresses, and other contact information.

FIGURE 5.2

The Homeschool World Web site is a good source of homeschool group information as you can see here.

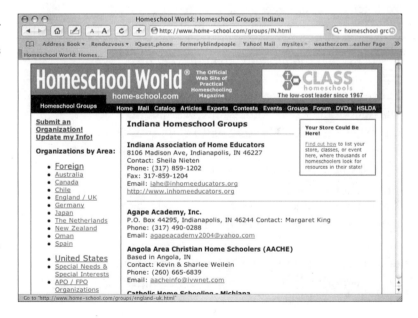

After you have identified groups that look interesting, contact the group for more information, such as what kind of group it is, when the next meeting is, what requirements to participate are, and so on.

Another option is to contact a homeschool association in your area (more about this in the next section).

Getting Involved with Homeschool Associations

Most states have a homeschool association. Most of these associations serve several purposes, such as representing the needs of homeschoolers with state government leaders, influencing the legislative process to benefit homeschooling, and to provide seminars and conventions for the homeschooling community.

A homeschool association can be an excellent resource for you in several ways.

Participating in a homeschool association can lead you to homeschoolers and homeschool groups in your area. In fact, most homeschool associations can put you in contact with groups in your area. For example, some associations divide a state into regions and have a representative for each region who maintains a list of groups in that region. These representatives can put you in touch with those groups.

A homeschool association can keep you informed about homeschool events in your state, including conventions or other special activities.

An association can keep you informed about significant legislation related to homeschooling that is being considered in your state. An association also attempts to influence such legislation for the betterment of homeschooling.

Most associations hold conventions—these conventions can be very useful to you and are discussed in more detail in the next section.

Many associations also hold seminars and other opportunities for you to learn more about homeschooling.

tip

You can use the Homeschool World Web site to find homeschool groups in your state. Use your Web browser to move to www.home-school.com/groups. Click the link for your state and you will see a page that is similar to the one shown in Figure 5.2.

note

A teacher affects eternity; he can never tell where his influence stops.
—Henry Adams

Finding a Homeschool Association

In what is probably becoming a familiar pattern to you, checking your homeschool network is one way to find out about homeschool associations in your area. (Are you starting to really see why it is so useful to have a homeschool network?) Just ask your fellow homeschoolers about any associations they participate in or of which they are aware.

And, you can use the Web to find associations in your area. You can use the same steps as you would to find homeschools, except this time search for "**homeschool association *yourstate***" where ***yourstate*** is your state. It is highly likely that the first link on the search results page will be the homeschool association for your state (see Figure 5.3). Click its link to visit its home page (see Figure 5.4).

FIGURE 5.3

If I lived in California (which I did earlier in my life), this search would have found homeschool associations in my state.

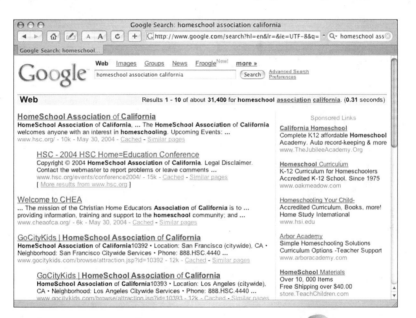

When you visit the association's homepage, you can explore all that it offers; be prepared, however, to spend some time here as most associations have quite a lot to offer.

tip

There are homeschool associations not associated with a state, but with some other region, such as part of a state or an area where several states come together.

FIGURE 5.4

As you can see on this page, homeschool associations offer lots of information, such as upcoming events, contacts, and so on, that you will find very useful.

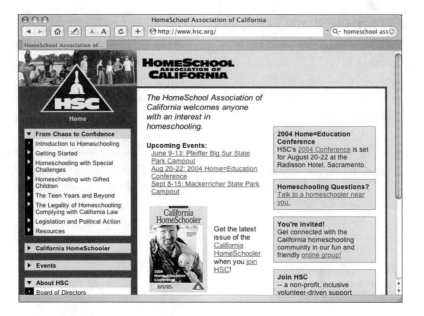

Participating in a Homeschool Association

There are several ways in which you can participate in a homeschool association, such as the following:

■ Take advantage of the information resources provided by the association. All associations provide a variety of information to you, which can be especially useful when you are getting started. For example, most publish periodicals that keep you informed about homeschooling activity in your state. Association Web sites typically have lots of "how-to" information that you can use along with contact information for homeschoolers in your area and information about homeschool events.

■ Attend homeschool conventions or seminars offered by the association (more on this in the next section).

■ Become actively involved in the association by volunteering your time to support the association's activities.

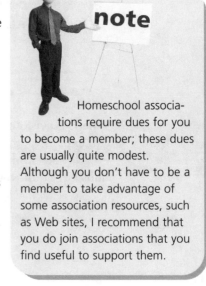

note

Homeschool associations require dues for you to become a member; these dues are usually quite modest. Although you don't have to be a member to take advantage of some association resources, such as Web sites, I recommend that you do join associations that you find useful to support them.

Participating in Homeschool Conventions, Conferences, and Seminars

Homeschool conventions, conferences, and seminars are a great way to expand both your knowledge of homeschooling and your personal homeschool network. These activities generally offer some or all of the following benefits:

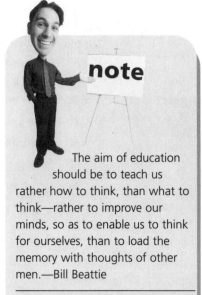

- **Seminars on specific topics**, such as teaching certain subjects or how to teach high school at home. These seminars provide very targeted information and allow you to hear from experts in various areas. Authors and publishers of homeschool resources, such as textbooks, are frequent speakers at such seminars. This can be a good way to identify resources you might want to use in your homeschool.

- **Vendor displays**. Most of these gatherings include vendor areas in which homeschool resource vendors, such as book publishers or retailers, display their offerings. This enables you to research resources "hands on" and it is a good way to compare similar resources from different sources. You can usually purchase items at these displays, typically at reduced prices (no shipping costs either!).

- **Homeschool group displays**. Often, homeschool groups will provide displays at which you can learn more about those groups.

- **Homeschool activity information**. There is usually information about homeschool activities at these gatherings, such as sports leagues, orchestras, and so on.

- **Networking opportunities**. Because these events include many homeschoolers in one place, they are a great way to build your homeschool network as you interact with exhibitors, lecturers, and attendees.

The aim of education should be to teach us rather how to think, than what to think—rather to improve our minds, so as to enable us to think for ourselves, than to load the memory with thoughts of other men.—Bill Beattie

Just a word of warning about attending a homeschool convention for the first time. You are likely to be overwhelmed at the sheer amount of information and activities available, especially if you are just getting started with homeschooling. If this happens to you, don't worry about it. Just try to get an overview of what goes on during such events and attempt to answer a specific question or two. It usually takes one or two of these events before you feel comfortable and learn how to get what you need from them. If possible, I recommend that you attend your first one with a more experienced homeschooler who will be able to "show you the ropes."

To find about upcoming homeschool conventions or other gatherings in your area, check your homeschool association's Web site or use your homeschool network (I bet you could have guessed this one!).

THE ABSOLUTE MINIMUM

Developing your own homeschool network is a very important part of homeschooling effectively for the many reasons that you learned about early in this chapter. You can build your own homeschool network by doing the following:

- Connecting with homeschoolers you already know.
- Finding a homeschool mentor.
- Participating in homeschool groups, both informal and formal.
- Becoming involved with homeschool associations.
- Attending homeschool conventions, seminars, and conferences.

6

PREPARING TO TEACH YOUR CHILDREN

After you have decided to homeschool and have started developing your homeschool network, it's time to start planning to teach. You should allow plenty of time before you are actually going to start a school year because there are lot of decisions and preparations to be made before you begin. Most homeschoolers start planning for the next school year as soon as the current one is complete. They often use the "summer" break to do the planning work needed for the next year and to gather the materials that will be needed. Over the next several chapters, you will learn about the tasks you need to accomplish before you say "School is in session."

Preparing for School

Homeschool, like traditional schools, is based on a year period of time for planning and assessment purposes; progress through a student's education is measured by grade level. There is lots of work you need to do to prepare for a school year; some of this work has to be done only once or periodically, while parts of the work are done annually or more frequently. The major tasks involved in preparing to homeschool are in the following table that includes the chapter in this book in which that task is covered.

Table 6.1   Major Tasks to Prepare to Teach

Task	When to Do It	Where It's Covered
Assess each student's education level	3-4 months before each school year	This chapter Chapter 17
Determine each student's personality and learning style	3-4 months before you start homeschooling, depending on the child's age	This chapter
Choose topics for the upcoming school year	3-4 months before each school year	Chapter 7
Design a curriculum for each topic	3-4 months before each school year	Chapter 7
Identify field trips to support your curricula	3-4 months before each school year	Chapter 7 Chapter 13
	As possible during the year	
Identify activities to support your curricula	3-4 months before each school year	Chapter 7 Chapter 14
	As possible during the year	Chapter 15
Identify outside classes or tutors for your curricula	3-6 months before each school year	Chapter 7 Chapter 16
Identify unit studies, if used	3-4 months before each school year	Chapter 7
Obtain and prepare teaching materials for the upcoming year	1-3 months before each school year	Chapter 7
Prepare a classroom	3-4 months before you start homeschooling	Chapter 8
Create and update lesson plans	1-2 months before each school year	Chapter 9
	As needed throughout the year	
Withdraw student from public school (if needed)	3-4 months before you start homeschooling	Chapter 10

A SCHOOL YEAR BY ANY OTHER NAME

Although homeschool is like "regular" school in that it is based on a school year, the definition of a year is really up to you. You can define what a school year is based on your personal preferences, such as the schedule you like to keep, vacation plans, and so on. As long as you meet your state's legal requirement regarding the number of days your students must attend school, how you schedule those days is up to you. Here are some options you can consider:

- **A traditional school year**. Homeschoolers who use this model keep to a traditional school year that starts in the late summer or early fall, has a Christmas break, has a spring break, and ends in the late spring or early summer. The summer months are off (for the students of course; homeschool managers use this "off time," which will be used for planning the next year).

- **Year-round school**. Some traditional schools use this approach, too. Instead of taking a large break during the summer, several longer breaks are taken throughout the year and school continues throughout the year.

- **Hybrid approach**. Some homeschoolers take longer breaks during the year and include a shortened summer break, which is still longer than all the other breaks during the year.

One of the great things about homeschool is that you can choose the schedule that best meets your family's needs. You can literally design your schedule the way you want it to be.

Assessing Your Students

In order to plan and teach effectively, you need to assess two fundamental aspects of each student. One is the student's current education level. The other is each student's learning style. Understanding these two factors will enable you to plan the topics you are going to teach and how you will teach those topics.

Determining Each Child's Current Education Level

The idea here is to get a relative baseline of where your child stands in terms of grade year. This will help you determine the topics you need to teach

> **tip**
>
> Speaking of breaks, another advantage of homeschooling is that you can easily plan family vacations at off-peak times for lower costs and fewer crowds. For example, you might take your summer vacation in early September when most public schools have started. You will be amazed at how much less such vacations cost and how much more fun they are because everything is less crowded.

and the resources you will use to teach those topics; because teaching materials are rated by grade, such as first grade, second grade, and so on, it's important that you know what your students' grade levels are. Figuring this out depends on how old your children are and if they are currently involved in an institutional school.

If your children are just starting their education, this task is relatively easy—your target grade level will be kindergarten. However, you need to take into account if your child can already read by the time you start your homeschool program. If a child can read relatively well, you will most likely want to consider that child as being ready for first-grade level materials when you start.

WHEN DOES SCHOOL START?

For people who decide to homeschool their kids from the beginning, it can be difficult to decide when to start a formal homeschool program. In reality, you can start as early as you'd like (see the next paragraph). However, most people start at the age when children would start attending kindergarten in their state; this is usually at 5 or 6 years old.

Homeschool actually starts as soon as you begin reading to your children. Studies show that children whose parents read to them frequently when they are very young will learn to read earlier than those who aren't read to as much. In the years when your child is an infant and toddler, read to them as much as possible. Think of this as homeschool preparatory work…

If your children are already in school, determining their relative grade levels is also easy because you know the grade level they completed most recently. However, you really shouldn't stop there. To have the best understanding of their actual grade levels, you should administer a standardized test. This will give you a better idea of your child's actual education level because the results of this test will tell you if your child is ahead of or behind the norms for his current grade level. This information will help you know if your child is ready to advance to the next grade or needs more work at the current grade level. To learn about standardized tests, see Chapter 17, "Evaluating the Progress of Your Students."

Determining Each Child's Learning Style

One of the great things about us humans is that each of us has a unique personality. One of the hard things about educating humans is that each person has a unique personality; a person's personality has a huge impact on how that person learns most effectively.

One of the best things about homeschooling is that you can tailor your homeschool program to match the individual personalities of your students. This is quite a contrast to an institutional school in which everyone in a class is taught with exactly the same methods and materials. For the kids who happen to be best taught with the institutional approach, this is fine. For those who would learn better in a different way, well, they just have to do the best they can.

Before you open your school for learning, you should take some time to understand each of your student's basic personality traits so that you can choose the kind of materials and teaching methods you should use to reach her most effectively.

Understanding the Basic Types of Personality That Impact Learning Styles

Explaining the complexities of personality types and learning styles would require a book of its own; in this brief section, I can only provide a very basic level of information on this somewhat complex topic. The good news is that you don't need to understand all the complexities involved to be able to adjust your homeschool program to the specific personality types of your children. That's because peoples' personalities can be well categorized by four general personality-type scales. When you understand where your child's personality fits on each of these scales, you will be well equipped to tailor your teaching materials and methods to that child's personality.

In the Myers-Briggs scheme, there are four basic elements of personality preferences. Each of these preferences is measured on a scale that has two "sides." Knowing where a person's tendency resides on each of these scales determines the person's overall personality type.

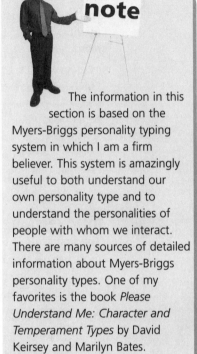

note

The information in this section is based on the Myers-Briggs personality typing system in which I am a firm believer. This system is amazingly useful to both understand our own personality type and to understand the personalities of people with whom we interact. There are many sources of detailed information about Myers-Briggs personality types. One of my favorites is the book *Please Understand Me: Character and Temperament Types* by David Keirsey and Marilyn Bates.

When dealing with personality types and preferences, people naturally think of their own types as "good" and other types as "less good." However, the purpose of personality types is not to judge or grade specific individuals, but to understand ourselves and other people better so that we can relate to one another more effectively. Or in this case, to be able to understand and teach people, namely your children, more effectively.

MORE ON PERSONALITY PREFERENCES

Notice I use the word "preference" when talking about personality types. That's because each of us has a behavior preference that is driven by our personality type. However, because we humans are so flexible and adaptable, we sometimes don't act in accordance with our own personality preferences. For example, someone who has a strong preference for introversion might realize that participating in a large social event is important for some reason and do so even though it wouldn't be tops on their list of fun things to do.

In some cases, such as institutional schools, people are taught that there are "good" and "bad" ways of learning or behaving to get rewarded. If the "good" way goes against a person's personality preferences, that person will sometimes learn to mimic the expected behavior in order to get the desired reward. Because of this, you can accurately assess someone's personality types based on one or two actions. You need to be able to either observe a person over a long period of time or use a personality test to accurately understand an individual's preferences.

Introversion Versus Extroversion

The first scale is the preference to be introverted or extroverted. Contrary to what most people think, this isn't really indicated by the amount a person talks or how "sociable" a person is. The real concept is whether the main source of a person's energy comes from within or from without themselves.

An extroverted person gains energy from external sources, such as people and other environmental stimulation. For example, an extroverted person becomes invigorated when he or she is around other people. The more extroverted a person is, the more external energy is sought. This is why extroversion is usually associated with people who talk a lot or who are the life of a party. Put an extraverted person in a roomful of people and he will naturally seek out energy from those people by interacting with them. Basically, extroverted people's focus is outside themselves because that is where their energy comes from. Put an extroverted person in a room by herself, and she will actually lose energy because of the lack of external stimulation. Put her in a room with a few other people and she will regain her normal energy level. A stereotypical example of an extroverted person is the politician or salesman who meets and greets everyone with whom they come into contact.

An introverted person gains energy from their internal world. Put an introverted person in a crowded room and that person will start losing energy. This doesn't mean that an introverted person will be unsociable, it just means that an introvert will have to expend energy to interact with other people. After a while, the introvert will get tired and will need to recharge his energy from his internal world. This is most easily done by being alone, which is why extremely introverted people tend to be viewed as loners. It isn't really that an introvert doesn't like or need to have relationships with other people, which we all need. It is just that being around people is draining to an introvert and they need to recharge by being alone frequently. A stereotypical example of an extreme introvert would be a bookworm who prefers reading to talking.

Sensing Versus Intuiting

The next scale measures the preference for sensing versus intuition.

The person who has a preference toward sensing is more focused on facts, such as those gained from direct observation using the senses (thus, the term "sensing"). Sensing people like things that "make sense" and are usually oriented more toward action than thought. A sensing person will assess his environment based on what can be seen, felt, and understood at the time. A sensing person tends to prefer that things are more direct, straightforward, and "to the point." Sensing people tend to prefer things in a linear fashion, such as stories in a straight narrative form. Sensing people tend to be focused on the here and now. As an example, a sensing person prefers a story that has a definite start, is at least somewhat grounded in reality, and has a definite end. An ultimate example of a sensing person would be the detective Sergeant Friday on the TV show *Dragnet*, whose famous line was "Just the facts, mam."

> **note**
>
> All these preferences are measured on a scale. For example, no one is perfectly introverted or perfectly extroverted. Each person has a preference toward a trait. And people have stronger or weaker preferences toward a trait. In the case of introversion or extroversion, someone who has an extreme preference toward introversion will need much more alone time to be re-energized than does someone who has only a slight preference toward introversion.

The person who has a preference toward intuition is more focused on thoughts and patterns than on specific facts about their environment. An intuitive person prefers to identify a pattern from which they can predict their environment rather than assessing the environment through their senses. Intuitive people make decisions based on their thoughts/intuitions about a situation as much as or more than whatever facts happen to be at hand at the moment. Intuitive people tend to be focused on the future. In contrast to a sensing person, an intuitive person tends to prefer a story that is complex and has fantastic elements to it. An example of an intuitive would be the character Gandalf of *The Lord of the Rings* who identified patterns from the occurrences around him.

Thinking Versus Feeling

This scale measures the preference of a person toward thinking or feeling.

A person with a thinking preference prefers things that are logical, rational, and that can be supported with valid arguments. A person with a strong thinking preference tends to make decisions based on logical arguments rather than how such decisions impact themselves or other people. People with a strong thinking preference can appear to be cold or indifferent because they are guided by logic and reason. An ultimate example of a thinking personality would be the character Spock on *Star Trek* who was totally devoted to logic and rejected all emotion.

A person with a preference toward feeling, on the other hand, prefers things that result in positive impacts on people; positive impacts are measured in terms of how something makes people feel. Because people with feeling preferences tend to be aware of and responsive to other people's emotions, they can be both pleasant to be around (because they are natural people pleasers) and very inspirational leaders. For example, the character of William Wallace in the movie *Braveheart* clearly had feeling preferences (his motivation was all about freedom for the people of Scotland).

Judging Versus Perceiving

The fourth preference is judging versus perceiving.

A person with a judging preference is one who likes things to be finished, a problem to be solved, a decision to be made, and so on. The judging preference leads people to want things closed, finished, and completed. People with a strong judging preference are more interested in the end than the journey. A businessman who is totally focused on the "bottom line" would likely have a strong judging preference.

A person with a perceiving preference is one who is more interested in the journey than the destination. They don't need to have things closed out or finished but are fine to continue a process until it no longer is interesting. The classic example of a person with a perceiving preference is an absent-minded professor who becomes totally enthralled in contemplating a problem without regard to any deadlines or other incentives to actually get it solved.

A fifth "scale" (it isn't really a scale), which is not usually included in personality typing, is the sex of the person. Although it isn't politically correct to state, there are biological and other differences between the sexes that result in the same personality preference being manifested differently in a male than it is in a female. And some preferences are typically stronger in one sex or the other. For example, in what likely isn't a surprise to you, females tend to have a much stronger feeling preference than males on average. (Some studies indicate that less than 10% of males have a strong preference toward feeling.)

Putting the Preferences Together

In formal personality typing, the four preference scales are measured and a letter representing each option is assigned to a person. The following abbreviations are commonly used:

- **Introversion versus Extroversion**. A person with a preference for introversion is given an "I" while an extrovert receives an "E."

- **Intuition versus Sensing**. An intuitive person receives an "N" (the I is already designated for Introvert) while a sensing person receives an "S."

- **Thinking versus Feeling**. I bet you can guess this one: A person with a thinking preference receives a "T" while a feeling person receives an "F."

- **Judging versus Perceiving**. People who want to close things out get a "J" while those who just enjoy the journey get a "P."

To identify a person's personality preferences, the four letters are grouped together. For example, my personality type is INTJ (which a common type for people who are authors, scientists, military strategists, and so on, but not common in the general population with less than 5% of people being INTJ). This means I have a preference toward introversion, am intuitive, prefer thinking to feeling, and do like things to be finished. Someone who is ESFP would be my opposite. They would be extroverted, prefer to base decisions on facts and sensing, be more concerned with feelings, and would be happy making progress even if the end was never reached.

In addition to the four letters, each type can also be labeled with a general description. For example, an INTJ is called a "mastermind" or "wizard"; an ESFP is called a "performer," and so on. In Table 6.2, you will see some examples of famous people

note

Remember that these are preferences and we all exhibit some characteristics from each scale. For example, even someone with a thinking preference can be quite considerate of other people's feelings. In fact, a healthy person recognizes her own personality type and realizes how her preferences can be weaknesses. For even someone with an extremely strong T preference can learn to be more considerate of other people's feelings.

If you do the math, you will see that there are 16 possible combinations of personality types (four traits with two options for each trait). This means that everyone is one of the 16 types. If you think that sounds too limited, remember that each trait is a scale of preference. Our uniqueness comes from the strength of our preferences in each area.

and their personality types. See if you can reconcile what you know about these people with the descriptions of the types I provided previously.

Table 6.2 Famous People and Their Personality Types

ISTJ-Inspector		
Harry Truman		
Queen Elizabeth	INTJ-Mastermind	
Dwight Eisenhower		
Thomas Jefferson	ESTJ-Supervisor	
Lyndon Johnson		
Elliot Ness	ENTJ-Field Marshall	
Bill Gates		
Margaret Thatcher		
ISFJ-Protector		
Jimmy Stewart		
Mother Teresa	INFJ-Counselor	
Mohandas Gandhi		
Tom Selleck	ESFJ-Provider	
George Washington		
Terry Bradshaw	ENFJ-Teacher	
Abraham Lincoln		
Payton Manning		
ISFP-Composer		
Johnny Carson		
Barbra Streisand	INFP-Seeker	
William Shakespeare		
James Harriot	ESFP-Performer	
Bob Hope		
Elvis Presley	ENFP-Journalist	
Paul Harvey		
Bill Cosby		

Table 6.2 (continued)

ISTP-Crafter	
Clint Eastwood	
Amelia Earhart	INTP-Scientist
Albert Einstein	
Carl Jung	ESTP-Promoter
Lucille Ball	
Chuck Yeager	ENTP-Inventor
Theodore Roosevelt	
Alfred Hitchcock	

Assessing a Child's Personality Preferences

To understand a child's personality preferences, you need to somehow assess your child in each of the scales. There are two primary ways to do this: observation or testing.

As you observe your children in everyday life, preferably without them knowing you are paying attention, you should be able to identify their preferences in the four personality characteristics by observing how they prefer to behave over time (again, this assessment needs to be based on a long period of observation, not just one or two choices). The following are some specific things to look for to help you assess your child's preferences on each scale:

■ The I or E preference is the easiest to determine because it is based on an obvious behavior. If your child likes to spend fairly long periods of time alone or if not alone, at least not interacting with other people, he probably has a tendency toward introversion. If your child prefers to play with others and seldom plays alone (if others are available), she likely is an extrovert.

note

Although personality preferences are developed at a very young age (some believe that these preferences are determined more by genetics—that is, we are born with our personality preferences—than any other factor), it is difficult to assess them until a child gets old enough to be able to independently choose from available options. And, some preferences are harder to determine than others. The easiest preference is introversion or extroversion because that becomes clear quite early in a child's life. The most difficult is the sensing versus intuiting preference because a person must be older before their preference on this scale becomes clearer.

- The S or N preference is the most difficult to observe and you likely won't be able to make a clear distinction about this until the child is a bit older (for example, 5 or 6). One of the most prominent characteristics of N children is that they prefer stories with fantastic elements, such as fantasy or science fiction and want to repeat those stories over and over. A sensing child, on the other hand, is more likely to prefer a straightforward adventure story. Sensing children also prefer games while intuitive children can spend lots of time just thinking about something or daydreaming.

- The T or F preference is also relatively easy to distinguish. If your child is a "people pleaser" and likes to do things just because she thinks it will make you happy, she likely has an F preference. If a child is likely to ask for a reason to have to do something and prefers to have things explained, the child likely has a T preference. Children with an F preference are likely to be interested in how events affect people while a T child is likely to be interested in how and why the event occurred. For example, if you read a story about a tornado hitting a town, an F child would likely be interested in the impact on the people in the town, while the T child would more likely be interested in how and when the tornado hit and what caused the tornado.

- The J or P preference can also be determined fairly easily. If your child likes things to be finished, he tends toward J. If your child enjoys the process of something as much or more than the results, she is likely a J. For example, if your child is driven to complete a puzzle, a J preference would be indicated. If a child enjoys working on a puzzle, but doesn't particularly care if it ever gets finished, he is likely a P.

JUDGING PREFERENCES

You can often get some idea about a child's personality preferences by observation. Following are some examples:

- Your child doesn't like to be alone. When everyone else leaves a room, the child immediately follows. Assuming the child isn't overly fearful of something, the child is likely an extrovert.

- Your child plays with other children for a while, but then will go off by himself to be alone (sometimes while playing his own game). The child is likely an introvert and needs alone time to recharge his batteries.

- Your child will start and enjoy puzzles, but gets distracted and seldom completes them. Likewise, the child starts a book, but stops in the middle and starts another one. This child likely has a perceiving preference.

- When you take your child somewhere, she likes to know where and when you are going. She also wants to know what is going to happen when you get there. This child likely has a judging preference.

- When you read your child stories about something bad happening to characters (real or not), your child is likely to become upset and worry about the characters. This child probably has a feeling preference. In contrast, if your child would rather understand how or why the bad things happened, the child probably has a thinking preference.

There are various types of tests that will measure someone's personality type more scientifically and objectively than you can do through observation. These tests are usually geared toward adults, but some are available for children. Until your child gets to age 10 or 11, I recommend that you rely on your observation to determine personality type. After that age, it can be useful to have each child take a formal personality test. Many of these can be taken online using the Internet. For example, you can go to www.advisorteam.com to take an online personality test (at press time, a basic test and results were free, but detailed analysis required a fee).

The results of such as test will determine both your child's personality type, such as ESFP, and the relative strength of his preference under each characteristic, such as how extroverted she is.

Teaching Based on Personality Preferences

Understanding your children's personality preferences will go a long way toward making you an effective teacher, especially in regard to how you teach a specific child. Here are some examples that show you what I mean.

Suppose you have a child who is introverted. This should tell you that you need to provide plenty of time for that child to learn independently; you can expect a strongly introverted child to be fairly self-directed. On the other hand, if your child is extroverted, you should spend more time interacting with that child directly, as well as arranging additional interactions through activities outside your home with other people.

tip

Extremely introverted children can really benefit from homeschooling. Introversion is often misunderstood as shyness or aloofness. When placed in an institutional setting, introverted children are often overlooked by teachers and picked on by more extroverted students. Additionally, being among lots of people all day can be extremely tiring for an introverted child.

Now suppose your child has a preference for sensing. You should expect to communicate with that child using lots of visual and audio stimulation and activity. On the other hand, if your child is more intuitive, providing opportunities for them to exercise their active imaginations will be of great benefit.

The whole point of assessing a child's personality is that you can use that information to design your homeschool program so that it plays to your child's strengths, thereby maximizing learning potential. A little bit of thinking and work in this area will go a long way to making your homeschooling experience the best that it can be.

caution

A child who has a dramatically different personality type than you do can be quite a challenge for you to teach effectively. It might be hard for you to understand such a child's motivations and behavior because they might not correspond to your own. For example, if you are intuitive and your child is sensing, you might get frustrated with your child's need to experience things to learn effectively. If you do have one or more children with personality types that are significantly different from your own (and you probably do), you should read more about your child's specific personality type along with your own to understand how you can better relate to them.

THE ABSOLUTE MINIMUM

Getting ready to homeschool takes more work than just buying a textbook and sitting down with your kids at the kitchen table. In this chapter, you learned some basic things you need to do to get ready for your homeschool.

- There are a number of tasks you need to do well before you begin a homeschool year. These include assessing your student's education level and personality, choosing topics, designing a curriculum, obtaining teaching materials, and so on.

continues

- Successfully completing these planning tasks requires that you make a good assessment of the students whom you will be teaching.

- The first step in assessing a student is to determine his or her education level. If you are starting a child's education in homeschool, this will be kindergarten or first grade. If you are transitioning a child from an institutional school, it will be the child's current grade level. For children who are past the second or third grade, you should also use a standardized test.

- One of the benefits of homeschooling is that you can tailor your child's education to her personality type and learning styles. There are a couple of ways to figure out your children's personality types: observation and testing. After you become familiar with your students' personality types, you will be able to plan their education and teach them much more effectively.

7

PLANNING SUBJECTS AND OBTAINING TEACHING MATERIALS FOR A SCHOOL YEAR

As a homeschool manager, it is up to you to select the subjects that you will teach each student during a school year. After you have selected these subjects, you need to prepare the curriculum that you will use to teach each subject (again, you will need to do this for each student, too). This involves researching the curricula that are available to you, deciding which you want to use, and obtaining any materials you need.

Choosing the Subjects You Will Teach in a School Year

In Chapter 6, "Preparing to Teach Your Children," you learned about assessing each student to determine his or her education level. This becomes your starting point for that student for the upcoming year. For example, if a student has completed the first grade level, you will be planning the second grade for the upcoming school year.

The first step in planning your school year is to select the subjects that you will be teaching each student during the upcoming year; the subjects define *what* you are going to teach. Initially, your subjects might be quite general, for example subjects like math, history, geography, science, and so on.

After you have selected the general subjects you will teach, you further refine those subjects to be more focused on a specific aspect of a subject you will be teaching, such as Ancient Egyptian History, Algebra 1, Biology, and so on.

Selecting subjects can be a bit intimidating at first. But, there are lots of resources available to you, including this book, to help you select appropriate subjects. Also keep in mind that there just aren't all that many general subjects from which you will choose, especially before a child reaches the junior high level (typically considered seventh grade).

As you contemplate the subjects you are going to teach, refer back to the legal requirements for your state (see Chapter 3, "Determining the Legal Requirements for Homeschool in Your Area"). If your state requires that specific subjects be taught, this will provide a good starting point for your selection of subjects for a specific year. Some states require specific subjects for specified grade levels, while others require that a general set of subjects be taught each year. You can refer to the HSLDA Web site for your state to determine if subject requirements are provided.

For example, consider New York's subject requirements (see Figure 7.1). As you can see in the figure, New York requires that specific subjects be taught and also provides the grades in which those subjects must be taught. All grades (K-12) must be taught the following subjects: patriotism and citizenship, substance abuse, traffic safety, and fire safety. In grades 1-6, the additional subjects required are arithmetic, reading, spelling, writing, English, geography, U.S. history, science, health, music, visual arts, and physical education. Although this is quite a list of subjects, the 1-6 grade subjects don't all have to be taught in the same year, although some of them (such as math) are likely to be taught each year at a different level.

FIGURE 7.1

Homeschoolers
in New York are
provided a set of
subjects that are
required for spe-
cific grade levels.

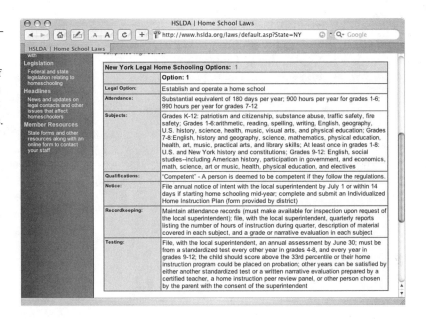

Utah is another state that requires specific subjects be taught, although the list of
subjects is not broken out by grade level, as is New York's list (see Figure 7.2).

FIGURE 7.2

Utah also
requires some
subjects to be
taught, but it
doesn't specify
the grade levels
in which those
subjects are
taught.

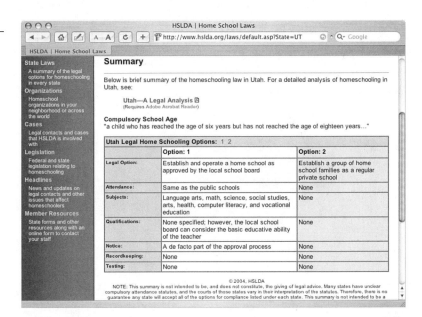

Although at first such subject requirements might seem burdensome to you, they can
actually be helpful—especially when you are just starting to homeschool because

you don't have to come up with a list of subjects from scratch. And, although these subjects are required, you are still free to choose how you teach the required subjects. The requirement is only for a general subject; your job will be to decide how you want to teach that subject and the kind of curriculum you will use to teach it.

You should consider such lists of subjects to be just what they are—basic requirements. You are free to add more subjects, and you probably will want to do so.

If your state doesn't require that you teach particular subjects, you are free to choose the topics that you believe should be taught. This can be more difficult initially, but choosing the general subjects for a school year likely won't be all that difficult for you, especially after the first year.

Table 7.1 provides a list of basic subjects by grade year that you can use as a starting point to plan a specific grade's school year.

> **tip**
>
> Just because your state doesn't have subject requirements is not a reason you can't take advantage of the subject requirements of other states. Check out some of the more regulated states' requirements to get an idea about what subjects are required. This can be a good way to build your list of subjects.

Table 7.1   Basic Subjects by Grade Level

Grade Level	Subjects
Kindergarten-2nd Grade	Reading/Phonics
	Math
	Arts
	Physical Education
3rd-5th Grade	English
	Math
	Science
	History
	Arts
	Physical Education
5th-8th Grade	English
	Math
	Science
	History/Social Studies
	Arts
	Physical Education

In addition to these basic subjects, you might want to add more subjects to suit your and your children's interests and values. For example, you might want to include Bible study on your agenda.

As you can see in the table, basic topics are general. After you have selected the basic topics, you can break them down into more detail, usually by grade level. For example, you should teach math at every grade level. Each year, the student progresses in difficulty as shown in the following progression from kindergarten through the third grade:

- Kindergarten: numbers, counting, simple addition
- First grade: simple addition and subtraction
- Second grade: multiplication, division, simple word problems
- Third grade: more advanced operations, charts, and graphs

tip

To get ideas about how you should break out general subjects for a specific year, you can research some of the curricula that are available for these topics. For example, if you want to get ideas about what kind of math you should teach at the fourth grade level, look at various fourth grade math curricula for ideas.

As the student enters the fifth and sixth grades, the topics become more complex and move into pre-algebra and algebra.

Your goal in this part of the planning process should be to develop the list of topics that you will teach each student in the coming year. A simple example is shown in Table 7.2.

Table 7.2 Example Subjects by Student and Grade Level

Student	Grade Level	Subjects
Rachel	Kindergarten	Reading/Phonics
		Math (Numbers, counting)
		Arts (Painting, drawing)
		Physical Education
		Bible study

Table 7.2   (continued)

Student	Grade Level	Subjects
Hans	3rd Grade	English (Literature, spelling, grammar)
		Math (Advanced operations, graphs, charts)
		Science (Basic life science)
		History (1700-1800 America)
		Arts (Piano lessons, basic music reading, performing arts)
		Physical Education (Soccer, baseball)
		Bible study
Jill	5th Grade	English (Literature, writing, spelling, grammar)
		Math (Pre-algebra)
		Science (Geology, astronomy)
		History/Social Studies (1700- 1800 America, geography)
		Arts (Violin lessons, ballet, performing arts)
		Physical Education (Gymnastics)
		Bible study

This list provides *what* you will teach and will provide general guidelines for the coming year.

As you plan subjects, there will be some that you can teach to children at the same time even though those children might be at different grade levels. History is a good example of this. You can choose the same general subject, such as Ancient Egypt, for each child. You can teach the subject to each child based on its own grade level. This makes preparation slightly easier, but it makes managing your classroom time much easier because you can teach more than one child at the same time. Of course, the specific way you teach that topic, such as the level and amount of work required, will be different based on the grade level of each child. This approach works for some subjects, such as history and the arts, much better than others, such as math (which is very difficult to teach to different grade levels at the same time).

tip

Teaching the same subjects to more than one child at the same time also makes activities more applicable to the group. For example, you can take field trips related to history together and each child will get something related to their particular course of study from the same activity.

The next step in the process is to break down those general guidelines into specific plans.

Building the Curricula You Will Use

Although the list of subjects is *what* you will teach, the curricula are *how* you will teach those subjects. You will need a curriculum for each subject for each student for each year.

What Is a Curriculum and Why Is It Important?

People often use the term *curriculum* for the book or books you will use to teach a subject. However, the term actually refers more generally to the methods and means you will use to teach a subject. Books are only one component of a curriculum. As you will learn in this section, there are many other aspects of a curriculum that you can use to teach more effectively.

The curricula you use are very important because they define how you will teach each subject, the coverage of that subject for a year, and the materials and means you will use as you teach. Developing a curriculum for a subject is the second most time-intensive part of planning for a school year (with lesson planning being the single task that will require the most time). It is extremely important because the effectiveness of the curriculum you create will play a major role in determining how well your children learn.

Identifying Academic Elements of a Curriculum

The core element of most curricula that you use is likely to be the academic elements; by that I mean the traditional aspects of school, such as textbooks, homework, and so on. These elements are important because they form the basis of understanding of most subjects. You can use other elements of a curriculum to build on this, but most subjects will have an academic element.

note

Genius without education is like silver in the mine.--Benjamin Franklin

You'll learn about selecting the academic elements of a curriculum in a later section in this chapter.

Identifying Experiential Elements of a Curriculum

As the old expression goes, "Experience is the best teacher." Fortunately, home-schooling enables you to make the most of this teacher by including lots of experiential elements in the curricula you use. Some of the experiential elements of a curriculum can include the following:

- **Field trips**. Field trips are a great way to make the academic part of a curriculum come alive for your students. Field trips can be included in the curriculum for almost every subject; including the obvious ones, such as history, science, and the arts; and the not-so-obvious ones, such as math. Chapter 13, "Planning and Taking Field Trips," explains how to use field trips in your homeschool in detail.

- **Music lessons, sports, service work, and other activities**. These activities add a great dimension to your homeschool experience. They teach many lessons and provide your students with the chance to put what they learn into practice in real-life situations. These activities are covered in detail in Chapter 14, "Incorporating Music Lessons, Sports, Service Work, and Other Experiences into Your Homeschool."

- **Home projects**. Projects around the house (or at someone else's house) can be an excellent way to help students exercise many of the subjects they are learning together and for a real purpose. For example, a home improvement project can teach students real-world applications of math and science. It also helps with organization and planning skills. See Chapter 15, "Incorporating Home Projects into Your Homeschool," for more information about using home projects in your homeschool.

Identifying Needs for a Tutor or Outside Classes for a Curriculum

In some cases, you might realize that you might not be qualified and have the desire to teach a specific subject. Or, you might want your children to have experiences being taught by other people. For these reasons, tutors and outside classes can be a valuable component of a subject's curriculum. In Chapter 16, " Including Tutors, Outside Classes, and Online Courses in Your Homeschool," you'll learn how to identify when you might want to take advantage of these resources and how you can go about doing so.

note

As your children advance in grade, you should expect to increase the use of tutors and outside classes, especially as they approach high school.

Understanding the Relationship Between Learning Styles and Curricula Choices

In the previous chapter, you learned about personality types and how they can impact learning styles. As you develop curricula, this knowledge becomes very useful because you can begin to tailor the curricula you use to match a child's personality type.

Suppose you have decided that one of your children is extroverted and sensing. That child will learn more effectively with lots of external stimulation rather than with a more academic approach. In this case, you can increase the use of "experience" in the curriculum and choose materials that are more active, such as interactive learning tools.

On the other hand, suppose you have an introverted child who is intuitive, has a thinking preference, and is judging (likes things to be closed out). Such a child will likely be able to learn quite well with a greater emphasis on a more academically focused curriculum with more independent learning.

When you consider personality types and learning styles, realize that these preferences are just that, *preferences*. Although you should tailor your curricula to your children's learning styles, it is best if you include some of all the elements for each child. For example, an introverted intuitive child will benefit greatly from experiences just like an extroverted child. Likewise, an extroverted child needs lots of time "in the books" to learn effectively. The point is that you should focus the primary direction of your curricula toward the child's personality type while not excluding other important elements.

Using Unit Studies

Unit studies are a special kind of curricula because they combine multiple subjects into one curriculum. You then teach all those topics by using the single unit study.

Unit studies are typically built around one topic, such as a period in history, a specific event, or even fictional or historical characters. The lessons that are built on those topics are designed to include multiple topics. For example, when my children were younger they were hugely interested in *The Little House* series by Laura Ingalls Wilder. One year, we used a unit study that was based on these books. Included in this curriculum were several topics including reading, grammar, history, and so on. Each lesson related to specific passages from one of the books.

There are a couple of benefits to unit studies.

One benefit is that they can hold some children's interest longer than dealing with subjects individually. For example, a child might not be interested in learning some aspect of math on its own, but placed in the context of something they are interested in, that same math might become much more interesting.

The other primary benefit is that you have a single source for several topics. This makes lesson planning and teaching easier and simpler because you have to deal with fewer resources.

Unit studies have a couple of drawbacks as well. One is that there aren't that many because it is difficult to package a variety of subjects into a single unit effectively. Another is that it can be difficult to find a single topic that will hold a child's attention throughout an entire year or even a substantial part of a year. For example, no matter how interested a child is in a particular topic, such as *The Little House* books, eventually, they will likely get tired of dealing with that topic, in which case the whole unit study becomes less effective.

note

As with life, variety is the spice of education. Adding variety to the subjects you teach and the curricula you use to teach those subjects will make learning more interesting and attention holding, while also making it more enjoyable for everyone. One excellent benefit of homeschooling is that there can be as much variety as you design in to it.

Developing a Curriculum

Once you have selected topics and understand the types of resources that are available to you, it's time to identify the curricula you need. As with the subjects you select, you will need a curricular for each topic for each student for the upcoming year. You should identify your needs using the subject list that you created earlier. Table 7.3 adds this information for one student to the subject table presented earlier in this chapter.

Table 7.3   Curricula Needs by Student and Grade Level

Student	Grade Level	Subjects	Curriculum Elements
Jill	5th Grade	English (Literature, writing, spelling, grammar)	Book club, grammar book, spelling book, write play script, various reading assignments (some related to 1700-1800 history and plays for field trips)
		Math (Pre-algebra)	Pre-algebra book
		Science (Geology, astronomy)	Geology text, astronomy class, field trips to museum, observatory, quarry

Table 7.3 (continued)

Student	Grade Level	Subjects	Curriculum Elements
		History/Social Studies (1700-1800 America, geography)	History text, nonfiction books from the period, living history museum field trip, vacation planning, map software
		Arts (Violin, ballet, performing arts)	Violin lessons, ballet classes and performance, field trips to local theaters
		Physical Education (Gymnastics)	Gymnastics class, conditioning program
		Bible study	Study of Genesis, Psalms

This planning will help you identify the specific materials you need to obtain, the outside resources you will use, field trips to plan, and so on. This planning will require creativity on your part and you can expect it to take some time.

This will also be an iterative process. As you start searching for resources, you will likely identify more specific curricula elements for topics; when you do, you should update your plan to make it more specific. Likewise, you might find that some of your ideas don't pan out and so you will need to adjust your plan by replacing them with ideas that do work. You should expect your curricula plan to change significantly during the planning process even up to and into the school year.

Understanding and Obtaining the Teaching Materials Available to Your Homeschool

A large element of your curricula plans is likely to be various teaching materials. These materials can include the following:

- **Books**. You are likely to need lots of books to support the various curricula you will use during each school year. These include textbooks, reading books, instructional books, references, and so on. Some of these you will probably purchase while others you will be able to borrow, either from individuals or from libraries.

- **Workbooks**. Many curricula include workbooks that contain exercises for students to complete. Workbooks can be useful up to middle school grades, such as kindergarten through fifth or sixth grade.

- **Videos and DVDs**. There are thousands of videos and DVDs that can be important elements of your curricula. These include documentaries, historical pieces, instructional videos, and so on. Some movies can also be very useful, such as some of the classic books for which movie versions have been made.

- **The Internet**. The Internet can be a very significant part of your curricula. From Web sites that provide reference material on any topic you can imagine to online courses that your students can take, you should consider Internet resources for your curricula needs. Additionally, the Internet is extremely useful in developing your curricula because of the many homeschool resources you will find there.

note

The object of education is to prepare the young to educate themselves throughout their lives.
--Robert M. Hutchins

Determining the Teaching Materials You Need

In your curriculum plan, you should identify the teaching materials you need. For example, if you refer back to Table 7.3, you will see that a number of resources will be needed for this fifth grade student such as a pre-algebra book, a history text, reading books that focus on the historical period being studied, a grammar workbook, and so on. Use your plan to make a list of materials you need for each student. This list will become your shopping list and you will be ready to start researching for the materials you want to gather.

Researching Available Materials

No matter what your teaching materials needs are, there are likely several options from which you can choose. The sheer number of possible materials, even for fairly specific subjects, might feel overwhelming to you at first. But with a little effort, you can winnow this set of possibilities down to a few that you will examine in detail.

Early in this book, you learned about building a homeschool network. Researching teaching materials is another area in which you network will be extremely valuable. Asking other homeschoolers in your network for recommendations for specific curricula needs is one of the best ways to discover

tip

When researching materials, consider materials in the same curriculum for future grade levels as well. Most curricula include teaching materials for several grade levels. If you can find a curriculum that you like that covers more than one grade level, you get the benefits of using consistent materials and there being less work for you to do in subsequent years because the choice of curriculum is already made.

what materials are available and to understand the strengths and weaknesses of those materials from the perspective of people who have actually used them. Frequently, asking about specific needs will quickly result in two or three options that you can research in more detail. Even better, you can usually borrow these resources for a short time so that you can evaluate them hands-on, which is the best kind of research you can do.

In addition to your homeschool network, there are several other sources that you will find very useful: the Internet, homeschool conventions and seminars, and homeschool publications.

On the Internet, there are thousands of Web sites for both publishers and retailers of materials that you can visit to get information about the teaching materials they offer (see Figure 7.3). For example, when researching these sites you can get extensive amounts of detail on a specific curriculum (see Figure 7.4). In Appendix B, "Homeschool Curriculum and Teaching Material Publishers and Retailers," you will find an extensive listing of these Web sites that you can use as a starting point for your own research.

FIGURE 7.3

On the Saxon Web site, you can research this publisher's offerings, which are very popular with homeschoolers.

Most homeschool conventions and seminars feature vendor display areas in which you can examine all sorts of teaching materials. This is very useful because you can often compare options for specific needs you may have. (Often, you can purchase these materials at discounted prices too.) One goal for many homeschoolers who attend these gatherings is to purchase a good portion of their teaching materials for the upcoming school year. For information that will help you locate conventions and seminars in your area, see Appendix A, "Homeschool Associations and Conventions by State."

FIGURE 7.4

This information on the Saxon fifth grade math curriculum includes the structure of each day's lesson, the number of daily lessons, and other useful information.

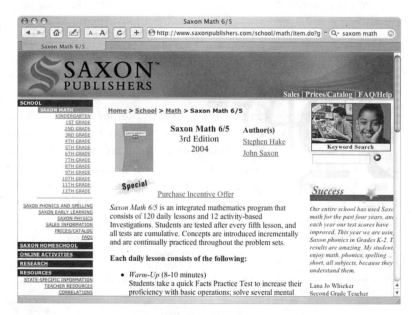

You can also get information about teaching materials via homeschool publications, both in paper (magazines and other periodicals) and online. These publications include reviews of materials and other information that you might find useful. To get started with these sources, see Appendix B.

Choosing and Obtaining Teaching Materials

As you research available materials, your goal is to choose materials that best match your needs. The following are some of the factors you should consider:

- How is the subject approached? Is the topic handled in the same way that I plan to teach it?

- Does the material teach the topic effectively?

tip

All publishers and retailers produce paper catalogs that can also be a good way to research what they offer. Simply contact the vendor or publisher to request a copy. And, once you get on mailing lists, you won't ever need to ask for a catalog again... because they will keep on coming.

- Are the materials clearly organized in a helpful way, for example in daily lessons.

- Are supporting materials, such as teacher's guides, available?

- Does the material play to my child's personality type and learning style or is it counter to them?

- Is the curriculum available for future years?

- How much does it cost?

As you make decisions, add your choices to the plan you created earlier. A partial example is shown in Table 7.4.

tip

When you select teaching materials, keep your personality type and learning style assessment of your students in mind. For example, if your standardized test results indicate that a child is performing at a very high percentile of her current grade level, you might want to get materials for the next higher grade level so the child will be challenged during the upcoming year.

Table 7.4 Teaching Materials for Subjects

Student	Grade Level	Subjects	Curriculum Elements	Teaching Materials
Emily	5th Grade	English (Literature, writing, spelling, grammar)	Book club	Borrow books to read from library as needed
			Grammar	Grammar: A Journey Through Grammar Land, Pt. 1
			Spelling	Sitton Spelling Workbook
				Sitton Spelling Source Book
			Period study (1700-1800)	American Revolution Battles and Leaders
				Founding Fathers DVD
				The Revolutionary War Memoirs of General Henry Lee
				Frontier Living: An Illustrated Guide to Pioneer Life in America

Table 7.4 (continued)

Student	Grade Level	Subjects	Curriculum Elements	Teaching Materials
		Math (Pre-algebra)	Pre-algebra	Saxon 6/5 Math Student Edition Teacher's Edition Solutions Manual Concept Posters Facts Practice Workbook

After you have developed your list of needed materials and have done the research to identify possible options, it is common that you will be able boil down the list of possibilities to one or two options. If your research leads you to one clear choice, you simply need to purchase or borrow that curriculum.

More likely, you will have two choices between which you need to decide. If that is case, go back to your research sources, again starting with your homeschool network. Try to find people who use each option so that you can compare your choices directly. If that doesn't help your decision, check out online resources, such as publisher Web sites and retail sites. If the choice still isn't clear, there probably isn't a significant difference between the options so you can make a decision based on other criteria, such as cost.

tip

Some retailers include user and other kind of reviews on their Web sites. These can be useful when you are selecting materials because the reviewers typically have actually used the materials you are researching in their own homeschool.

Although most publishers produce curricula in many subjects, don't think you need to use the same publisher's curricula for multiple subjects that you are teaching. It is common to mix and match among publishers for different subjects. You can also switch among publishers from year to year for the same subject. However, you need to be aware of any gaps or overlaps in coverage of the material between the materials from different publishers and different grade levels. Ideally, you will stick with a curriculum from a single publisher for a subject for its entire course because this gives you the most consistency from grade level to grade level. Of course, you can always supplement that curriculum with supplemental materials.

After you have decided upon materials for a subject, you need to obtain those materials. Often, you will need to purchase them. Like other things you buy, you can get the same materials from different sources. Start with the publisher's Web site to get cost information. Then explore retail sites on the Web; if you live in a larger city, you might also be able to find a bookstore that specializes in home-school materials (but it is usually easier to find specific materials on the Web). Check out Appendix B for the Web sites for some publishers and retailers that you might find useful.

With some good luck, you might be able to borrow teaching materials from someone in your home-school network. For example, another home-schooler might have the curriculum material you need, such as textbook, but currently not have a child at that grade level. This presents a good opportunity for you to borrow the material for your school year.

Your goal should be to have all of your teaching materials on hand at least a month before the school year. This will enable you to learn about your materials and get them organized for the upcoming year.

note

As you identify materials, make sure you identify any companion materials that are available. For example, some textbooks have companion workbooks, teacher's guides, and so on. You need to obtain these companion items in addition to the teaching materials themselves.

Learning About Your Teaching Materials

After you obtain the teaching materials for a subject's curriculum, you need to spend some time with those materials to get familiar with them. Specifically, examine the materials to answer the following questions:

- How is the material designed to be delivered? Is it broken out into daily lessons or larger chunks?

- How long is each session expected to take?

- What kind of work is the child expected to do?

- Do I have all supplemental materials that I need, such as the teacher's guide or student workbooks? If not, you will need to get them before the school year starts.

tip

If you have more than one child, you often can reuse materials. This is useful because it is easier on your wallet, and planning becomes simpler because you are already familiar with the materials.

- How do supplemental materials, such as a teacher's guide or answer key fit in?

- What kind of other materials will I need to use the materials? For example, are special kinds of paper needed? Do I need special writing instruments or other tools, such as rulers, compasses, and so on? Make sure you identify and obtain any materials like this before you start teaching.

- Does the material really match my expectations of it? Occasionally, especially if you haven't been able to examine materials directly, you will end up with materials that aren't what you expected. Don't hesitate to return such materials and replace them with materials that do match your needs. You should never use materials just because you have them.

- Do the materials I obtained really cover the subject or will I need to supplement the materials with materials from different sources?

Organizing and Preparing Teaching Materials for Your Homeschool

As you get familiar with your teaching materials, organize them so that you know where everything is. Here are some ideas that might help you with this task:

- Store materials for the upcoming school year grouped by student and by topic.

- Separate the materials that you will use from those used by your children.

- Make the materials that your kids will use easily accessible to them.

- When you organize the materials for a subject, keep any supplemental materials with the primary ones. Make sure that additional materials, such as special paper or tools, are also easily available when they will be needed.

- If the storage space in your classroom is limited, keep the materials you will need over the first couple of months in your active storage (you'll learn about

note

You'll learn about the kinds of storage and organization areas you need in your homeschool classroom in the next chapter.

this concept in the next chapter). Keep the other materials in your archive storage. As you move through the school year, you will need to shuffle materials so the materials you are using are readily available to you.

- Consider creating a catalog or listing of the materials you have. This is especially useful when you teach more than one child over a number of years. This list can help you keep your materials organized over a long period of time. Even after just a couple of years of homeschooling, you are likely to have quite a collection of materials and it can be hard to remember exactly what you have.

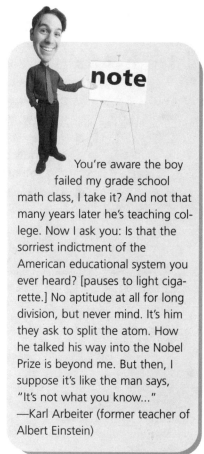

note

You're aware the boy failed my grade school math class, I take it? And not that many years later he's teaching college. Now I ask you: Is that the sorriest indictment of the American educational system you ever heard? [pauses to light cigarette.] No aptitude at all for long division, but never mind. It's him they ask to split the atom. How he talked his way into the Nobel Prize is beyond me. But then, I suppose it's like the man says, "It's not what you know..."
—Karl Arbeiter (former teacher of Albert Einstein)

THE ABSOLUTE MINIMUM

In this chapter, you learned about two of the critical tasks you need to do before each school year: choosing the subjects you will teach and obtaining the teaching materials you will use to teach those subjects.

- The subjects you choose for a year will drive the rest of your planning work. You need to identify subjects both generally, such as math, and more specifically, pre-algebra.

- After you have selected subjects, you need to figure out how you will teach those subjects. You do this by developing a curriculum for each subject.

continues

- As you build curricula, consider unit studies, which can be an interesting way to combine topics into a single unit (thus, the term *unit* studies).

- As you develop your curricula, you will break each curriculum down into more specific levels of detail. This detail will help you identify teaching materials you need to obtain (don't forget that a curriculum is more than just teaching materials; it can also include experiences and activities).

- When you know what teaching materials you need, you can research the materials available with the goal of choosing and obtaining the materials you will actually use.

- After you have obtained your teaching materials, you will need to spend some time learning about them to prepare for the upcoming school year.

- Keeping your materials well organized will help you run your homeschool more efficiently and effectively.

8

Preparing a Classroom in Your Home

To homeschool effectively, you will need some place in your home to homeschool. Ideally, you will have a room in your home that is dedicated to your homeschool. However, if you don't have such a room available to you, you shouldn't let that prevent you from homeschooling. You can homeschool effectively with a very modest classroom that might do double duty as a kitchen or dining room. Even so, you will get better results and have a more enjoyable experience if you have the space and tools dedicated to your homeschool. The good news is that developing a homeschool room is fun and doesn't have to cost a lot of money. The bad news is that, well, there isn't any bad news on this front actually.

Developing a Home Classroom

Homeschooling is, no doubt, a somewhat serious task for you; after all, it is very important as to how your children will grow and become capable adults. This requires a certain amount of discipline on your part; the place where you home-school will have an impact on the effectiveness of your efforts. If your homeschool area is too casual, it will be harder for your children to take the effort as seriously as they should.

No matter how much space you can devote to homeschooling, try to make that area as dedicated to your school as you can. Make it a real schoolroom because it will help your kids understand that you are providing them with a real education and aren't just messing around.

There are several steps you should consider when establishing and equipping your schoolroom:

- Choose a location
- Create a layout
- Create workstations
- Build a homeschool library
- Add a computer and the Internet
- Add audiovisual equipment
- Create storage and archival areas

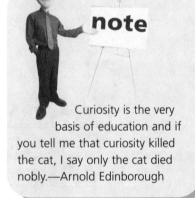

note

Curiosity is the very basis of education and if you tell me that curiosity killed the cat, I say only the cat died nobly.—Arnold Edinborough

Choosing a Location

The location of your schoolroom is important because its location has an impact on how effective you can be there. As you consider where to conduct school, ponder the following suggestions.

If you can, dedicate a room in your home to your homeschool. Almost any room will do; ideal candidates are a moderately sized bedroom, a den, a basement, or other place that is separate from the home's main living areas. There several reasons why this is the ideal situation. First, homeschooling takes a lot of room. You will have lots of materials to deal with, such as books, papers, projects, and so on. You will spend less time moving your materials around if you have enough room to store them properly; this leaves more time and energy for teaching and learning. Second, you won't have to set up and tear down at the start and end of each school day. This will also help you have more time for school itself. Third, having an area that is distinct from the living areas in your home will help your children take it more seriously and understand that when they are in the school room, it is time to work on school. Fourth, being able to isolate the schoolroom from the other living spaces in your home will make it easier to prevent distractions.

Unless you have a large home with areas you don't currently use, you likely won't have much of a choice about where to locate your homeschool; you will use a room that isn't being used for some other purpose that you can't live without. However, if you have some options regarding location, consider the following factors:

- **More space is better**. You really can't have too large an area for your school.

- **Distractions are distracting**. Homeschool kids are still kids and if your homeschool is subject to lots of outside distractions, you might have to deal with distracted students.

- **Light is important**. A room that is well lighted is obviously important; if it has lots of natural light, that can be even better (unless that light comes through lots of windows with interesting things to look at outside!).

- **Storage is king**. You will have a lot of materials to store. A room with a closet, bookshelves, or other storage areas will make it convenient to keep your homeschool materials accessible and organized.

- **Holes are inevitable**. As you homeschool, you will invariably need to post things on the walls, such as maps, posters, and so on. This will inevitably lead to some minor damage to the walls, which, fortunately, is easily repaired when your school days are done.

- **Doors are good**. If your schoolroom has doors that you can use to shut it off from the outside world, it will help your students stay focused.

Although being able to have a room dedicated to your homeschool is ideal, it isn't a requirement. You can use any area in your home for homeschool that has enough room in which you and your students can work. Some people use their dining room or other place that has at least a table at which you can work. If this is your situation, be aware that you will still need storage areas and unless you are extremely dedicated about getting everything out at the start of each day and putting it all back again at the end of the day, it will be impossible to eliminate the signs of a homeschool in that room. (For example, if you have and use a formal dining room, that isn't a good option for a homeschool.)

If you can't dedicate a room in your home to school, you will need to dedicate some area in your home for storing the books, papers, projects, and other fallout from running a homeschool.

Creating a Layout

After you have selected a location for your homeschool, create a plan for the space. You will need to account for the following features:

- **Workstations**. You will need places for your students to work and for you to teach.

- **Homeschool library**. Books? You'll have them! Your homeschool should have plenty of places to store the books you will use during a school year. Plus, you will need to accommodate reference books and other resources that you use throughout your homeschool's existence.

- **Computer area**. I strongly urge you to include a computer in your homeschool. You will need an area in which to locate it and its peripheral devices, such as a printer.

- **Audio-visual equipment**. There are many resources available on cassette, videotape, and other means. It can be helpful to have equipment to present these materials in your schoolroom.

- **Storage**. Your going to need storage—as much of it as you can carve out for your school. In addition to storing the materials you are actively using, you will need someplace to store files or materials you have already used for documentation purposes.

- **Project table**. Projects are likely to be an important part of your homeschool. If you can put a large work surface like a table in your schoolroom, you will have an easier time working on projects.

- **Couch or other comfortable sitting area**. Reading to your students and having them read to you is an important part of their education. An area where you can sit close to one another while reading makes it easier for everyone to hear, and it is just plain nice to be able to be close to your kids while you read.

note

This list of features is idealized and represents a "dream" schoolroom. You can get by with fewer features; this list provides you with a "dream" schoolroom to give you something to shoot for.

Although not required, it can be helpful if you actually draw up a plan for your schoolroom so you know where everything should go as you prepare the room. This plan can be quite simple (see Figure 8.1). Just identify the location of all the major features. If you make the room to scale, you can save yourself some work moving furniture around (it is a lot easier to move a paper desk than it is a real one!).

FIGURE 8.1

A simple plan for your home-school room will help you equip and organize it—this room has been designed for three students.

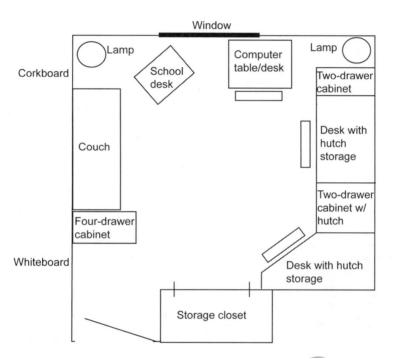

Creating Workstations

A workstation is just an overly complex term for a desk or other area where someone can work, hopefully comfortably, and with good access to the resources they need. You will need two kinds of workstations in your schoolroom: one for the teacher and one for each of the students who will be in school at the same time.

Creating Learning Stations

For any parent, one of the most common pieces of advice to help their children be serious about school work is to have a place dedicated to that work. Homeschool is no different. You should have a desk for each student in your classroom. A desk can be as simple as a small table or as elaborate as a desk/hutch combination with shelves, built-in lighting, and other niceties. Check out the usual sources for this kind of furniture, such as furniture stores, office supply stores, and school equipment suppliers. For example, you can easily find companies on the Web that sell "real" school desks for a modest price (see Figure 8.2).

tip

It usually isn't hard to find actual desks that public or other schools are discarding. These tend to be ideal for homeschool as well as usually quite cheap. To locate some of these, take advantage of your homeschool network, search for school desks on the Web, or contact a local school furniture supplier. You might also find them at yard sales.

FIGURE 8.2

School desks like these are an efficient way to add learning stations to your schoolroom.

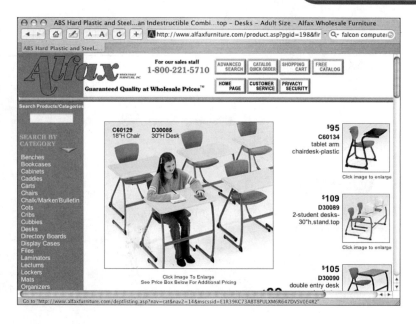

So you'll need to provide each child with his or her workstation that includes a writing surface, comfortable chair, good lighting, and hopefully, some storage for books and other materials—a desk with an overhead hutch is ideal for this (see Figure 8.3).

Creating a Teaching Station

You will also need a place to work while grading tests, planning for school, and so on. Ideally, you will include a workstation for yourself along with one for each student. If possible, use a desk with a storage hutch or other storage area so you can keep your teaching materials separate from student materials.

note

Your kids will also need to post things on the wall from time to time. Consider adding a couple of cork boards to the walls in your school room to make this easy for them to do and to save some wear and tear on your walls.

FIGURE 8.3

This desk includes drawers, an overhead hutch, and room for a computer.

In addition to a desk, you also will need to provide the space and equipment to instruct your students. There are lots of things you can use, such as a whiteboard, blackboard, easel and paper, overhead projector, and so on. You need to be able to present information to your kids, and these are ideal tools to do so.

If possible, mount a corkboard or other surface on a wall to which you can attach maps, timelines, and other things to which you will refer. (Of course, if you don't mind a few holes in the wall, you can tack stuff directly to it.)

note

I have never let my schooling interfere with my education.—Mark Twain

Building a Homeschool Library

No matter how much you take advantage of experiences, the Internet, and other nontraditional teaching tools, your homeschool will involve books, and a lot of them. You are going to need shelves to hold both the books that your students are working with during the year along with reference books you might want to keep in the school room at all times. You can't have too much room for your homeschool library and you are bound to fill up your bookshelves sooner than later! The more bookshelves you have in your schoolroom, the more convenient accessing the materials you need will be. At the least, you should provide a place for the books your students will be using in the current week or month. Ideally, you will be able to keep all the books you will need for a year in your schoolroom with current materials.

tip

Developing your home-school room can be a great home project in which you can involve your kids. They can help you design the room's layout, choose objects to go in it, and help with the work that is required to put it together. You can start homeschooling before you even have a place to home-school in…

In addition to the specific materials you will use as part of each subject's criteria, consider adding the following books to your homeschool library:

- Dictionary
- Thesaurus
- World atlas or map
- U.S. atlas or map (or other country if you live in a different one)
- Encyclopedia

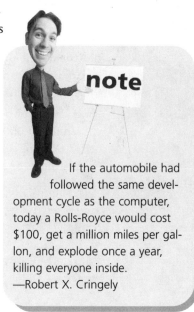

tip

If you take my advice and equip your schoolroom with a computer, you can get many of these resources in electronic format, which offers several benefits. Many of these references are also available on the Internet for free.

Adding a Computer and the Internet to Your Classroom

A computer with Internet access is essential to a homeschool for a number of reasons, including the following:

- You can access most of the reference information you will ever need, both for your students as part of the learning process, and for you to plan and conduct your homeschool.
- Enable your children to learn valuable computer skills that they will need throughout their life.
- Your students will be able to use word processing and other software to do their work.
- Use educational software, such as typing programs, electronic encyclopedias, reading games, and so on.
- Take part in online courses.
- Keep in touch with friends and family all over the world.

note

If the automobile had followed the same development cycle as the computer, today a Rolls-Royce would cost $100, get a million miles per gallon, and explode once a year, killing everyone inside.
—Robert X. Cringely

Choosing a Computer

There are two basic types of computers from which you can choose; those that run the Windows operating system and those that run the Macintosh operating system. Either type will provide everything you need for your home-school.

It is likely that the most important consideration when choosing a computer for your homeschool is cost. When it comes to buying a computer, there are two basic schools of thought regarding how much you should spend. One is to spend as much as you can afford so you get a computer that will be able to run the newest software for as long as possible. The other is to spend as little as possible and just pay for the minimum capabilities you need today, recognizing that you might have to replace the computer before too long.

Either approach will work. Most new computers will provide all the processing power you need and will be capable of running any software that you want to use in your homeschool.

A good Windows computer system can be purchased for $1,000 or less (see Figure 8.4). You can get an Apple eMac for as little as $799 or an iMac for as little as $1,299 (see Figure 8.5).

caution

Be leery of purchasing extremely low-cost computers. If there aren't hidden costs (there usually are), you might get substandard equipment that will be more trouble than it is worth in the long run. Try to stick to reputable companies; you might pay a bit more, but you are also likely to have better results.

note

If you are intimidated by all the specifications provided for most computers, you don't really need to be. The fact is that most new computers you can purchase, unless you ignore my advice and go for the cheapest ones, are quite capable of doing everything you will need to do for school. Expensive machines are needed for processor and resource intensive applications, such as video editing or high-end games.

Be aware that most computer suppliers offer educational discounts. While these are typically offered through traditional schools, some companies, such as Apple, recognize homeschools and will provide an educational discount to you as long as you provide some limited proof that you actually homeschool.

Connecting Your Classroom to the Internet

The Internet provides access to more information and other resources than you can imagine. (If you have read any of this book, you likely have noticed several references to valuable Internet resources. These are just the start.) In addition to resources you can use while teaching your children (for example, online museums, reference resources, online courses, and more), there are lots of Web sites that will help you plan and run your homeschool. Plus, the Internet enables you to communicate with other homeschoolers via email.

note

To check out Falcon computers, visit www.falcon-nw.com. To explore Macintosh computers, visit www.apple.com.

Many public libraries feature computers that you can use. Most of these have Internet access. If you can't afford to own a computer, you can still take advantage of their capabilities by visiting your local library.

FIGURE 8.4

Falcon Northwest produces excellent computers and matches them with superb support.

FIGURE 8.5

If you are a Mac fan, an eMac or iMac is an excellent choice for a home-school computer.

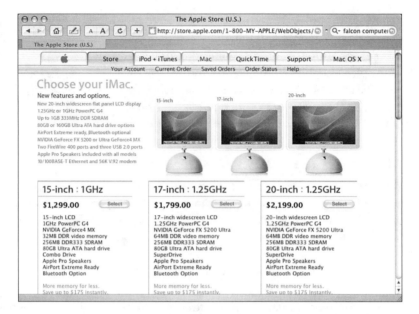

For these reasons and more, it is extremely helpful to include Internet access on the computer in your schoolroom. There are three basic ways you can connect your computer to the Internet:

- **Cable**. If you have access to cable television service in your home, the odds are that you can also take advantage of cable Internet access. This is among the fastest ways to connect, which is useful when you are accessing information rich Web sites (for example, those that include online video and interactive information) and download-ing files. Plus, your Internet connection is always active so you never have to wait for your computer to connect. Check with your cable provider to see if it offers Internet service.

note

One excellent Internet Service Provider that pro-vides access through a variety of means is Earthlink. You can con-tact Earthlink at www.earthlink. net.

Fortunately, all operating systems include a Web browser and email program so if you have a com-puter, you have these two tools already.

- **DSL**. DSL, which stands for Digital Subscriber Line (in case you were wondering), offers excellent performance over standard phone lines. While not quite as fast as cable access, it is fast enough to enable you to make full use of all Internet resources. DSL availability depends on your home's relative location to the phone infrastructure. Check with your local phone company or Internet service provider to see if DSL is available in your area.

- **Dial-up**. This method enables your computer to communicate over standard phone lines. It is available from just about every home (because just about every home has telephone service) and it is also relatively inexpensive. However, this connection method is quite slow, which means it will take a long time to download files and some of the Net's more interesting sites won't work well at all.

If you can afford the service and it is available to you, try to get cable or DSL Internet access. The payoff in usability will be well worth the cost of the service.

Stocking Your Computer with Software

There is software available that can do just about anything you can imagine. Fortunately, your software needs for a homeschool computer are relatively mild:

- A Web browser, such as Microsoft's Internet Explorer or Apple's Safari

- An email client, such as Microsoft's Outlook Express or Apple's Mail

caution

You should monitor your children's access to the Internet. Most kids won't intentionally look for problem areas, but accidents can happen. You can install filtering software on your computer that will attempt to block access to undesirable sites. However, the best protection is your watchful eye.

tip

One advanced feature you might want to consider including in your computer is a drive that is capable of creating DVDs and CDs. These drives have many purposes, including allowing your kids to create their own movie projects and audio CDs.

There are many reference resources available at no cost on the Internet. For example, you can access an online dictionary at www.dictionary.com.

- A word processor, such as Microsoft Word
- A drawing program, such as KidPix
- A typing program, such as Typing Tutor
- Educational games (there are too many to list)
- Reference software, such as dictionaries and encyclopedias

Adding Audio-Visual Equipment to Your Classroom

There are thousands of DVDs, videotapes, cassettes, and audio CDs available today that you will find valuable additions to your curriculum. These include documentaries on DVD, such as Ken Burns' seminal *The Civil War* miniseries, to instructional programs to foreign language lessons on CD. To take advantage of all these types of resources, you'll need to equip your schoolroom with the following equipment:

- Television
- VCR
- Cassette deck
- CD player
- DVD player

A good way to get the audio-only equipment is to add a boombox to your schoolroom. Of course, you probably already have a television, VCR, and DVD player in your house. You can also use these for school, but it can be more convenient to add inexpensive versions to the schoolroom. For example, you can get a small television with a built-in VCR for relatively little money.

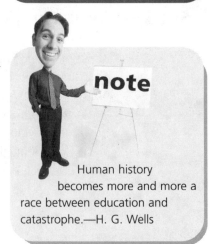

caution

You should also protect your computer from viruses and hackers by installing an anti-virus program and putting your computer behind a firewall (which is a device that keeps people on the Internet from accessing your computer without your consent).

tip

If your homeschool computer includes a DVD and CD drive, which it will likely have unless it was extremely cheap or is very old, you can use the computer to watch DVDs and listen to CDs.

note

Human history becomes more and more a race between education and catastrophe.—H. G. Wells

Creating Storage and Archive Areas

From the textbooks you include in your curricula to supporting resources such as videotapes and DVDs to completed projects and homeschool documentation, you will need to handle lots of "stuff" related to your homeschool. When designing your homeschool area, you need to include lots of storage room.

There are two basic kinds of storage you'll need to homeschool. One type is for the materials that you are using in the current school year; I call this "active storage" because you are actively using it. The other type I call "archival storage" because you use it to archive the materials that you aren't currently using.

Creating and Maintaining "Active Storage"

Your active storage areas should include the following:

- Bookshelves for textbooks, workbooks, and other printed materials
- Filing cabinets for storing current and completed assignments and tests
- Drawers for storing pencils, scissors, rulers, and other tools
- Shelves for storing supplemental materials such as DVDs and CDs
- Shelves or drawers for storing projects
- Shelves and drawers to store your teaching materials

If you have more than one student and don't live in a huge home, the battle for enough storage space is one that you will likely fight throughout your homeschool career. The key to winning this battle is to keep your homeschool well organized.

If you find yourself running low on active storage space before you get to the end of a school year, you will need to move completed work from your active storage to archival storage.

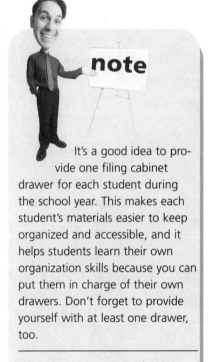

note

It's a good idea to provide one filing cabinet drawer for each student during the school year. This makes each student's materials easier to keep organized and accessible, and it helps students learn their own organization skills because you can put them in charge of their own drawers. Don't forget to provide yourself with at least one drawer, too.

Education is not received. It is achieved.—Author Unknown

Creating and Maintaining "Archival" Storage

Maintaining your homeschool documentation is very important for a number of reasons, which you will learn about in detail in Chapter 12, "Documenting Your Homeschool." In fact, you'll basically want to keep everything your children do during their homeschool career. And, you will often reuse curricula items over the span of different years so you will also keep many of the teaching materials that you acquire.

Unless you have a very large schoolroom, you probably won't want to use up active space with documentation and teaching materials that you aren't using. To store these items, you should identify an archival storage area in which you can store and organize completed school materials along with teaching materials that you won't be using during the coming school year.

Basements and attics are often good locations for this kind of storage. You typically will place items you want to archive in boxes and them place those in your archival storage area.

Like all other storage, keeping these materials well organized is important so that you can easily find them when you need them. If you store materials in boxes, label the boxes clearly.

One important factor to consider when choosing an archival storage area is the environmental conditions. For example, if you have a basement that tends to get wet or become humid, you probably don't want to store papers and books there because they can get ruined in those kinds of conditions. Similarly, be careful about what you store in an attic, where the temperature is likely to be almost as extreme as the outside. You probably don't want to store items that can be damaged by heat in your attic because in the summer time, most attics get very warm.

If you do choose an archival storage area that is subjected to some amount of moisture, consider using sealable plastic storage boxes to store your materials. While considerably more expensive than cardboard boxes, they do offer much better protection from the elements, especially from water and damp conditions.

The Absolute Minimum

A space in which to teach is an important element of your homeschool program. Hopefully, you will be able to dedicate a room to your homeschool, but you can get by with a shared space if you don't have a room you can dedicate to this purpose. As you create a homeschool space, keep the following points in mind:

- There are a number of factors you need to consider and tasks you need to do to create your homeschool space. Fortunately, this can be a fun project and doesn't have to be terribly expensive.

- Choose a location for your schoolroom that isn't subject to lots of distractions from daily life. A room with a door is ideal because you can separate it from the rest of the house.

- You'll save yourself time and effort planning the location of things in your room and then arranging your furniture and other equipment if you create a simple plan for your room on paper or on computer.

- You'll need to create a workstation for each student along with one for yourself.

- What would a school be without a library? The answer is not much. Your homeschool will need a library in which you can store and organize your teaching materials and provide references that you'll need.

- A computer with Internet access is an extremely useful addition to your homeschool room. You don't need anything really fancy; most current computers will more than meet your homeschool needs.

- To take advantage of supplemental resources, such as videos and audiocassettes, consider adding a television and boombox to your schoolroom.

- Homeschool involves lots of stuff; you'll need room to store the stuff that you are currently using and you'll need even more room to store items that you aren't using in the current year. Plus, you will need to keep most of what you have done as part of your homeschool for documentation purposes.

9

CREATING LESSON PLANS AND SCHEDULES

You've no doubt heard the expression that time is of the essence (I'm not sure what it is the essence of, but apparently, that isn't important). When it comes to having an effective homeschool, planning and managing time is indeed of the essence. Because there are so many neat and interesting things you can do in a homeschool, you'll never have enough time to do everything that you want to do. Plus, there are all the things you have to do, like making sure that you teach all the topics you have planned for a year. Planning your time effectively is critical to achieving your goals over a long school year (which actually won't seem so long once you are up to your neck in it). Two tools you can use to help you plan and manage your time are lesson plans and schedules.

What Are Lesson Plans and Why Are They Important?

A lesson plan breaks down a curriculum for a topic into "pieces" and relates those pieces to a student for a specific period of time. In other words, a lesson plan is a map that shows you how to get to your goal for a student—completing a curriculum in the allotted time, such as a school year—from where you are at the moment. Lesson planning is how to make sure that you get through all of the material you need to cover with a student within the time you have designated for this purpose.

Lesson planning is critical and is one of the most time consuming tasks you will do to both plan for an upcoming school year and conduct your school throughout the year. You use lesson plans to identify when you will be covering each part of a curriculum for each student. As you move through the year, you will use your lesson plans to measure your progress and to make adjustments for the rest of the year— should things go not quite as you had planned them.

Before you get into the detail of a lesson plan, you will need to define your school year; this tells you the overall time frame over which you need to plan. After you have done that, you can map your curricula onto the school year via the lesson plans you create.

Your starting point to develop a lesson plan is the set of subjects for each student, along with the curriculum you developed in your previous planning.

The mechanics of how you develop a lesson plan are mostly a matter of personal preference. There are several options; you should try one or more of them to see which suits your working style best:

- **A lesson plan book**. You can find these at most places where homeschooling supplies are sold. These books consist of blank, ruled pages for each day of the year. You will need one of these for each of your students.

- **A daily calendar**. If you use a paper calendar, be careful to make sure you have one that has enough room to write a substantial amount of detail in each day's space.

- **A computer calendar**. A computer calendar application is a good way to create lesson plans. In addition to making it easy to make changes as you go, you can usually share the calendar electronically so everyone can see it. You can also print out multiple copies.

note

His lack of education is more than compensated for by his keenly developed moral bankruptcy.—Woody Allen

Defining Your School Year

In order to start the process of lesson planning, you need to know how much time you are planning for; in other words, what is a school year for your homeschool?

First, determine the total number of school days in your school year.

There are two factors you need to consider when making this determination. One is the number of instructional days required by your state. Even the least-regulated states have a requirement for the minimum number of days of instruction for the school year. Typically, this is 180 days, but some states require more, some fewer. This is the minimum number of days for which you must plan. (If you don't remember where to get the minimum number of instructional days for your state, see Chapter 3, "Determining the Legal Requirements for Homeschool in Your Area.")

The other factor you need to consider is the number of days that will be required to move through the longest curriculum that you have planned for the upcoming school year. If that "longest" curriculum will require less than the minimum number of instructional days, it won't be a factor in defining your school year. If it will require more days than the minimum, its length will determine the length of your school year. For example, suppose your state requires a minimum of 180 days of instruction. When you examine your curricula for the upcoming year, you find out that one curriculum, say algebra, will require 200 days of instruction to complete. Your school year would then need to be 200 days long.

Be aware that you should expect different curricula to require different amounts of time to complete, and that many won't "come out even" with the school year. Also, some curricula aren't designed to last the entire year, but might be intended for only a couple of months of instruction. There is no requirement that you must be doing the same set of curricula for a student every school day, and the odds are that you won't. You will complete some curricula while you are still working on others. Your lessons plans might call for starting some curricula sometime during the year, say successively after you complete another one, or concurrently.

After you have determined which is more days, your state's minimum number of days of instruction or your longest curriculum, you will know the total number of days in your school year. This becomes the total number of days for which you must create lesson plans.

Planning Your School Year

After you have determined the number of days in your school year, you will need to decide how you want to achieve that number of days by planning your school year. You know that the year has 365 days available for school. You also know the number of instructional days in your school year. Now you need to decide how you will lay out those instructional days over the 365 that are available to you.

Earlier in the book, you learned that one of the nice things about homeschooling is that you can determine exactly how your school year is laid out. Although most homeschoolers generally follow a typical school year consisting of nine months of school weeks that are Monday through Friday followed by two off days—there is no reason you have to do it this way. You might want to plan longer school weeks, say Monday through Saturday, to make the school year shorter or to allow for more breaks through the year.

Speaking of breaks, the number and length of breaks you want to take during the year is another area over which you have control. Traditional schools usually have long breaks at Christmas time and in the spring with a very long break over the summer months. You might want match this general plan. Alternatively, you might want to allow for more frequent but shorter breaks during the year and skip the traditional summer vacation (the basic concept of year-round school).

As you plan your school year, make the following decisions:

- **How many and which days of the week will be school days?** In most cases, you will likely decide to have school on the five weekdays, but in some circumstances, you might want to choose something different. For example, suppose that your spouse works Tuesday through Saturday. You might want to match that schedule in your school so that all your family has the same two "off" days during the week.

- **When and how long will breaks be?** Looking at the calendar, decide when you will want school to be "closed." This includes breaks (for Christmas or vacations) and holidays that you want to take off (for example, Memorial Day).

- **When will school start?** Determine the date on which your school year will begin. In addition to defining the start of your school calendar, this determines when you need to have all your planning and preparation work completed.

> **note**
>
> When you are laying out your school year, don't forget about any family vacations you are planning. You can define your school year to make your vacations more convenient, less expensive, and less crowded. For example, you might want to plan a week or two break in late September or early October so your family can take a "summer" vacation when there are fewer people doing so. Of course, you can also plan your vacation so that it is actually part of your school year, too (see Chapter 13, "Planning and Taking Field Trips").

WHAT'S A SCHOOL DAY?

How many hours school will require each day should depend on the curricula you have defined for each day. Some days will be longer and some might be shorter depending on that day's lesson plan. Like traditional schools, school days will tend to be shorter for early grade levels and gradually get longer as topics increase in number and complexity.

Be aware that most states define a minimum number of "instructional hours" for a school day. A typical number is three hours. This might seem odd to you because most schools have days that consist of more than three hours. But remember that days in traditional schools are filled with a lot more than just instructional hours. There is the time to get to and from school, the administrative activities (taking roll for example), the time between classes, recess and other breaks, lunch, and so on. The actual number of hours a student spends "learning" in a traditional school is usually quite a bit fewer than the total number of hours in a school day.

Homeschooling can be much more efficient than a traditional school because you can eliminate much of the time that is wasted in traditional schools. You may find that you can get a lot more accomplished in fewer hours than can be done in a traditional school.

Even so, you need to make sure that you can document that you have spent the required number of instructional hours on the required number of days. It is highly likely that you will spend more time than is required, but you need to be able to demonstrate that you have met at least the minimum requirements. You will learn how to document your school days later in this book.

Creating and Maintaining a Homeschool Calendar and Schedule

Now that you know how many days of instruction (school days) you will have in a year, when the school year will start, and when the breaks will be, you are ready to create your homeschool's calendar.

Your homeschool calendar is important for a couple of reasons. In addition to helping you determine which days of the year you will be having school, you will need some way to keep track of all the activities that are inevitably part of your family's life, both related to school and not. These include field trips, music lessons, sports, and so on.

How you maintain a calendar is up to you. You might want to use a paper calendar or you might prefer an electronic one. How you do maintain a calendar doesn't matter as much as making sure that you create and maintain one.

note

The real object of education is to have a man in the condition of continually asking questions.—Bishop Creighton

Even if you prefer an electronic calendar, which offers several benefits such as the ease with which you can make changes, you should create and post a paper calendar so that everyone in the family has access to it. Of course, if yours is a high-tech family, you can also make an electronic calendar available to everyone as well by posting it on the Web.

Taking your calendar of choice, start on the first school day of the year and move through the remainder of the year marking each day that will be a school day until you have accounted for the total number of school days that you have determined to be required for the school year.

Flexibility is important. It is a good idea to include several more days of school than you actually plan to do so that you can make up any days on which school doesn't happen as planned. In traditional schools, these are often called "snow days." Although you won't need to skip school because of snow, there are other reasons that you might need to skip school on a day on which you had planned to have it. If you have some of these days built-in, you can skip them when needed without throwing your entire plan off. If you don't end up using them, you can always stop school earlier than planned—no one will complain about that!

Creating Lesson Plans

After you have identified the school days in your school year, you will be ready to start planning what you will be doing on each of those days. This is where lesson planning comes in to the equation.

You will need to create a lesson plan for each student for each school day. This plan determines what you will teach and when you will teach it throughout the year.

As you start to create a lesson plan, refer back to your list of subjects and curricula for each student for the coming year; an excerpt of a sample subject/curriculum list is shown in Table 9.1.

Table 9.1 Extract of a Subject/Curriculum List for a Student

Student	Grade Level	Subjects	Curriculum Elements	Teaching Materials
Grace	5th Grade	English (Literature, writing, spelling, grammar)	Book club	Borrow books to read from library as needed
			Grammar	Grammar: A Journey Through Grammar Land, Pt. 1

Table 9.1 (continued)

Student	Grade Level	Subjects	Curriculum Elements	Teaching Materials
			Spelling	Sitton Spelling Workbook
				Sitton Spelling Source Book
			Period study (1700-1800)	American Revolution Battles and Leaders
				Founding Fathers DVD
				The Revolutionary War Memoirs of General Henry Lee
				Frontier Living: An Illustrated Guide to Pioneer Life in America
		Math	Math— 5th Grade Level	Saxon 6/5 Math
				Student Edition
				Teacher's Edition
				Solutions Manual
				Concept Posters
				Facts Practice Workbook

In this example, two subjects are shown: English and Math. English has several curriculum elements for which you have to plan while Math has only one.

Depending on the specific curriculum you are planning and the materials you are using, lesson planning can be relatively simple or a bit more complex.

For example, as shown in the previous table, you can see that the math curriculum for the student for the upcoming year is pre-algebra and that the teaching materials for that subject have been selected. Usually, a formal curriculum (such as Saxon Math) will already be broken out into a number of lessons. Most of the time, these lessons are designed to correspond with a school day (see Figure 9.1). When a curriculum is provided like this, lesson planning is much simpler because you just map each lesson in the curriculum onto the day on which you will teach it.

In other cases, such as the English curriculum shown in Table 9.1, there will be a number of elements that make up that curriculum and some of the teaching materials you use won't be already divided into convenient lessons. In these situations, lesson planning will require a bit more thought on your part. You will have to organize and plan the elements of the curriculum (planning the lessons) so that you are able to get the student through all of them during the school year.

FIGURE 9.1

The first page of this table of contents for a Saxon Math curriculum shows that it is divided into many lessons (120 total) that are targeted to be delivered each school day.

Choose the first curriculum for which you will create a lesson plan and get to work. Pick the simplest curriculum first, such as one with a single element with teaching materials that are already organized into lessons. Get out your homeschool calendar and begin to plan each lesson of that curriculum for a specific day.

Creating a Lesson Plan: A Simple Example

As a simple example, suppose I am developing the lesson plan for the student shown in Table 9.1. Further, suppose I am starting with the Math curriculum because I know that the teaching materials (Saxon in this example) are already laid out in lessons. Creating a lesson plan involves identifying the specific lesson for each day of the school year.

To start, I would open my lesson plan book or electronic tool and begin with the first day of the school year (for this example, I am starting school on September 6) on which I will be teaching the Math curriculum for this student. I would identify a lesson from the Math curriculum for each day. The resulting lesson plan might look something like Table 9.2.

Table 9.2   Example of a Lesson Plan for the Math Curriculum for a Student

Day	Date	Subject/ Curriculum	Lesson Number and Topic	Estimated Time
Mon	September 6	Math	Lesson 1, Sequences and Digits	60 min
Tue	September 7	Math	Lesson 2, Even and Odd Numbers	60 min
Wed	September 8	Math	Lesson 3, Using Money to Illustrate Place Value	60 min
Thu	September 9	Math	Lesson 4, Comparing Whole Numbers	60 min
Fri	September 10	Math	Lesson 5, Naming Whole Numbers Through Hundreds, Dollars, and Cents	60 min
Mon	September 13	Math	Lesson 6, Adding One-Digit Numbers, Using the Addition Algorithm	60 min
Tue	September 14	Math	Lesson 7, Writing and Comparing Numbers Though Hundred Thousands, Ordinal Numbers	60 min
Wed	September 15	Math	None, field trip	N/A
Thu	September 16	Math	Lesson 8, Subtraction Facts, Fact Families	60 min
Fri	September 17	Math	Test on Lessons 1-8	45 min

The process would be continued throughout the school year until all the lessons in this curriculum are accounted for by being planned for a specific day.

While the example lays out a lesson each day, there will likely be some gaps in this pattern through the year. For example, some days might be consumed with other activities, such as field trip, in which case the math lesson might not be done because there wouldn't be time for it. In Table 9.2, you can see that on September 15, a field trip has been planned and so no math lesson will be presented for that day.

Creating a Lesson Plan: A More Complex Example

Now let's take a look at how you might develop a lesson plan for a curriculum that isn't quite as cut and dried as the Math example. For this example, we'll do some lesson planning for the English curriculum, part of which is shown in Table 9.3.

Table 9.3   Part of an English Subject/Curriculum List for a Student

Student	Grade Level	Subjects	Curriculum Elements	Teaching Materials
Grace	5th Grade	English (Literature, writing, spelling, grammar)	Book club	Borrow books to read from library as needed
			Grammar	Grammar: Grammar Basics
			Spelling	Spelling Workbook
				Spelling Source Book

In this extract, there are three curriculum elements of the subject, which is English. Each of the elements needs to be planned. Some elements, like Grammar, might include teaching materials that provide lessons while others, for example the Book club, might not.

The lesson plan for English for this student would need to address each of these elements by creating the "lessons" associated with those elements with each school day. The resulting lesson plan might look something like Table 9.4.

Table 9.4   Example of a Lesson Plan for the English Curriculum for a Student

Day	Date	Subject/ Curriculum	Lesson Number and Topic	Estimated Time
Mon	September 6	English/Grammar	Lesson 1, Grammar Concepts	30 min
Mon	September 6	English/Spelling	Words to Live By: Week 1, Lesson 1	30 min
Mon	September 6	English/Literature (Reading for book club)	The Chronicles of Narnia, Chapters 1-2	30 min
Tue	September 7	English/Grammar	Lesson 2, Parts of Speech	30 min
Tue	September 7	English/Spelling	Words to Live By: Week 1, Lesson 2	30 min
Tue	September 7	English/Literature (Reading for book club)	The Chronicles of Narnia, Chapters 3-4	30 min
Wed	September 8	English/Grammar	Lesson 3, More on Parts of Speech	30 min
Wed	September 8	English/Spelling	Words to Live By: Week 1, Lesson 3	30 min
Wed	September 8	English/Literature (Reading for book club)	The Chronicles of Narnia, Chapters 5-6	30 min

Table 9.4   (continued)

Day	Date	Subject/ Curriculum	Lesson Number and Topic	Estimated Time
...				
Wed	September 15	English/Grammar	None, field trip	N/A
Wed	September 15	English/Spelling	None, field trip	N/A
Wed	September 15	English/Literature (Reading for book club)	None, field trip	N/A

This process would be continued until all the curriculum's elements were mapped onto the days on which they will be taught.

Putting Together All the Lesson Plans for a Student

It is a good idea to include lots of field trips, sports, music lessons, and other activities into your homeschool program. As you do so, you will need to account for these activities in your lesson plans as well. In the examples in the previous sections, you can see that a field trip has been scheduled for September 15. On that day, there are no lessons planned for Math or English. However, you would expect to have follow-up lesson plans if you were going to have student's write a report on the experience; or, you might have them do preparation work before the field trip, such as reading about some of the processes used in a factory you will be visiting. In that case, the preparation activities would also appear on a lesson plan.

You continue creating lesson plans for each subject and curriculum for a student until you have accounted for all of the curricula for all of the subjects.

Next, you need to put all of your lessons plans together to form the set of lessons plans for that student for the year. This involves combining the lesson plans by school day so you generate a complete set of plans for each day of the school year. Combining the Math and English example lesson plans from the previous section would look something like Table 9.5.

note

The lesson plans used as examples in this chapter are very simplified and only account for one full subject and parts of another. Your lesson plans will probably need to cover three to seven subjects per day.

Table 9.5   Example of a Combined Lesson Plan for Math and English for a Student

Day	Date	Subject/ Curriculum	Lesson Number and Topic	Estimated Time
Mon	September 6	Math	Lesson 1, Sequences and Digits	60 min
Mon	September 6	English/Grammar	Lesson 1, Grammar Concepts	30 min
Mon	September 6	English/Spelling	Words to Live By: Week 1, Lesson 1	30 min
Mon	September 6	English/Literature (Reading for book club)	The Chronicles of Narnia, Chapters 1-2	30 min
Tue	September 7	Math	Lesson 2, Even and Odd Numbers	60 min
Tue	September 7	English/Grammar	Lesson 2, Parts of Speech	30 min
Tue	September 7	English/Spelling	Words to Live By: Week 1, Lesson 2	30 min
Tue	September 7	English/Literature (Reading for book club)	The Chronicles of Narnia, Chapters 3-4	30 min
Wed	September 8	Math	Lesson 3, Using Money to Illustrate Place Value	60 min
Wed	September 8	English/Grammar	Lesson 3, More on Parts of Speech	30 min
Wed	September 8	English/Spelling	Words to Live By: Week 1, Lesson 3	30 min
Wed	September 8	English/Literature (Reading for book club)	The Chronicles of Narnia, Chapters 5-6	30 min
...				
Wed	September 15	Field Trip to Acme Factory	Field Trip	7 hours
Wed	September 15	Math	None, field trip	N/A
Wed	September 15	English/Grammar	None, field trip	N/A
Wed	September 15	English/Spelling	None, field trip	N/A
Wed	September 15	English/Literature (Reading for book club)	None, field trip	N/A

As you combine lessons plans for the various curricula, it is likely that you will need to make adjustments to account for too much or too little class time, an activity such as a field trip, or other interactions among the curricula plans. For example, you might discover that the expected time for your lessons on a day requires too many hours or doesn't require enough to qualify as a day of instruction. You should expect to adapt to changes like this as you build the full set of lessons plans for a student.

Continue this process of combining and refining lesson plans until you have an entire school year's worth of daily plans laid out for each student.

If this seems like a lot of hard work, that's because it is. Planning an entire year of school for one student takes a lot of time, effort, and thought. If you need to do this for more than one student, the job only gets bigger. However, creating lesson plans is critical to being an effective homeschooler. If your first lesson plans seem to take forever to develop, don't worry, you'll get much faster with experience because you will develop a good sense of what you need to do for specific topics.

note

If you are teaching more than one student at a time, which is likely to be the case, you will also need to account for the effect of one student's lesson plans on another student. For example, one student's activity on a day might impact the ability of another student to get through the allotted lessons.

AN OPTIONAL APPROACH

Although it is usually a good idea to plan an entire school year at a time, that might not be the way you want to approach this. Some homeschoolers do detailed lesson plans based on shorter periods of time, such as a month or a week. In that case, the curricula are divided up into larger chunks, such as the number of lessons that need to be completed per month, to ensure that the entire curriculum is completed during the school year. Then, detailed lesson plans are created for only that month's worth of lessons (or week's worth if weekly lesson plans are used).

This approach breaks the planning process into smaller chunks that are spread throughout the year, depending on how lesson plans are being generated. One downside is that you will be creating lesson plans during the school year rather just updating existing plans, which can add more work to an already busy schedule. If you develop lesson plans for an entire school year, you typically do your lesson planning during one of your breaks.

Updating Lesson Plans

No matter how well you plan, it is inevitable that things will change as you start to carry out your plan. You might find additional activities that you want to do. Or, lessons might take less time or more time than you planned. Occasionally, the teacher might be ill (sometimes a spouse or older student can substitute teach, but sometimes not) and the planned activities for a day don't get done. As you move through a school year, you will have to make adjustments to your lesson plans to ensure that any unanticipated events don't prevent you from reaching your goals. You should set aside a time each week, such as one of your "weekend" days to review and update your lesson plans for the upcoming week.

Besides telling you what you need to do each day, your lesson plans are also a critical tool to document your progress and to help you manage your homeschool effectively. You'll learn more about using and maintaining lesson plans in Part 3, "Managing a Homeschool," of this book.

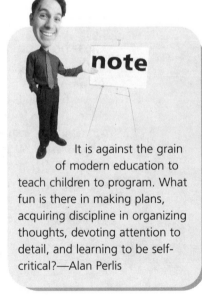

tip

As you create lesson plans, it is a good idea to schedule in some slack days so that you can use these days to catch up in areas in which you might fall behind. If you are still on track when you reach a slack day on the schedule, you can either move the slack day to later in the year, in case you need it then, or take a day off.

note

It is against the grain of modern education to teach children to program. What fun is there in making plans, acquiring discipline in organizing thoughts, devoting attention to detail, and learning to be self-critical?—Alan Perlis

THE ABSOLUTE MINIMUM

Planning your time effectively is a critical element of homeschooling. You do this by creating lesson plans that guide you through the school year. These plans define the activities you need to accomplish each day of the year to complete all of the material you have identified for each subject you are going to teach during the year. Creating lesson plans is the single most important planning activity that you need to do for your homeschool. The detailed planning activities for a school year include the following tasks:

- Define your school year
- Plan your school year
- Create and maintain a homeschool calendar
- Create lesson plans
- Update lesson plans as the school year unfolds

10

TRANSITIONING A CHILD FROM PUBLIC OR PRIVATE SCHOOL TO HOMESCHOOL

If you start your kids' education in homeschool, good for you. (And by the way, you can skip this chapter.) If your kids are already in a public or private school and you have decided to change to homeschooling, good for you, too! Starting homeschooling with children that have already been in public or private school can be very similar to starting kids out in homeschool, or it can be a bit different depending on your specific situation. In this chapter, we'll take a look at some of the possibilities.

Understanding the Reasons for Transitioning from "Regular" School to Homeschool

If your child is already in school and you have decided to homeschool him or her, your reasons for doing so probably fall into one of the following two categories:

- **My child is not doing well in school**. For a variety of reasons, some children just don't do well in institutional schools. Sometimes, the school itself is just not very good for a variety of reasons. Or, it may be that your child's personality and capabilities just don't match an institutional school environment well. While it might be more common to think that the child has a problem, it might be just the opposite. It might be because a child is just not challenged enough to remain interested. After all, schools are generally geared toward the "average" or just below average students. If you have an exceptional student, it is possible that your child is just not interested because the pace is too slow. Children can also have problems in school for social reasons, like not fitting in or getting mixed up with kids who don't have the same values you do. Deciding to homeschool a child who is struggling in an institutional school might just be the best decision you have ever made.

- **My child is doing well in school, but homeschooling will be better for our family**. You might know people who have homeschooled their children, or you might have thought about all the benefits of homeschooling and decided that it is for you and your children. Homeschooling offers many benefits for kids, even if they do well in institutional schools.

Both situations can lead to certain challenges for you as you transition a student from institutional schools to homeschool. The specific challenges you will face depend on the personality of the child you are transitioning and the reasons you have decided to homeschool. Some possible challenges and suggestions for dealing with them are described later in this chapter.

Withdrawing a Child from Public School

If your child attends public school, you will need to formally withdraw that student from the public school system so that the school knows it is no longer responsible for your child. If you fail to do this, you might have to deal with truancy issues when your child fails to attend school.

How you formally withdraw a child from a public school varies by school district. In general, you should submit a formal letter to the school system's superintendent that informs the school district of your intention to withdraw your student. In most cases, you don't need to go into lots of detail. Just a simple statement that you are withdrawing your student from the school district will suffice. You should also include the option you are exercising, which legally allows you to withdraw your child. This will make it clear to the school district that you understand exactly what you are doing and that you also understand you are within your legal rights to do so. Ideally, you should quote the part of your state's education regulations that allow you to homeschool. A sample letter is shown in Figure 10.1.

tip

Although most public school administrators will be reasonable with you as long as you comply with the law, you might run into one who is not. It is in those situations that you need to make sure you fully understand your state's education regulations in regards to homeschool. Public officials can sometimes be intimidating; knowing your rights will provide you with the confidence you need to be able to handle them. See Chapter 3, "Determining the Legal Requirements for Homeschool in Your Area," for information about determining what your state's educational regulations are.

FIGURE 10.1

A formal letter to withdraw a student from public school doesn't have to be complicated.

Before you create and submit such a letter, you should check with your public school district to make sure you understand what its specific requirements are so that you can make sure that you do things "by the book." For example, you might be required to complete and submit some type of form to be able to legally withdraw your child. Be as compliant as you can to make the transition easier on everyone.

Withdrawing a Child from Private School

When it comes to withdrawing a child from a private school, you don't have any legal obligations to explain what you are doing, unless you have some sort of contract that specifies how you can withdraw your student from the school. If you are withdrawing a student during a school year, it is likely that you will have to live up to any financial commitments you have made to the school for that school year.

> **note**
>
> Even if you live in a state that doesn't require that you provide notification when you homeschool, you should still submit a withdrawal letter to the public school from which your child is withdrawing. This will help prevent any interference from the school, whether that interference is well intentioned or not.

Although not required, you should formally inform the private school about your decision as well so there is no ambiguity about the situation. Obviously, when you are dealing with a private school, you don't need to justify yourself with regards to your state's education regulations. But, you can still avoid potential problems by being clear and upfront about your intentions. Besides, it is the appropriate thing to do, in case the school is holding a slot open for your child.

Helping a Student Make the Change from Public or Private School to Homeschool

The degree of difficulty your child experiences in his or her transition from institutional schools will depend largely on the child's age and personality and the relationship you and your child have. The younger the child is when you make the transition, the fewer issues you are likely to deal with. Similarly, if you and your child have a good, close relationship, it is less likely that you or your child will have problems. If your child is having behavior problems, particularly those associated with a group (such as hanging around with the wrong crowd), you are more likely to have issues when transitioning that child to home-school.

Although there is no way to account for every possible issue your child might have with a transition to homeschool, the remainder of this section explains some of the more common issues and suggests some things you can do to deal with them.

Dealing with Social Anxiety

The most common issue your child is likely to have with being homeschooled comes under a catchall of what I call "social anxiety." The basic root of this comes from children's fears that they will no longer have any contact with other kids or that they will no longer be able to have their friends. (In some cases, like when your child has been associating with kids that you prefer they don't, this is one of the reasons you are homeschooling!)

If your child is older and has been in institutional schools for a long time, peer pressure has likely taught your child to think in "group-think." In this mode of thinking, whatever the crowd is doing is "in" and whatever they aren't doing isn't in (or "cool" to use another word for it). You child might express this as "I don't want to be weird." While homeschooling is growing rapidly, it is still possible that your child doesn't know many homeschoolers and might consider people who homeschool to be weird (translated different, which is naturally bad under group-think!).

If you have any issues with transitioning your child to homeschool, this type of issue is the most likely one you will experience. Unfortunately, you can't convince a child who is locked into the "group-think" social structure of institutional schools that homeschool will be better. But, you can do several things to reassure such a child about homeschooling:

- Help your child remain in contact with his or her friends (at least those who aren't a negative influence on your child). See a later section in this chapter for ideas about how to do this.

- Use your homeschool network to locate other homeschooled kids with whom your child might become friends. Make it possible for your child to regularly spend time with those other homeschoolers. Not all that time has to be doing

> **note**
>
> If your children are young, say less than nine years old, the odds are that they are going to be so thrilled to be able to spend more time with you that you won't have any transitional issues to confront. Likewise, this is true even if you have an older child who doesn't fit in with the crowd or who has experienced any of the number of traumatic events that are common to the institutional school experience.

homeschool activities either. Homeschool kids benefit just from hanging around and having fun, too.

- In addition to letting your child hang out with other homeschooled kids, arrange to have your child to "interview" some of these kids to get their perspectives on the pros and cons of homeschooling.

- Emphasize how much more fun and freeing homeschool will be than institutional school. Focus on things like field trips, fewer hours in the school day, more flexibility, and so on.

- Demonstrate how they will be able to move as fast as they can to get their work done. And when they're finished, they're finished—unlike institutional schools in which they are required to be in certain places (translation: classrooms) for a set amount of time—regardless of whether anything valuable is happening or not. Many kids, especially those with active minds, get bored with institutional schools. Homeschool will be less boring for these kids because you will design the learning to match the child's capabilities.

- You might be able to help some kids by explaining that you are just trying homeschooling for a period of time, say, for a school year. Tell them at the end of the year, you will evaluate what has happened to see how it has worked for everyone. This can help kids not feel trapped into something that is going to continue forever. The odds are that you and the child will have great success so it is highly unlikely this evaluation will lead to returning the child to an institutional school.

If your child is extremely tied into the "social scene" at school and suffers from a group-think addiction, your explanations might not help too much. If that is the case, you might just have to bear with your child as he or she struggles with the transition. If you stay the course, I believe that your child will eventually grow to accept and even value homeschooling. But, in the worst cases, that acceptance can take some time so you need to be patient. It can take some time for a child to break free of the group-think way of life.

After this sometimes painful transition, your child will begin to think more independently and over time will come to not look for other people to direct his or her thinking or actions so much (and when they do, they will naturally look to you instead of other children).

Dealing with Increased Flexibility or Lack of Structure (Depending on One's Point of View)

Someone who has been in an institution for a large part of their life, such as a traditional school, gets used to having a rigid structure that includes someone telling them what to do and when to do it (even if they don't like that part of it so much). When a child moves to a homeschool, that rigidity largely goes away. Some children will really take to this lack of rigidity very well; though it might cause some anxiety in others.

In both cases, you can help your child with this aspect of the transition by making sure you take your homeschool as seriously as you want them to take it. You can convey this in a number of ways, including the following:

- Maintain a room dedicated to homeschool.

- Make sure they have a schedule that they know you expect that they keep—it's up to you to make sure they keep it.

- For the first month or two, keep school hours as regular as you can; introduce flexibility gradually to give your child a chance to get used to it.

- Act like a teacher/coach while school is in session. Make sure you conduct yourself like a teacher or coach when you are teaching rather than a parent. This will help your child get accustomed to you in this role.

- As you establish the proper homeschool environment, you can gradually "release the reigns" as your child begins to accept and learn to operate in greater independence.

Dealing with the Need for Separation from You

Depending on your child's age and personality, they might have a greater need for independence than others. As you might expect, this situation is more likely with older children, but it can apply to even extremely independent children. Until they understand how homeschooling works, children might experience some anxiety about having to spend too much time with their parent (that being you).

This issue is rather easily dealt with by emphasizing the independent aspects of homeschooling. For example, especially for older kids, you can allow them times of mostly independent work. You should also consider creating a study area outside of the homeschool room, for instance in a bedroom. This will allow the child to separate himself or herself when needed.

note

Extremely introverted children will have a greater need for independence than extroverted children will. Introverted kids often find ways to "be alone" when they are at school or traveling to or from it. Because they will be at home all the time, they might think you are going to "be in their face" all the time.

Dealing with the Need for Separation from Siblings

Another of the great things about homeschooling is that it fosters very close relationships between the siblings who are homeschooled. Although this is a good thing, some children might see this as a bad thing, especially if there is a large age difference between siblings. ("I have to spend all day in the same room with him!")

Over time your children will come to enjoy spending time together so this is another issue that is more one of perception than reality. Still, it can be a serious concern for a child who is dealing with the anxiety that a switch to homeschooling can bring.

Because you are likely to be teaching all of your children at the same time, it isn't practical to keep them separated, nor should you really try. However, you should provide some degree of separation between siblings if they express the need for it. The best way to do this is to create some independent study areas in your home where kids can work on their own from time to time.

Helping a Child Keep in Touch with School Friends

If your child has been in an institutional school for awhile, he probably has some friends. Removing a child from the school environment obviously presents challenges for your child maintaining these friendships simply because of the realities of no longer spending most of the day in the same place.

You can expect that over time, your child will develop friendships with other homeschoolers and that their friendships with school friends will gradually fade somewhat. This is an inevitable part of the transition just because of the physical separation and the lack of commonality of the school experience (except for those kids who have strong connections outside of school, such as in clubs or other activities).

In the short term, you should help your child remain in as close contact with her friends as you can (assuming the friend is someone you want your child to remain in contact with of course). Here are some ideas:

- If your child participates in an activity with a friend, keep them in that activity.
- Allow your child to invite his friends over to your home regularly.
- Provide email access to your child so she can keep in touch that way.
- Include "schooled" friends in homeschool activities.

■ Answer questions your child's friends or their parents might have about homeschooling. This can make homeschooling more comfortable for everyone.

■ Take your child to school events that don't interfere with your homeschool, such as sporting events in which their friends participate.

THE ABSOLUTE MINIMUM

If your kids are already in an institutional school, there are several things you need to be aware of to help them make the transition from public or private school to homeschool.

■ There are two general types of reasons for transitioning kids from public or private schools to homeschool. One is that kids are not doing well in those schools; homeschooling can be a great help to most of these kids. The other is that while the child is doing fine in school, you believe that they will do better in homeschool. Kids from either "situation" can experience some issues in making the transition.

■ Before you start homeschooling, you need to formally withdraw your child from school; this is especially important if your kids are currently in public school.

■ There are a number of issues that can crop up when you switch a child to a homeschool. Patience and time usually cures most of these. For the others, there are some relatively simple actions you can do to make the move easier on everyone.

■ No one likes to lose his or her friends, including your child. If they have school friends, do what you can to keep your child in touch with their friends.

PART III

Managing a Homeschool

IN THIS CHAPTER

- Run a homeschool
- Develop daily and weekly schedules
- Understand important aspects of teaching
- Use current results to update future schedules

11

CONDUCTING HOMESCHOOL CLASSES EFFECTIVELY

After you have developed your lesson plans, obtained and organized your teaching materials, and you have done all the other planning work needed to get ready for school, the day will come when it is time to get started. Although the first day of homeschool is likely to cause you some anxiety because it is both an important activity and something you haven't done before, don't worry about it too much. If you have planned as I suggested in the previous chapters, those plans have prepared you to do an excellent job of homeschooling. And because you control your homeschool, you can always make adjustments as you go. Think of homeschooling as an adventure or journey rather than a destination. Like all journeys, you will have successes, failures, and unexpected happenings along the way. That is part of the fun of homeschooling.

Running a Homeschool

Homeschooling your kids is a major undertaking. Depending on the number of children you have and their grade levels, teaching your kids at home can easily be more than a full-time occupation. When your children are at lower grade levels, you can expect homeschooling to require a bit less of your time. As they approach middle school, you can expect the time required to increase because you will need to teach them a greater quantity and complexity of material, but they won't be ready for lots of independent work. As your students approach high school, the time you spend actually teaching them will start to decrease again as the amount of independent work they do increases and as you more than likely will start to include outside classes and tutors in your homeschool.

Because it is such as major undertaking, you should expect that your homeschool will consume the majority of your available time each week. Thus, it is very important that you manage your homeschool effectively to ensure that you accomplish your goals.

In some ways, running a homeschool is similar to running a business. You will need to carefully manage your schedule, supervise your students, measure your progress, maintain documentation, and make sure you are making progress toward your goals.

> **note**
>
> No plans are perfect. Know from the start that you will regularly need to make changes to your plans as you move through the year. Real life never quite matches our plans, no matter how well developed they are. As you learn from your homeschooling experiences, you will figure out what works for your homeschool and what doesn't.
>
> ---
>
> Perfection is a road, not a destination. Every time I live, I get an education.—Burk Hudson

Developing Weekly and Daily Schedules

Among the most important tools you will use to manage your homeschool are daily and weekly schedules. These schedules will help you determine the specific activities you need to accomplish each day. They also help you measure your progress; the results of that progress assessment will determine any changes that are needed to your plans.

The first step in creating a weekly schedule is to refer to the lesson plans you have created for each student (see Chapter 9, "Creating Lesson Plans and Schedules"). Each lesson plan should define the material you need to teach on a daily basis along with the estimated time each curriculum element will require per day. An example showing a couple of days from a lesson plan, including two subjects for a single student, is shown in Table 11.1.

Table 11.1 Example of a Student's Combined Lesson Plan for Math and English

Day	Date	Subject/ Curriculum	Lesson Number and Topic	Estimated Time
Mon	September 6	Math	Lesson 1, Sequences and Digits	60 min
Mon	September 6	English/Grammar	Lesson 1, Grammar Concepts	30 min
Mon	September 6	English/Spelling	Words to Live By: Week 1, Lesson 1	30 min
Mon	September 6	English/Literature (Reading for book club)	The Chronicles of Narnia, Chapters 1-2	30 min
Tue	September 7	Math	Lesson 2, Even and Odd Numbers	60 min
Tue	September 7	English/Grammar	Lesson 2, Parts of Speech	30 min
Tue	September 7	English/Spelling	Words to Live By: Week 1, Lesson 2	30 min
Tue	September 7	English/Literature (Reading for book club)	The Chronicles of Narnia, Chapters 3-4	30 min

As you can see, a lesson plan goes along way toward helping you know what you need to do for a particular student on a daily basis.

If you have only a single student, creating a daily schedule from your lesson plans is a relatively simple task because all you need to do is to decide the order in which you will cover the lesson plan elements and the time of day that you will do each part of the lesson plan. If you have more than one student, creating a daily schedule becomes both more of a challenge and more necessary.

To create a daily schedule, you need to map all of the activities required for each student on each day (from your lesson plans) onto the hours of the day that you are going to conduct school. Then, you need to add other activities that impact your schedule, such as medical appointments, non-school activities, and so on. As you can imagine, juggling all these requirements can tax one's creativity.

tip

For best results, create your daily schedules a "week at a time" before the start of each week. If you try to create them too far in advance, you will end up needing to make lots of changes as you go. If you try to create them each day, you will have a harder time making sure you get everything done in the allotted time.

You can begin with the amount of hours of instruction you have planned for your homeschool; this will likely be greater than the number required by your state's education regulations, assuming you have set reasonable learning goals for your children. The total number of hours of instruction for each student can be determined by totaling the time you have estimated for each student in their lesson plans. The greatest number of hours for any student will determine just how many hours you will need for each school day. For example, if the lesson plans for one student call for 5 hours of work while the plans for another call for 6, you will need to account for 6 hours of school in your schedule for that specific day.

Now, take the maximum number of hours and lay them over a daily schedule, such as in the example shown in Table 11.2. (It can be helpful if you also note the student whose lesson plan generated that number of hours, but it isn't terribly important.)

note

It is highly unlikely that the total number of hours required for each student in your homeschool will be the same each day. You should expect that some children will have a longer school day than others at different points in their homeschool careers.

Table 11.2 Maximum Number of Hours Needed Each School Day

Day	Date	Maximum Number of School Hours
Mon	September 6	6 (Jill)
Tue	September 7	5 (Emily)
Wed	September 8	6 (Jill)
Thu	September 9	6 (Grace)
Fri	September 10	5 (Emily)

tip

Although it usually isn't a problem if students finish their school day at different times, you should usually have the same start time for everyone. This makes the preparation time for the day more efficient because you won't have to try to get some students ready for the day while teaching others.

Next, pick the time you want to start school. This will depend on how early you want everyone to get up; a typical start time might be 8 a.m. It is usually a good idea to keep the start time consistent so that everyone knows when they are expected to be ready for school. You can let the end of school fluctuate from day to day depending on the day's workload and other activities that occur.

Build the schedule for each day based on that day's lesson plans for each student and other activities that need to happen. Create a matrix based on the maximum number of hours needed for each student that will show each student's activities as well as activities that affect everyone throughout the day as shown in Table 11.3.

Table 11.3 Daily Schedule Matrix

Day	Date	Maximum Number of School Hours	Time	All	Jill	Emily	Grace
Mon	September 6	6 (Jill)					
Tue	September 7	5 (Emily)					
Wed	September 8	6 (Jill)					
Thu	September 9	6 (Grace)					
Fri	September 10	5 (Emily)					

Now you will need to map the requirements of each student's lesson plan to a specific time on the schedule you create. This can require some juggling on your part when you have more than one student because some lesson plan elements will require your total attention. You have to make sure that you don't schedule elements like these at the same times.

As you create the detailed schedule for a day, you will define what should be happening during each hour of school for each student. A partial example is shown in Table 11.4.

Table 11.4 Daily Schedule Matrix in One-Half Hour Increments

Day	Date	Maximum Number of School Hours	Time	All	Jill	Emily	Grace
Mon	September 6	6 (Jill)	8:00 a.m.		Math	Math	English/Phonics
			8:30 a.m.		Math	Math	English/Reading
			9:00 a.m.		English/Grammar	English/Grammar	Math
			9:30 a.m.		English/Spelling	English/Spelling	Math
			10:00 a.m.	Break			

Table 11.4 (continued)

Day	Date	Maximum Number of School Hours	Time	All	Jill	Emily	Grace
			10:30 a.m.		English/ Literature	Geography	Science
			11:00 a.m.	Lunch			
			11:30 a.m.	History			
			12:00 p.m.	History			
			12:30 p.m.	Exercise (PE)			
			1:00 p.m.		Geography	Typing	Chores
			1:30 p.m.		Social Studies	Science	
			2:00 p.m.		Social Studies	Chores	
			2:30 p.m.		Science		
			3:00 p.m.		Chores		

As you develop your daily schedules based on your lesson plans, keep the following points in mind:

- **Spread yourself around**. Some segments will require your full attention. Don't schedule more than one of these segments at the same time. Schedule independent study segments for other students when you know you will need to be devoting all of your attention to one student.

- **Start and finish early**. As the day goes on, everyone gets tired and tends to lose focus. Plus, you will have other activities to account for, such as chores, medical appointments, and so on. Because getting school done should be your highest priority, start school as early as you can so that you can finish as early as possible. This will leave the rest of the day for other activities.

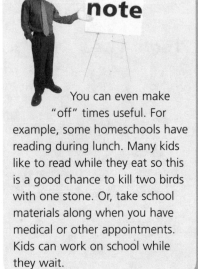

note

You can even make "off" times useful. For example, some homeschools have reading during lunch. Many kids like to read while they eat so this is a good chance to kill two birds with one stone. Or, take school materials along when you have medical or other appointments. Kids can work on school while they wait.

■ **Give yourself and your students a break**. Your homeschool day will be more successful if you include breaks. The number and frequency of the breaks you plan will depend on the age of your students. Younger kids will need more frequent breaks than older students. Breaks also give you a chance to catch up if something takes longer than you scheduled.

■ **Include exercise**. Whether you count it as an official subject (which you should), everyone needs some physical activity each day. Although most kids will be active on their own, I recommend that you get them in the habit of doing some regular exercise each day. Ideally, you will create an exercise "lesson plan" for your students.

> **note**
>
> Education is not to reform students or amuse them or to make them expert technicians. It is to unsettle their minds, widen their horizons, inflame their intellects, teach them to think straight, if possible.
> —Robert M. Hutchins

■ **Vary the routine**. As they say, variety is the spice of life. Although establishing and keeping a schedule is vitally important, everyone will benefit from some variety. Move topics around the schedule from day to day. Use field trips and other activities to break up things.

Teaching Your Students

When that first homeschool bell rings, it will be time to put your plans into action. In the beginning, this might cause you and your students some anxiety, but like most other activities, experience will give you confidence which in turn will alleviate any anxiety you or your students might feel. After a few weeks, homeschooling will become a natural part of life and the jitters you may have experienced at the start will become a thing of the past.

One important factor in successful homeschooling is the seriousness with which your students view their education. You largely determine this by how seriously you view and plan their education. For example, if you have a room dedicated to homeschool, it is easier to establish homeschool as a serious endeavor; when you are all in the school room, students will know that school is in session and they need to be about the business of being educated. If you have mapped out each day's activities based on detailed lesson plans and have all the materials you need on hand, the odds of being successful are much greater. If, on the other hand, you don't really have a clear plan for each day, you will likely flounder.

You should typically allow some time before the formal school day starts for your own preparation. You'll need to review the day's schedule and make sure you have all materials needed for the school day ready to go. You might also need to make some modifications to the day's schedule based on what happened on the previous day. For example, you might need to include some additional work if something that was scheduled to be completed on the previous day wasn't quite finished.

A good time to do this preparation can be when your children are eating breakfast, getting dressed, and so on. You should usually allow 30 minutes or so for your own preparation. If you need more than that, your schedules probably aren't planned using sufficient detail. Your preparation period shouldn't require much time or effort on your part.

tip

Your prep time for the next school day can be done at the end of the preceding day. This has several benefits, such as less pressure on you because the start of the school day doesn't depend on your getting your planning work done. The downside is that you will likely be tired from the current school day and might not want to the plan the next.

When the scheduled start time arrives, gather all your students in the schoolroom. It can be helpful to have a short group activity to get everyone in the school mode at the same time. Some homeschoolers may have a Bible reading period, or the reciting of the pledge of allegiance, or other activity in which everyone can participate.

When you have everyone's attention, get them started on the day's activities. If you have more than one student, hopefully, you have planned some independent activities for the older students while you work with the younger ones. Get the independent learning activities started, and then turn your attention to the younger students who need your full attention.

As you work through the school day, your lesson plans, schedules, and curricula should provide the structure you need to keep things moving along. Let your planning work pay off by using it to guide what you do throughout the day.

As you will learn early in your homeschooling career, you don't have to be the world's best teacher to have great success in educating your children. The teaching materials that you use in your curricula will do much of the teaching for you. (If they don't, they aren't very good materials, are they?) Your role as a teacher is to help your students work through this material, to help with questions, and so on. The fact is that you don't need to be an expert in all the topics you teach in order to teach those topics effectively. The people who create the teaching materials you use are experts on the topics (hopefully!); your job is to help your students use these materials to learn.

Understanding the Basic Teaching Options

I've mentioned several times through this chapter that there are independent types of study or curricula; this means, of course, that there are also dependent types of curricula. These options are the two basic types of teaching you will use.

An independent curricula is one in which you don't really do much except to plan and schedule the appropriate activities on the appropriate subjects. The actual learning will take place when the child works through the teaching materials for that curriculum on their own. The teaching materials you use will provide all the instruction that is required. For independent curricula, your job as a teacher is really more one of being an administrator or overseer. Your job is to make sure that the student is making the required progress through the materials. You will also need to evaluate your child's progress along the way, administer tests that are part of the curriculum, and so on. And you will need to be able to help your child find answers to any questions that might pop up along the way.

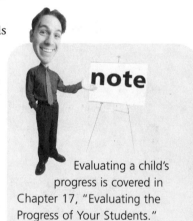

note

Evaluating a child's progress is covered in Chapter 17, "Evaluating the Progress of Your Students."

When you think about independent learning, don't limit yourself to the idea of a child simply plodding through a book. There are many ways to learn independently such as interactive programs on CD, video or Web-based courses, and so on.

Dependent curricula is one in which you act more like a "teacher." You will be directly involved in instructing the child. Sometimes this will involve simply reading to the child, while during other periods you might be using a whiteboard or blackboard to explain material to your child. You also might administer verbal tests or lead your child through other kinds of exercises.

Which type of teaching you do for specific subjects depends on several factors.

One of the primary factors is the age of your students. Younger children will have more dependent curricula (which makes sense given that it takes a more mature child to be able to work independently). As a student ages, the focus will shift more toward independent curricula. (This is a good thing if you have more than one student because dependent curricula require more attention from you during a school day.)

Somewhat related to age is a student's reading ability. A requisite to learning independently is the ability to read. Simply put, a child must be able to read to be able to effectively learn independently. (That is a bit of an overstatement because video and audio curricula elements can help even non-readers learn well on their own.) Of course, reading ability is not just a matter of age. Some children read at earlier ages while others read at a later age.

Another is the nature of the subject being taught. Some topics, such as math, lend themselves more to independent learning, especially beyond the first or second grade level.

READING IS FUNDAMENTAL

I hate to use that cliché, but it is definitely true when it comes to homeschooling. Your goal for all of your students should be to get them reading as soon as they are able. The earlier a student learns to read, the more independently they will be able to work. More importantly, however, is the fact that being able to read well will have a tremendous impact on your child's ability to learn. And, reading is perhaps the most basic skill your children need to master to be successful in further education, their careers, their own families, and life in general.

Your curricula design for all your homeschooled students should include, and even focus on, reading as a primary topic for all early grades. You really can't emphasize reading too much in the early stages. The better a child reads, the better they will be able to learn.

Your reading curricula should include several elements. Phonics should be a subject for all students through the first several grade levels. You should also spend plenty of time reading to your child and having your child read to you as they learn to read. And, some topics have side benefits of helping your children learn to read better, such as history in which one of the most effective ways to learn is by reading good historical books.

That said, realize that some children will read earlier and better than others. The ability to read is dependent on many factors, including the following:

- **Native intelligence.** The more native intelligence a child has, the more likely they are to be able to learn to read earlier in their lives. However, because a child doesn't learn to read early doesn't mean that child isn't intelligent. Intelligence is only one factor toward determining reading ability as you can see from this list.

- **Exposure to reading**. Many studies have documented the fact that children who are read to from a very young age and exposed to other people reading in a home has a major influence on that child's ability to read. You should start reading to children as soon as you want to, but by the time they approach a year, you should be reading to them on a daily basis. In addition to the learning benefits that come later, reading to your children is a great way to spend time and bond with them.

- **Personality type.** Some personality types "take" to reading much earlier and faster than others. Children with Intuitive personalities are much more likely to learn to read earlier than are those who learn toward the Sensing type. Because Intuitive children dwell in the realm of ideas and thought, reading is a much more compelling activity. A Sensing child will probably be more drawn to things they can experience. Similarly, Introverts are also more drawn to reading than Extroverts simply because an Introvert will be energized by the alone time spent reading, while an Extrovert will naturally seek out greater external sources of energy. As with intelligence, personality type doesn't necessarily determine how well people learn to read, but it can have a major impact on when people learn to read and how long it takes them to do so.

- **Learning disabilities**. Some learning disabilities, such as dyslexia, have a major impact on a child's ability to learn to read. If a child has a very difficult time learning to read, you should have that child tested to make sure that they don't have a learning disability.

- **Effective teaching**. Although it is probably obvious to you, I will state it anyway: Your children's ability to learn to read will be impacted by how well you teach them. Fortunately, there are lots of excellent reading curricula from which you can choose. And even more fortunately, a big part of teaching your children to read is simply to read to them, which also happens to be fun to do.

note

Interestingly, the Perceiving and Judging personality preferences can have an interesting impact on how a child reads. Because people with Judging preferences like to close things out, children who have this preference are more likely to finish books they start to read. Someone with a Perceiving preference, on the other hand, will be more likely to start books, but won't be compelled to finish them. Someone with a Perceiving preference might like to have several books going at the same time and jump between them on a whim. The Judging type of person is more likely to read only one book at a time.

One of the things that parents often wonder about is at what age a child should be able to read well on their own. If you check with the "experts," you'll find that there is a wide range of expectations. Some will tell you that a child should be able to read well by 4 or 5 years of age. Others will say that 7 or 8 years is a more reasonable expectation. Because the ability to read is influenced by so many variables, including those in the previous list, there isn't really a defined age by which a child should be able to read. Some children will be reading well by 4 while others might not master reading until 8 or 9. And, some people just can't read as well as others do. Recognizing when your child has a reading problem and when they are reading according to their personality and capabilities is an important distinction.

Adjusting Your Teaching Style to a Child's Age and Learning Style

As you can no doubt guess, a child's age has a major impact on how you teach that child. The younger a child is, the more intensely you will need to interact with that child. As children age, it is natural for them to learn more independently. And, as they approach young adulthood, it is also natural that they will seek to gain some separation from you. (This is where you can really benefit from outside classes and tutors; you'll learn about these tools in Chapter 16, "Homeschooling with Tutors, Outside Classes, and Online Courses.")

Way back in Chapter 7, "Planning Subjects and Obtaining Teaching Materials for a School Year," you learned some basics about personality types and preferences. Understanding a child's personality style is more important to you than it is in teaching that child effectively. The more you can adapt your teaching style to a child's personality preferences, the more effective your homeschool will be. Let's take a look at some simple examples to make this concept clearer.

Suppose you have a child who is an extreme Extrovert. (Remember this means that the child will be energized externally.) An extroverted child will be seeking his source of energy, which is outside himself. This is often manifested in talking; the more extroverted a person is, the more likely he is to talk. An extreme extrovert will talk "all the time." This means that you will need to provide more external stimulation for such a child. An extroverted child will need interaction with other people to be able to learn more effectively. For example, if you give an extroverted child a book and expect him to sit alone and read it for hours on end, you will probably be disappointed. After a length of time, the child will need to re-energize, which means interacting with people. On the other hand, an extroverted child will learn effectively through interacting with you, such as with questions and answers, group discussions, and so on.

note Because of their need to take energy from their environment (often by talking), extroverted children often have problems in traditional school settings because they tend to "disrupt" class. The traditional response to such students is to "clamp down" and make them tow the line. Of course, this leads to less opportunity for the extrovert to be energized, leading them to seek more opportunities and "act out." This cycle can continue indefinitely; in extreme cases, the child can be forced out of school altogether (hopefully to homeschool!). A more effective approach is to provide opportunities for the extroverted child to interact with others. She will then be energized and will have less need to interact, ego, she will be able to "control herself."

As an opposite example, suppose you have an extremely introverted child. (In case you have forgotten, an introvert is someone who is re-energized from the inside.) An introvert will be worn out by interacting with other people and will be energized by being alone with their thoughts. Give an introvert a book and a quiet place to read it, and you will have one happy introvert on your hands. On the other hand, expecting an introvert to constantly interact with others, such as in group discussions, might lead you to frustration. Interacting with people tires introverts, meaning they will need to have "quiet" time to refresh themselves.

Be aware that it is as important to understand your own personality preferences as it is to understand your children's. This is especially important when a child has dramatically different preferences than you do. As an example, suppose you have a strong Sensing preference and your child has a strong Intuitive preference. You might tend to view that child as passive or a daydreamer. Your own preference might lead you to try to teach that child as you prefer to learn, which will tend to be with more sensory input and by doing defined exercises. An Intuitive child will learn more effectively through independent reading, stories, and "thinking." An Intuitive child will likely quickly grow bored with workbooks and repeated exercises while a Sensing child would learn quite well through such activities.

> **note**
>
> The great thing about homeschooling is that you can tailor how you teach students to their preferences, helping them learn more effectively and making it a better experience all around. For example, introverted students are ideal homeschoolers as are extroverted students. That's because you can teach them according to their own preferences.

Significant differences between your own personality type and your children's types are a likely cause of frustration for everyone and can be a major roadblock to learning. If you don't account for those differences as you teach, your ability to teach your children will be impacted negatively.

Hopefully, you will take the time to try to determine and understand your preferences and your children's early in your homeschool career. This will go a long way to making you a better homeschool teacher. If you don't take the time to do this early and you have one or more students whom you just can't reach, a lack in understanding of and not accounting for the differences in personality preferences might be the culprit.

And remember that personality preferences are just that—preferences. We all act both according to and contrary to our personality preferences at different times.

Preferences are simply the way people choose to be or act given no reason to be or act otherwise.

Also, the more extreme a personality preference is, the more it will drive a person's behavior. For example, someone with only a slight preference toward introversion will not seem that different than someone with only a slight preference to extroversion.

Teaching Multiple Students at the Same Time

Unless you have only one child whom you are homeschooling, a challenge you will face is managing more than one student at the same time. This sometimes difficult balancing act can be likened to one of those plate jugglers in the circus who spins plates on top of long poles and has to keep moving back and forth among the plates to prevent them from slowing down and falling to the ground. While "juggling" several students won't be quite that frantic, it still can be a challenge.

Sometimes, you will involve all of your students in the same activity at the same time. Examples of

In fact, one important purpose of education is to help children learn to act appropriately even when the appropriate action is opposite to their personality preference. This helps the student become well rounded and able to excel in any situation. For example, introverted students need to learn how to function well when interacting with other people in group situations. Extroverted students need to learn to control their need to interact at times.

this are when you are reading (such as history), doing projects, and so on. In this case, you don't really have to think about jumping around to each student because each one is doing more or less the same thing (perhaps at different levels or for slightly different purposes).

Much of the time, however, each student will be working on his or her own curricula element. The only real way to handle this is to avoid scheduling more than one dependent activity during the same period of time. For example, if you have three students, have two of them working on independent activities while you work with the third student's dependent activity. This enables you to focus your attention where it is needed the most. As a student moves from independent to dependent activities, you will shift your attention accordingly (just like the plate juggler when one of his plates is about to fall).

If you can't avoid scheduling more than one dependent activity at the same time during the school day, you may need to shift some activity out of the allocated time and move something outside of school into the school day. For example, if you assign daily chores to your children, you might need to have one child work on chores while you are teaching another and then switch.

There are several activities that you can include in most days' school schedules to give you some flexibility when you have a large number of dependent activities to accomplish. A few suggestions follow:

- Chores
- Exercise
- Reading
- Video or audio courses
- Educational computer or other games
- Typing

Having Students Teach Other Students

If you have been reading the quotes included in the Notes throughout this book, you read a quote that said "to teach something is to learn it twice." You can take advantage of this to both help your students learn and to help you manage multiple students.

note

Much of the social history of the Western world over the past three decades has involved replacing what worked with what sounded good. In area after area—crime, education, housing, race relations—the situation has gotten worse after the bright new theories were put into operation. The amazing thing is that this history of failure and disaster has neither discouraged the social engineers nor discredited them.—Thomas Sowell

If you have children with different age ranges, older students can help teach younger ones. This benefits the older students in that they gain practical experience in teaching a topic to someone else, which also helps them learn more about that topic along with the skills needed to teach someone else. You get the benefit of help with younger children who need more dependent learning activities.

For example, if you have an older student who reads well, that student can read to a younger student who doesn't read so well. In turn, the younger student can read to the older student. Similarly, more experienced math students can help younger students with basic math exercises and so on.

Having students teach other students also helps with the maturation process and can provide additional closeness in the sibling relationships.

There are several things that you need to be careful of when you have students teach one another. First, make sure that you don't overburden older students with teaching the younger ones. Each student should have a full load of work to do for himself. Students helping other students should be a relatively small part of the older student's school day. Because this can be such a help to you, there might be the temptation to over do it. Second, some siblings just don't get along well for whatever reason. It isn't a good idea to have one child teach another when they don't get along well much of the time. Third, you need to remain responsible for the results of the process so that you don't put too much pressure on the teaching student. For example, you should be responsible for administering tests and evaluating progress.

note

Real education should educate us out of self into something far finer; into a selflessness which links us with all humanity.—Nancy Astor

Updating Future Schedules Based on Current Results

As you work through each school day, occasionally things will go just as you planned them. When this happens, be happy and content in a job well planned and well done. Sometimes, things won't go quite as planned. You might not get through all of the material that you planned for that day or something might come up that prevents you from accomplishing all of the goals you set for the day. Or, even though a student might have made it through the planned material for a topic, you might decide that she really didn't learn what was needed and some additional work is needed.

At the end of each school day, you need to assess the progress of each student compared to the plan and schedule you created. Where goals were not accomplished, you need to update future schedules to enable those goals to be met. Because you probably created full schedules to begin with, this might require that you do some schedule juggling to keep everything on track.

Suppose that a student was only able to get through one-half of a day's math lesson in the allotted time. You will need to make up the other half of the lesson somehow. You might decide to do it "after school" or you might adjust the next day's schedule to include additional math work. If the next day's schedule is already full, this might bump work to the next day as well.

tip

If you find that you don't meet your schedules most or even much of the time, you might be scheduling too much. Or, you might need to find more efficient ways of getting things done.

Because things don't always go as planned, you should include some "slack" or makeup time in your schedules. For example, you might want to include an hour or two on the last school day of the week for makeup work. If no makeup work is needed, you can let out school early that day or plan for another activity or project during the slack time.

caution

Be mindful of getting very far behind schedule. It can be tempting to let things go and plan on picking them up the next day. Too much of this and you might find yourself way behind schedule with a mountain of catchup work to do. You should make sure you are back on your original plan on at least a weekly basis.

THE ABSOLUTE MINIMUM

All of your planning and preparation starts to pay off when you hit the classroom and get to work. Running a homeschool is no small task and requires all the dedication and effort that any other significant undertaking does. As you move into the classroom, consider the following points:

- You need to develop and maintain daily and weekly schedules. Schedules are essential in knowing what you need to do and how well you are making progress toward your goals. They are also essential for managing your time throughout your busy homeschool days.

- There are many ways to teach you children. You will be helping your students learn independently and dependently. You also need to account for each student's personality types; you'll be even better off if you understand your own personality type, too.

- Managing multiple students at the same time can be a challenge. You can meet that challenge by planning your schedules carefully and by having older students teach younger ones.

- As you work through school days, you need to adjust future schedules based on current results. Include some slack or makeup time in your weekly schedule so that you don't get behind.

12

Documenting Your Homeschool

When you homeschool, you will be doing lots of work. Documenting the work you do might seem like adding more work to your already busy schedule, which it does, to be frank. However, documenting the work you do for homeschooling is very important for a number of reasons. If you set up a good system and are consistent with the documentation that you keep, you will find that the additional work you have to do is well worth it.

Understanding Why Documenting Your Homeschool Activities Is So Important

Planning and scheduling are tasks you do to prepare to homeschool effectively. Initially, your planning work identifies what you need to do. As you develop lesson plans and then schedules, you determine how well you will achieve your homeschool goals.

Documenting your homeschool is an equally important, but less time consuming, part of running a homeschool effectively. While planning and scheduling look to the future and present respectively, documenting looks to the past. Documenting your homeschool is important for a number of reasons, including the following:

- Documenting helps you measure your progress so you know if you are meeting your goals.

- Documenting your homeschool enables you to see where you are ahead or behind in your plan. You then can make needed adjustments to your future plans and schedules to keep your homeschool on track.

- Documenting your homeschool will help you realize just how much you have accomplished.

- Documenting your homeschool helps you keep a portfolio for your children; this is sometimes required if you plan to transition them to public or private high school; it also can be useful for some college admissions and scholarship applications.

- Documenting your homeschool enables you to prove that your children are being educated. This is important so that you can demonstrate that you are meeting all your state's schooling requirements, should you ever be challenged. Some states require regular reports from you; you will use your documentation to create these reports.

Education is when you read the fine print. Experience is what you get if you don't.—Pete Seeger

Keeping Homeschool Records

Keeping current records on your homeschool activities should become a natural part of your homeschool work. As you work through the school year, there are several kinds of documentation you should produce, including the following:

- Daily records
- Weekly records
- Other records

Keeping Daily Records

You document the results of each school day as you complete that day. As you learned in the previous chapter, you need to understand what you have accomplished each day to make adjustments to your plans for future days. When you do this, you can also create the daily documentation you need to maintain your homeschool. Fortunately, this doesn't require that you do very much additional work.

You should have a daily schedule for your homeschool that guides your daily activities. Your schedules might look something like Table 12.1. With just a couple of additions, you can also use these schedules to document your homeschool work.

Table 12.1 Daily Schedule Matrix in One-Half Hour Increments

Day	Date	Time	All	Jill	Emily	Grace
Mon	September 6	8:00 a.m.		Math	Math	English/ Phonics
		8:30 a.m.		Math	Math	English/ Reading
		9:00 a.m.		English/ Grammar	English/ Grammar	Math
		9:30 a.m.		English/ Spelling	English/ Spelling	Math
		10:00 a.m.	Break			
		10:30 a.m.		English/ Literature	Geography	Science
		11:00 a.m.	Lunch			
		11:30 a.m.	History			
		12:00 p.m.	History			
		12:30 p.m.	Exercise (PE)	Aerobics	Aerobics	Aerobics
		1:00 p.m.		Geography	Typing	Chores
		1:30 p.m.		Social Studies	Science	
		2:00 p.m.		Social Studies	Chores	
		2:30 p.m.		Science		
		3:00 p.m.		Chores		

There are a number of ways to use a schedule like the one in Table 12.1 to document your homeschool. One way is to add a column to record the accomplishments for each scheduled activity. An example of this is in Table 12.2. Here, I have taken the schedule for a specific student and added a column for the work that student completed for that day. In most cases, this should be the same work that the lesson plan had scheduled for that topic on that day. When there is an exception, you should note that exception as well.

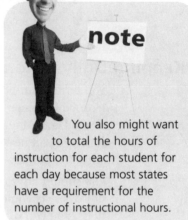

note

You also might want to total the hours of instruction for each student for each day because most states have a requirement for the number of instructional hours.

Table 12.2 Daily Schedule Matrix with Results Documented

Day	Date	Time	All	Jill—Planned	Jill—Completed
Mon	September 6	8:00 a.m.		Math	Saxon Math Lesson 1, Sequences and Digits
		8:30 a.m.		Math	Lesson 1, Grammar Concepts
		9:00 a.m.		English/Grammar	English/Grammar
		9:30 a.m.		English/Spelling	Words to Live By: Week 1, Lesson 1
		10:00 a.m.	Break		
		10:30 a.m.		English/Literature	The Chronicles of Narnia, Chapters 1-2
		11:00 a.m.	Lunch		
		11:30 a.m.	History		The History of the Roman World, Chapter 1
		12:00 p.m.	History		
		12:30 p.m.	Exercise (PE)	Aerobics	1/2 hour complete
		1:00 p.m.		Geography	Geography Level 2, Lesson 1, Day 1
		1:30 p.m.		Social Studies	Fundamental of U.S. Government, Chapter 1, pages 1-15
		2:00 p.m.		Social Studies	
		2:30 p.m.		Science	Basic Life Sciences, Lesson 1, Day 1

Total Hours of Instruction: 6

You should maintain similar documentation for each student.

When a lesson isn't completed as planned, you would note that as well. This would indicate that you need to plan when that lesson would be completed, such as during the next day, in the weekly slack time, or other time. When you document the period in which the work was completed, you would show that the work was completed at that time.

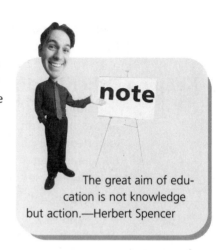

note

The great aim of education is not knowledge but action.—Herbert Spencer

Keeping Weekly Records

Your daily records will form the bulk of the schedule-based documentation for your homeschool. However, as you wrap up each week, you might want to keep notes covering the following:

- Total the number of hours of instruction for each student for the week.
- Total the number of days of instruction for the week.
- Calculate the average number of hours of instruction per school day per student (divide the total number of hours by the total number of days).
- Make a note of significant milestones, such as the completion of a curriculum.
- Note any work that wasn't accomplished during the week (of course, you would need to carry such work forward to make sure it gets completed).

Keeping Test Documentation

In addition to documenting the progress made toward your goals, as measured by your lesson plans and schedules, you will need to evaluate the progress that your students are making through the education you are providing. You do this through tests and other evaluation materials. The results of such testing also become very important parts of your documentation. While you can document the work you have done, tests and similar tools enable you to evaluate the results of that work. Keeping results of the tests your children complete is important so you can be assured that your children are being well prepared for life and also to demonstrate that your homeschool is working effectively. (This might be the case if you have to report to state officials or if your homeschool is ever challenged in some legal forum.)

You'll learn about the various types of testing that you can use to evaluate your students in Chapter 17, "Evaluating the Progress of Your Students." For now, just know that you need to keep the results of all testing that you do, whether it is testing that is built into many curricula or it is formal standardized testing that measures your children's education levels compared to national standards.

Keeping Other Documentation

In Chapters 13-16, you'll learn about incorporating various experiences into your homeschool through field trips, projects, activities, tutors, outside classes, and other experiences. Each of these activities should also be documented; you should add that documentation to the schedules, lesson plans, and test documents that you collect. In each of those chapters, you'll learn how to document those various experiences so that you can capture them as part of your homeschool documentation.

For example, you should include projects in your homeschool. There are many kinds of projects that you might find useful (you'll find some home project examples in Chapter 15, "Incorporating Home Projects into Your Homeschool"). Projects can include many types of activities such as writing and producing skits, designing and building things, writing reports, and so on. Each of these types of projects lends itself to various kinds of documentation. In the case of building something, you should keep any plans that you create as the project is underway. During the project and when it is completed, take photos of the item as it is being built. These plans and photos could become the documentation for that specific project.

Organizing and Archiving Your Homeschool Documentation

As you create and collect homeschool documentation, you will probably be surprised at the amount of material your homeschool will generate. Organizing that documentation and making it accessible is as important as its collection. After all, if you can't find the documentation in which you are interested, it probably won't do you much good.

There are two basic kinds of documentation. One type is *active documentation,* which relates to the current school year. This includes your current lesson plans, schedules, progress assessment, test results, project documentation, and so on. The other type, which I call *archived documentation*, relates to school years that have been completed.

Both types of documentation are important for your homeschool.

Keeping Your Active Documentation Current and Organized

Back when I explored creating a schoolroom in Chapter 8, "Preparing a Classroom in Your Home," I mentioned that you will need different types of storage space, including storage for teaching materials, school supplies, and so on. When it comes to documentation, storage space becomes critical because you need to be able to access your documentation throughout the year.

Active documentation that you need to consider storing includes the following:

- Lesson plans
- Schedules
- Test results
- Lessons, worksheets, and other documents that your students produce
- Project documentation
- Reports written by your students
- Field trip documentation
- Grades provided by you and outside tutors and classes
- Documentation of service and volunteer work
- Documentation of music or sports activities

There are number of ways to organize your active documentation.

Lesson plans are usually maintained in books or on worksheets. Schedules are usually maintained via a planning calendar or large-size daily calendar. Because these items are so closely related and are also used daily during the school year, you need to keep them easily accessible. In most cases, you will want to keep them on a bookshelf or in a file drawer that you can access easily.

Other types of documentation should be collected as it develops. Most documents to be archived are in hard copy format. Create a filing system for these documents that organize this material in some meaningful way. To keep things organized, you might want to dedicate a file folder for each type of documentation in the previous list. You then can place these folders in a file cabinet to keep them organized and to make it easy to add documentation to the appropriate folder as soon as you receive it.

note

If you prefer to maintain all your documentation on a computer, for example if you use a calendar program to create schedules, you should make sure you back up any digital documentation periodically or print hard copies in case your computer fails (which they do once in a while).

caution

Organizing and maintaining documentation might be one of the tasks that you might be tempted to procrastinate over. I highly recommend that you don't procrastinate. Remember setting up a system to keep your documentation organized is much easier before you have much of it to sort and file than it is after you have a lot on your hands.

There will be other types of documentation you will want to store, including

- **Recordings of musical recitals**. Consider placing these on CD or DVD for easy storage and access.

- **Trophies or other awards related to sports programs**. If your child wants to keep a trophy in her room, you can always take a photo of it and keep the photo as documentation.

- **Certificates of completion**. Any time your child receives a certificate of completion or appreciation for an activity, keep a copy with your homeschool documentation. If the child wants to keep or display the original certificate, just make a copy for your homeschool records.

- **Photo album or scrapbook**. A photo album or scrapbook is a great way to keep documentation related to activities such as vacations or home projects. Again, if you have digital photos, you can organize and keep them on a DVD.

- **Grades, test results, and other academic results**. You should also keep any documentation related to the evaluation of your student's progress. You won't need to refer to this documentation very much, but it is especially important if your homeschool should ever be challenged or if you are required to report progress to state officials.

If you have more than one student, you should keep each student's documentation separate from the others. This will result in some duplication of storage space, but will be a great help in making sure that you keep adequate documentation for each student.

You should also train your students to help you keep your documentation organized and complete. Each student should know where to store worksheets, tests, and other items on which they work. For example, when a student completes a worksheet, they should have a folder in which they place that worksheet. Similarly, they should have folders for test results, grades, and so on. Enabling your students to organize their own documentation will teach them

> **tip**
>
> Most new computers enable you to burn DVDs. DVDs are a great way to document your homeschool. In addition to photo, video, and audio records of events and projects, you can also store electronic versions of your documents on them.

> **tip**
>
> If you have enough space, dedicate a drawer in a file cabinet to each student.

organization skills and will prevent you from having to do more work. (That's one of the great things about homeschooling. There are many ways to accomplish multiple goals at the same time.)

Whatever organizational system you develop and use for your homeschool, make sure it has enough room and is easily accessible. The more difficult your organization system is to use, the less likely it is that you will keep your documentation in order.

Archiving Your Homeschool Documentation

No matter what you do during a particular school year, one aspect will be a constant. At the end of the year, you'll have a lot of material related to your homeschool activity. The odds are that you won't have room to keep the documentation related to every school year in your homeschool room—besides you probably don't want to do that even if you do have room because there will simply be too much material.

At the end of each year, you should take time to review, evaluate, and archive the documentation you have accumulated during the year. The primary goal of this task is to prepare the documentation for "long-term" storage (or archival storage). You should archive any material that you won't need in the upcoming year that has long-term value as part of your total homeschool documentation.

After the school year ends, take some time to take the following steps:

1. Review the documents, projects, lessons, and everything else associated with your homeschool year.

2. Place each item into one of the following groups:

   - **Useful for next year**. Some of the material will apply to the next school year, such as lesson plans for a specific grade level. You'll want to include this material in your preparations for that year.

   - **Documentation of the current year**. Much of the material will be useful only for documenting what you did for the current year. In other words, it won't have any function in the upcoming year. You'll want to keep most of this material in your archive.

   - **Material that has served its purpose**. Some of the material you will accumulate during the year just isn't worth keeping for documentation, or any other purpose for that matter.

Some of the material that falls into the second category will be in a form that doesn't lend itself to archiving. Projects are the most obvious example. If your students have constructed things during the year, you might not want to store the actual video of the project, but rather write a brief description of it.

Include this project documentation in your archive; what you do with the project itself is then up to you.

3. Move the material that you will use the following year back into your active storage areas.

4. Dispose of the material that you don't want to reuse or to add to your archive.

5. Archive the rest of the material.

Archiving material requires that you organize the material you are archiving. One way to do this to provide a box for each student for the school year. Place all the archived materials into this box, and then move the box into your archival storage area. If you have organized documents into file folders, just place the file folders into the box in the same order that you had them in the file cabinet.

Be careful that you archive materials in a safe place. You don't want them to be exposed to water or other conditions that can damage the materials. If you include videotapes, audiotapes, or other magnetic media, be careful about heat.

Label the boxes clearly with the student's name and school year. Seal the box properly and move it to your archival storage area. As you add boxes to your archive, keep them organized as well to make it easier to find the material when you need it later. For example, you might divide the area into sections and dedicate one section to each student.

There are several situations in which you might need to access your archived documentation.

- **To help with future school years**. Much of the material you archive can be helpful as you teach other students.

- **To defend your homeschool**. If your homeschool is ever formally challenged, your archives will be very helpful in defending it.

- **To prepare a portfolio**. You'll learn about this in the next section.

caution

Many materials degrade over time, especially magnetic media such as videotapes and audio-tapes. Consider placing the content of these items on CD or DVD, which will likely hold up better over time. If you print your own photos, you also need to make sure that they aren't exposed to moisture or light, as either of those conditions will degrade the images substantially.

note

Education is a private matter between the person and the world of knowledge and experience, and has little to do with school or college.
—Lillian Smith

Documenting Homeschool Accomplishments with Portfolios

As a homeschool student approaches a transition to a public or private high school or college, a portfolio can be an excellent way to demonstrate what the student has accomplished. Similar to an artist's portfolio, a homeschool student's portfolio provides examples of the student's work. Its purpose is to demonstrate that the student has been well prepared and that she has achieved significant accomplishments.

In addition to helping with the application of a student into a high school or college, portfolios can also be useful in other situations, such as when a student applies for a scholarship or other type of competition.

Creating a portfolio isn't difficult if you have followed some of the advice in this chapter, especially about keeping your homeschool archives organized and in good condition.

To create an archive, perform the following steps:

1. Review your archives for the student for whom you are creating a portfolio.

2. Locate and extract any records that indicate the accomplishment of goals or evaluation of the student's capabilities. Examples include standardized test results, grades or other evaluations received from teachers or tutors, awards of accomplishment, and so on.

3. Identify accomplishments that might not have resulted in a formal milestone (such as grade or award), but that indicate the student's capabilities. Examples of this might be documentation of a project involving the student, something describing the sports and other activities involving the student, and so on.

4. Gather all the material you have extracted from your archives.

5. Decide how you want to present the portfolio. There are many options. You might want to create a scrapbook that includes all the materials you have collected. You might decide a video presentation is the way to go. Or, you might choose to use a combination of media.

6. Prepare the portfolio you have planned.

tip

If you create a portfolio on CD or DVD and your student performs music, consider using the student's music as the soundtrack. Of course, make sure that you give the student credit so anyone who views or hears it will know.

As you create your student's portfolio, keep the following points in mind:

- Viewers or readers won't have a lot of time. Make sure your student's portfolio can be understood in just a few minutes. In many cases, an evaluator will only have a few minutes to look over the material. So make sure your portfolio can be viewed quickly. Use summaries wherever you can to present the most information about your student in a relatively short period of time.

- If you create a high-tech portfolio, such as one on CD or DVD, make sure you provide a low-tech backup in case the recipient doesn't have the knowledge or technology to view the high-tech version.

- It's never too early for a resume. Build a resume for your child and include that early in the portfolio, perhaps as the first page if your portfolio is in book form.

- Create your portfolio so that you can have multiple copies. You are likely to have to use the portfolio in different situations at the same time (for example, suppose your child is applying for two scholarships at the same time). Make your student's portfolio relatively easy to copy and keep a couple of copies on hand.

Although you probably won't need a portfolio until the eighth grade or later, there isn't any reason you can't start it earlier. This is a good idea because a good portfolio can be a rather large project and can take some time. Because of that, portfolio creation can be a good project to work on when you are on a school break.

tip

Consider the creation of a portfolio as a homeschool project. Students can exercise a number of skills, such as planning, organizing, and creating.

THE ABSOLUTE MINIMUM

As you learned early in this chapter, documenting your homeschool activities is important for a number of reasons. When you think about documentation, consider the following points:

- There are several types of documentation you will need to keep, including daily and weekly records, test results, project documentation, and so on. Basically, if you do something as part of your homeschool, you should document it in one form or another.

continues

- Homeschool produces a lot of documentation. You need to organize and store this documentation. Active documentation applies to the current school year. Archival documentation relates to previous years, but it is also useful for a number of purposes.

- As a student approaches high school, consider creating and maintaining a homeschool portfolio for that student.

13

PLANNING AND TAKING FIELD TRIPS

You've probably heard the expression that experience is the best teacher. In many ways, this is true. Field trips are very valuable because they provide the opportunity for your students to experience many different things and thereby take advantage of the "best teacher." There are many ways you can incorporate field trips into your homeschool; field trips might be one of the best things about homeschool.

Adding Field Trips to Your Homeschool

Field trips are a great addition to your homeschool for a number of reasons, including the following:

- **Improved learning**. Field trips are a great way to make the lessons you are teaching to your students more real; this helps them see the practical applications of their education.

- **Broadened horizons**. You can use field trips to expose your children to all sorts of experiences.

- **Opportunities for socialization**. Many of your field trips will be done in conjunction with other homeschoolers. This provides a great chance for your kids to interact with other homeschooled kids.

- **Interrupted routine**. Field trips are a great way to add variety to your homeschool and are a great way to break up the routine of school.

- **Lots of fun**. Field trips are fun for both students and their teachers (in this case, you!).

When it comes to field trips, homeschooling provides much more flexibility than field trips taken by traditional schools. Because you will likely have a much smaller group, you will be much less of a burden to the places you visit than would traditional schools. For the same reason, homeschool groups often have access to areas that are off limits to traditionally schooled kids. Because your schedule isn't driven by the clock as much as those of traditional schools, your field trips can have greater depth to them.

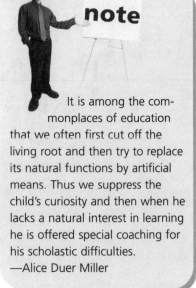

note

It is among the commonplaces of education that we often first cut off the living root and then try to replace its natural functions by artificial means. Thus we suppress the child's curiosity and then when he lacks a natural interest in learning he is offered special coaching for his scholastic difficulties.
—Alice Duer Miller

Identifying Potential Field Trips

The field trips that you take are limited only by your imagination. Although it is impossible to list all the possible field trips there are, here are a few examples to get you thinking about the possibilities:

- Historical sites (see Figure 13.1)
- Zoos and aquariums

Visiting a site like the battlefield at Gettysburg is a great way to bring history to life.

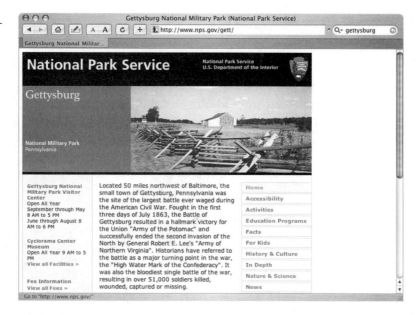

- Parks and nature sites
- Businesses and factories
- Theaters and symphonies
- Museums (see Figure 13.2)

FIGURE 13.2

Children's museums, like the excellent one in Indianapolis, also make excellent field trips.

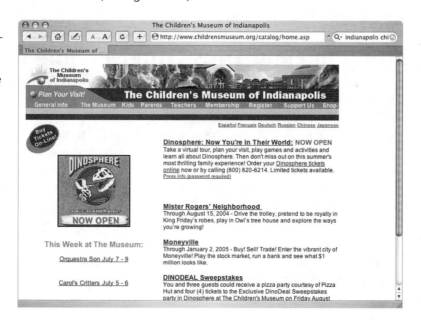

- Government facilities
- Airports, bus stations, train stations, and other transportation sites
- Media outlets, such as television and radio stations, newspapers, and so on

To get the most benefit from them, field trips should tie to your lesson plans in some way. There are two basic ways to relate a field trip to your lesson plans.

One way is to review upcoming lesson plans and choose a field trip that ties directly to those plans. One of the easiest examples of this is history. As you review your history lesson plans, you can identify historical sites that directly tie to specific lessons. Or, you might be studying social studies and decide to take a field trip to the office of someone who is running for a political office.

The other way is to adapt lesson plans to a field trip that you want to take. For example, you might not plan to cover some historical event in upcoming lesson plans, but a good opportunity to visit an interesting historical site related to that event pops up. In such a case, you might create a "mini" lesson plan about the historical event that takes advantage of the field trip.

Although it is best if a field trip ties directly to your current lesson plans, don't let this become a hard and fast rule. Some field trip opportunities will pop up without you being able to link them directly to your current lesson plans. Sometimes, this kind of field trip turns out to be the best kind.

When it comes to participating in a field trip that you have identified, there are two basic options. You can participate in a field trip that someone else has planned or you can plan a field trip yourself.

Participating in Field Trips Other People Plan

One of the great things about having a homeschool network is the field trips that will become available to you. Whether you participate in formal or informal networks, field trip opportunities and invitations will regularly come to your attention.

The best thing about field trips that someone else plans is that you usually don't have to do much of the planning work required. Although someone does the planning work, that doesn't mean that you should plan on not being responsible for anything. Any field trip takes a lot of work; you should help with this work even if you aren't in charge of the field trip.

When you receive a field trip invitation, evaluate the opportunity with the following points in mind:

- Does the field trip fit into my lesson plans? If so, figure out how you can best use the field trip to benefit the lesson.

- If it doesn't fit into my lesson plans, can I create a lesson to take advantage of it? Some field trips are worth taking even if you have to create some lesson plans to incorporate them into your homeschool.

- If the field trip doesn't really fit into my school plans, should I take it anyway? Some trips are just a lot of fun or they provide opportunities for learning without necessarily directly relating to the topics you are teaching.

- Do I have the time and money (if applicable) to participate?

- Are the people planning the field trip responsible and do we get along? Some people are good at planning and conducting field trips and some aren't. A poorly planned and executed field trip might not be worth the time or money it can require.

If you are invited to participate in a field trip, make sure that you inform the person who is planning the field trip about your decision whether you participate or not. Planning a field trip is often heavily dependent on the number of people participating so keeping the planner informed is very important.

If you accept an invitation, inform the planner about the number and ages of the students who will be attending. If you want to participate as well, make sure that you let the planner know. (You will often attend homeschool field trips along with your kids.)

Next, make sure you obtain and read any information that is provided for the field trip. This information usually includes details such as the date, time, location, transportation arrangements, cost, and so on. Pay particular attention to any response dates, such as when any money is due.

If you will be available, offer your assistance to the trip's leader. There are usually lots of tasks associated with a field trip. Being a responsible homeschooler means that you are willing and able to pitch in.

After that, follow any instructions that are provided to you. For example, make sure you show up on time, have met any financial obligations, such as purchasing tickets (most of the time, the planner will do this for you).

note

If you have any questions about a field trip to which you have been invited, make sure you ask the trip planner for details. If you have a question, it is likely that other folks do, too.

Make sure you arrive at the location for the field trip on time. Many field trips require that the group keep a schedule. Being late can cause problems for the group or might mean that you don't get to participate.

During the field trip, support the trip leader in any way you can. Help that person keep any eye on kids, communicate with personnel associated with the field trip location, and so on. Field trips are usually group functions; be as helpful as you can be to the group.

After the field trip is complete, make sure you understand any follow-up obligations. At the least, a thank you note to the trip's planner is called for. Later in this chapter, you'll learn about some of the ways you can integrate the field trip into your homeschool.

Planning for a Field Trip

Give and take is part of the homeschool life. Although you will no doubt participate in field trips that other people organize and run, you should also be prepared to plan field trips in which others can participate. And, someone might not be planning a field trip that interests you. In any case, at some point you are likely to want to plan and conduct a field trip yourself. This requires the following steps:

1. Decide what field trip you want to plan.
2. Plan the field trip.
3. Coordinate the field trip with other homeschoolers.
4. Conduct the field trip.

note

If you know a field trip will cause behavioral problems for one of your students, don't take that student on the field trip and cause the experience to be unpleasant for others. For example, if you have a high-energy child and the field trip requires several hours of inactivity, it probably isn't a good option for you.

Tis education forms the common mind;
Just as the twig is bent, the tree's inclined.
—Alexander Pope

Identifying a Field Trip

The first step is deciding on the field trip you want to take (see Figure 13.3). As you saw earlier in this chapter, there are many possibilities.

First, decide on the general type of field trip you want (again, in most cases, this should be based on some aspect of your lesson plans). Do you want to have a nature experience? Do you want to explore a historical site? How about taking a tour of a business? Or, maybe you want to see a play and take a backstage tour?

Second, decide how much time and money you want to invest. If there is a suitable destination close to you, you won't have the time and expense required to travel long distances. If not, how much time and expense are you willing to invest?

Third, do some research to determine if the destination you have selected supports "formal" field trips. In public places, such as parks and museums, this isn't hard to find out. For other destinations, such as businesses, you will have to dig a bit deeper to find out if the destinations are viable options.

After you have selected a destination for your field trip, it's time to get to work.

tip

If you identify a field trip destination that you would like to visit but that isn't within your time and expense limitations, consider planning a vacation so that you can visit that site. You'll learn more about how vacations and field trips can be integrated later in this chapter.

FIGURE 13.3

Design and manufacturing facilities, such as the Rolls-Royce turbine engine facility located in Indianapolis, can be excellent destinations for field trips.

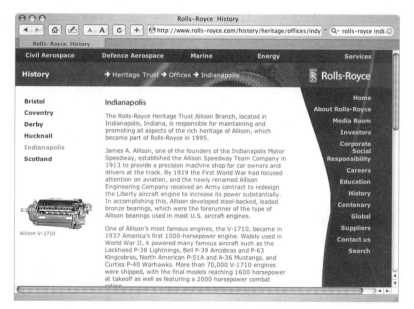

FIELD TRIPS AND BUSINESSES

Businesses can be some of the best field trip destinations. A field trip to a business can give your students a fascinating view into how some of the subjects they are learning about actually apply to the real world. They also help kids explore possible career options.

Many businesses support tours, such as field trips, because they make for good public relations. In these cases, arranging a field trip is usually straightforward.

For those businesses that don't support field trips in a formal way, you might have to work a bit harder to make it happen. If you'd like to visit such a business on a field trip and you know someone who works there, that person should be your first contact. He can either help you plan the field trip or can put you in touch with the person to whom you need to speak to make the appropriate arrangements.

If you don't know anyone who works at a facility, contact that organization's public relations department. They will be able to help you make arrangements.

Some organizations that do not formally support field trips might be willing to have you visit when they know that it will be a relatively small group of homeschoolers. Companies are often willing to provide one-time tours without needing to have a formal visit program in place, especially for homeschoolers, who have a reputation for being pleasant to host.

Planning a Field Trip

There are two general types of field trip destinations you will visit.

One type is where your field trip doesn't require (or benefit from) formal support from someone at the location. At these locations you control most aspects of the field trip and the responsibility for making it work the way you want it to. The benefit of this type of field trip is that it doesn't require that you coordinate your field trip with anyone at the destination and you are free to conduct the field trip as you see fit (within the confines of the location's rules, of course). That benefit is also a drawback in that you will be responsible for everything about your field trip and won't have support, such as that you would get from a staff. Destinations of this type include national and local parks, zoos, and other "public places."

The other type of field trip is where you do get support from the destination by being able to take

tip

Even if your destination doesn't offer formal support for field trips, consider contacting people involved in managing it to see if they offer behind-the-scenes tours or other activities that aren't provided for the general public. These sorts of opportunities are sometimes not well advertised, if they are advertised at all. Homeschool groups can often take advantage of these kinds of opportunities because of the relatively small size of the groups.

"official" tours or by participating in specific programs. These types of trips require a bit more planning and coordination on your part, but that additional work is often well worth it because you will have access to the people who run the facility and who know its operations better than you. Formal field trip support usually includes activities that aren't available to the general public such as backstage tours, behind-the-scenes demonstrations, and so on.

The planning you need to do for both types of field trips is similar, but there are a few minor differences.

1. If you are visiting a supported site, determine who the coordinator for your trip will be. This person will be very important to you as you plan the trip and during the field trip itself. If you will be managing the field trip on your own, locate any resources about the destination that will help you plan your trip, such as a Web site or information pamphlets.

2. Determine the logistics of the field trip, such as the date, start time, end time, and so on. If you are going to receive support from the site you are visiting, the start and end time will likely be defined by your trip coordinator at the site. There might be only certain windows of opportunity you have or there might be special programs or days you will want to take advantage of.

   Some destinations require that you have tickets or only have a certain number of "slots" available on any given day. Others will allow field trips only on certain days or for special events. These types of limitations will often be the driving factor when you plan the logistics of a field trip.

   When you visit a destination that will provide formal support for your field trip, one important question you need to ask is if there are group sizes that you need to consider. Sometimes, you need a group of at least a certain number to take advantage of special opportunities. In other situations, you can only take advantage of such opportunities with groups less than a certain size. This information will be very important if you intend to invite others to participate in your field trip.

3. Plan the itinerary for your field trip, which should include a general schedule of events. Also, think about key learning opportunities that you want to stress.

note

Most places that support public and private school field trips will also support homeschool field trips. In fact, sometimes homeschoolers have better access to a facility than public or private schools do. That's because homeschool groups are much smaller than groups from those organizations and therefore are easier to handle. Plus, because homeschool groups are not part of a large system, organizations don't have to worry that any additional opportunities will become expectations for future field trips.

4. If you need to purchase tickets or make reservations for the field trip, do so. (This step depends on how many people will be attending, so you need to decide if you will be inviting others on your field trip before you can do it.)

5. Create a document that includes all the information you have collected about your field trip. This will be useful enough for yourself, but if you have involved other homeschoolers in your field trip, this document becomes an essential means for communicating important information to them.

6. Decide how much, if any, preparation you want to do for the field trip. For example, if it doesn't closely relate to upcoming lessons that you have planned, you might want to include some special lessons to prepare students for the field trip. If there are books or other information relating to the destination, have your students start reading that material well before the field trip date. (Web sites are usually very good sources of information about field trip destinations.)

7. If you are going to want your students to complete some work as a result of the field trip, such as a report or worksheets, prepare the work that you are going to want them to do.

Coordinating a Field Trip with Other Homeschoolers

Field trips are usually more fun and meaningful if you involve other homeschoolers. This can be as simple as inviting one or two other homeschool families to come along or it might as formal as providing an invitation to a formal homeschool group. Whenever you involve other people, you need to be prepared to coordinate your trip with them.

The first step is to find out who else wants to attend. Unless it will be a very informal trip, you probably want to prepare an invitation that explains all the specifics of the trip. In your invitation, ask for a formal response by a specified date. If you need to purchase tickets or make other financial commitments for a field trip, I recommend that you ask people to provide the

tip

If you use email, try to get email addresses for everyone who will be attending. Sending emails is the best way to communicate information about the field trip to the group because you will only need to create one message to send (rather than having to make phone calls for example). Make sure you tell people that you will be using email to communicate about the trip so they know to keep up with their email.

required monies with their responses. This helps ensure that you won't end up footing the bill for other folks unnecessarily.

The number of people that you will want to invite depends on several factors. First, do you need a group to be at least a certain size or less than a certain size to have access to special opportunities? Second, how much coordination are you willing to do? The larger a group gets, the more work you need to do. Third, is there a "natural" group that makes sense for the trip you are planning? For example, if you are planning a field trip to a theater for a matinee and backstage tour and you know several families that have a specific interest in the theater, that group would be a natural fit for your field trip.

If you will need help on your field trip, make sure you ask for volunteers in your invitation. If possible, get specific people to commit to specific tasks.

Also, if you need other adults to attend with you, make that clear on the invitation as well (specify whether other parents are required to attend or not). Most of the time, you will want a parent to attend from each family so that you aren't responsible for all the kids on the trip; plus, you might enjoy some adult company!

After your response date passes, create a list of everyone who will attend along with contact information including phone numbers and email addresses. If you need to purchase tickets or make reservations, do so.

Make sure that you communicate any changes to the plans as soon as possible. This is where email addresses come in handy because you can efficiently communicate even with a large group.

tip

In some cases, you will need to purchase tickets for the entire group (for example, to make sure everyone can sit together during a play). In some situations, people will be able to purchase their own tickets. I recommend that you have people be responsible for their own tickets whenever possible. This makes life easier for you and reduces the chance of misunderstandings among the group related to money.

Most email programs enable you to create a mailing list (sometimes called a *distribution list*), which is a group of email addresses. You can send a message to everyone in the group by addressing a message to the list. As soon as you know who will be attending the field trip, create a mailing list for the attendees to enable you to communicate important information easily.

Conducting a Field Trip

When the day comes for your field trip, be prepared to have a great time! Here are some pointers to make sure that you do:

tip

One of the neat things about a field trip to a business is that you will often receive free samples of the product that the company produces. This can include food items, paper products, and so on.

- **Be punctual and expect others to be the same**. Whether you are "hosting" a field trip or just participating in one, being on time is always important. Many field trips require that you keep to a schedule, especially one that is supported by the destination.

- **Be prepared**. Make sure you have everything on hand that you will need to make the field trip a success. If you are going to be outside, bring along sunscreen, bug repellant, or other items you might need. Cameras, still or video, are always a good idea so you can document your field trip. If your students will need to take notes or do other work on the trip, make sure that you bring along any supplies they will need.

- **Treat your coordinator well**. If you have one, your coordinator will be doing work on your behalf. In addition to just being the right thing to do, treating this person well will often encourage them to go the extra mile for your group.

- **Manage the kids in your group**. Any group of kids can get "enthusiastic" when on a field trip. It is your responsibility to make sure everyone behaves properly so your group can have a great trip.

note

I am entirely certain that twenty years from now we will look back at education as it is practiced in most schools today and wonder that we could have tolerated anything so primitive.—John W. Gardner

If you take field trips to destinations that support them and they have had both homeschool and "regular" school groups participate, don't be surprised if your homeschool group gets special attention. In general, homeschool groups behave much better and are much less work to support than traditional school groups. Plus, homeschool groups generally have a less rigorous schedule to keep. All these factors tend to make homeschool groups much better to work with than those from public or private schools. (For example, most public school groups are woefully unsupervised because they usually have only a teacher and one or two volunteer parents to a large group of kids.)

Documenting a Field Trip

Before you take a field trip, think of some ways to document your field trip. This is useful for documentation purposes and it can be useful for follow-up work that you might require your students to complete, such as a field trip report. Here are some ideas to help you do this:

- **Photos**. Pictures are a great way to document a field trip. Consider providing each student with a single use or disposable camera (see Figure 13.4). In addition to being quite inexpensive, you don't have to worry about them becoming lost.

FIGURE 13.4

Single use or disposable cameras are a great way to have kids document a field trip.

- **Video**. A video camera is another great way to document a field trip. Designate a camera operator for the day so that you are free to manage the field trip. The downside of using a video camera is that they are expensive and on a field trip there are usually lots of opportunities to lose or damage one.

- **Notes**. Providing your students with a simple notepad or sketchpad is also a good way to have them document the field trip. Of course, you need to make sure they understand what kind of notes or sketches you want them to make!

- **Programs, maps, or pamphlets**. If your field trip destination provides programs, maps, brochures, or other documents, take some copies home with you as documentation of your trip.

- **Exercises**. If you have developed exercises that you want students to complete during the field trip, they can also serve as your documentation of the trip.

After you have completed a field trip, have your students complete any work you planned for the trip, such as writing a report or completing exercises. Consider having each student prepare a mini-report or scrapbook page for the trip by using photos they captured during the trip, along with captions or written descriptions.

Including Vacations in Your Homeschool

For homeschool families, vacations are often the ultimate field trip. The great thing about using a vacation as a field trip is that your kids will be learning without even realizing it! There are many ways to plan and take a vacation that includes lots of learning opportunities while your family has a fun and relaxing time (see Figure 13.5).

FIGURE 13.5

There are many vacation destinations, such as Discovery Cove in Florida, that are both great fun and highly educational.

The following list provides just a few examples to get your creative thought processes going:

- Study of almost any historical event can be greatly enhanced by a visit to important sites related to that event. For example, study the Civil War and then plan a vacation that includes visits to actual battlefields (see Figure 13.6). Or, when American history is being studied, plan a trip to Washington D.C.

FIGURE 13.6

It isn't hard to find Civil War battlefields to visit.

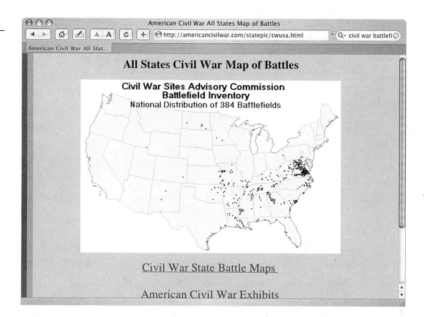

- Trips to oceans and beaches can include many activities that support biology and other science topics. Exploring tide pools is a great way to study marine biology. Taking a whale-watching boat trip is a great way to observe marine animals in their natural habitats.

- "Re-create" a journey taken by earlier generations. Many famous journeys can be made much more real with your own recreation. For example, a study of the westward expansion of the United States can be much better understood with a drive across the Great Plains or by following the Oregon Trail.

- Learn about geology and other physical sciences by taking a trip to the Grand Canyon and other geologic wonders.

- Include stops on a vacation to visit areas where famous inventors, writers, politicians, and others lived to help students gain a better insight into those people (see Figure 13.7).

FIGURE 13.7

Sites such as Lincoln's Boyhood Home are excellent side trips during vacations; they are so enjoyable your kids might not realize they are learning something.

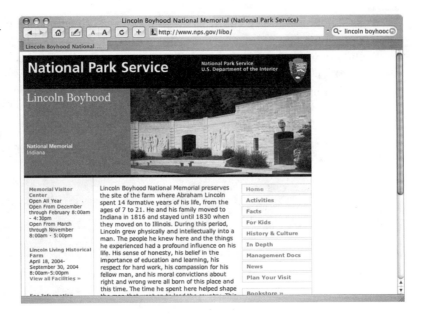

- Language studies can be greatly enhanced by visiting areas in which that language is spoken. For example, if your homeschool plans include Spanish, include a vacation to Mexico or other area where that is the dominant language. There is no better way to learn a language than being among people who actually use it.

note

Education is what survives when what has been learned has been forgotten. —B. F. Skinner

THE ABSOLUTE MINIMUM

Field trips are a great addition to your homeschool. In addition to being highly educational, they are also fun and provide socialization opportunities for your kids. Plus, they help break up the routine of school and everyone will benefit from that.

- There are many kinds of field trips you can take. In addition to the obvious destinations, such as zoos or aquariums, there are many others you will find valuable such as to businesses or national parks.

- Participating in field trips other people plan is a good way to interact with other homeschoolers, and you don't have to do as much work. Even so, you should volunteer to help if any help is needed.

- Planning your own field trip will require some effort on your part, but the results will be well worth your work. One of the most important aspects of planning a field trip is coordinating and communicating with others whom you invite to participate on your field trip.

- You should document field trips you take. One easy way is to provide students with cameras so they can take their own pictures. There are other ways, too, such as using a video camera or having your students take notes or make sketches.

- Family vacations can become the ultimate field trip. Your kids might be having so much fun, they won't even realize that school is in session.

14

Incorporating Music Lessons, Sports, Service Work, and Other Experiences into Your Homeschool

To be a well-rounded student, a child needs more than just academic work. There are a number of additional activities that you should consider adding to your homeschool program, including music, sports, service work, and several others. In this chapter, you'll get an overview of how to expand your homeschool to include these important activities.

Music and Your Homeschool

Music should be part of every homeschooler's education for a several important reasons. One is that an appreciation of music can provide lots of enjoyment throughout a student's life. There is no better way to develop this appreciation than to learn to read music and to play an instrument. These music skills will add pleasure and depth to your children for the rest of their lives. A second important reason is that the study of music has been shown to help students develop effective thought patterns that can benefit them in other areas, most notably mathematics because music and math are so closely related. Third, learning to play a musical instrument is an excellent way for children to practice and learn the benefits of discipline over an extended period of time.

There are a number of ways in which you can add music to your homeschool:

- Appreciating music
- Attending concerts and other music performances
- Reading music and playing an instrument

Appreciating Music

At the most basic level, you should include music in your homeschool at the "appreciation" level. This includes activities such as the following:

- Include regular periods of listening to a variety of music. You should expose your kids to all kinds of music including classical, jazz, folk, and so on. (Of course, some forms require more discernment and discretion, especially rock music.)

- Study composers and other musicians to understand their life and impact on the world. The Web can be especially useful for this purpose as there are numerous Web sites dedicated to lots of musicians (see Figure 14.1). In addition to getting biographical and other information about them, you can often listen to samples of their music online.

tip

One nice thing about music is that you can listen to it anywhere. Even if you don't want to include formal listening sessions during the school day, you can easily equip you kids with a portable music device so they can listen while they do chores or at other times.

As you study various musical instruments, pay close attention to how your students react to the instruments that you study. Their reactions can indicate instruments that you might want to explore teaching them to play.

FIGURE 14.1

When you study musicians, the Web comes in very handy.

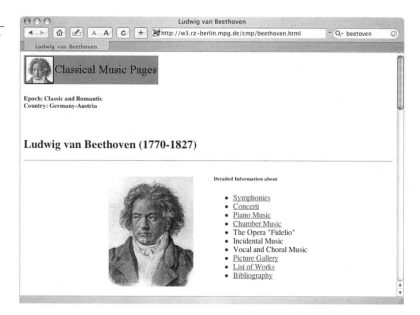

■ Study the musical instruments used in the various forms of music to which you listen. As with musicians, the Web can be a fountain of information you can use (see Figure 14.2).

FIGURE 14.2

Any instrument you can think of probably has a Web site dedicated to it.

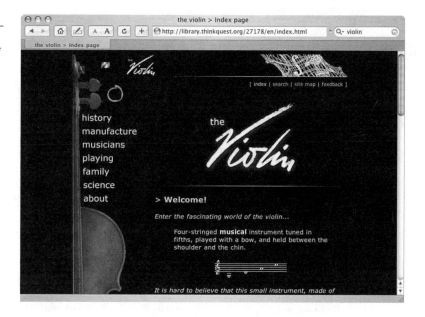

■ Begin a basic study of music itself by helping students learn to recognize notes, musical terms, and other parts of the music world.

Attending Concerts and Other Music Performances

In the previous chapter, you learned about the benefits of including field trips in your homeschool. When you are exploring music, field trips can be especially meaningful. Consider taking fields trips to concerts in you area. If you look for them, there are likely to be many free or low-cost concerts available to you. Also consider attending music festivals at which you can usually hear a large variety of artists play.

> **note**
>
> There is plenty of great software that can help in your study of music. You can find software that focuses on any aspect of music appreciation, including those that enable kids to make music with computer-simulated instruments.

Many symphonies and other musical venues offer matinee performances and other special events geared toward students. These often include the performance and additional educational activities. In some cases, the symphony will offer students the chance to experiment with many types of instruments. They also interact with the musicians to ask questions or watch them play up close.

Learning to Read Music and Play a Musical Instrument

Playing a musical instrument seems to be lots of fun and is a great way to express yourself musically. (It's confession time; unfortunately for me, I never learned to play a musical instrument and basically have no musical ability whatsoever. I think I missed out on a lot!) Like other things, it seems to be much easier for children to learn a musical instrument when they are young than it is for those of us who didn't learn to do so until we were older.

In addition to the fun of being able to play music, learning an instrument is a great way for children to develop and practice discipline. Playing an instrument also helps children learn to express themselves artistically.

Most students should participate in music lessons at some point in their life. The form and duration of this experience depend on the child's preferences and abilities, but most children will benefit from some form of musical training.

How to choose an instrument for a child is beyond the scope of this book (not to mention being beyond the scope of my knowledge), but it is likely that if you have exposed children to music through music appreciation and concert attendance, they will develop a preference for at least one instrument.

Of course, practicality has to come into the decision, too. If a child chooses an instrument for which you can't find a teacher, that probably isn't going to work.

After you and your child have selected an instrument, you will need to find an instructor for that instrument and sign up for music lessons. In your hunt for a music teacher, consider the following sources:

- **Your homeschool network**. The odds are that someone in your network is using a teacher for the instrument you are interested in or at least knows someone who is.

- **Instrument retailers**. Instrument stores can often put you in touch with an instructor.

- **Music schools**. Colleges or universities with music programs can be good sources of music teachers. These teachers can be instructors at the school or might be students, which is especially appropriate when your children are first learning an instrument.

- **Local musical groups**. Symphonies and other musical organizations can also be useful when you are looking for a music teacher.

- **Yellow Pages**. You can also search for teachers in your local Yellow Pages or other directory.

- **The Web**. A Web search might also be a way to find the teacher you need.

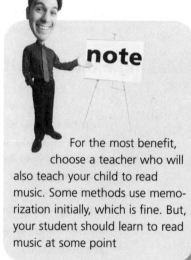

tip

You don't have to buy most musical instruments because you can rent them instead. This is especially good in the cases where an instrument you selected turns out not to be the right choice for your child. An excellent source of rental instruments is The Knapp Music Company; its Web site is http://www.knappmusic.com/.

note

For the most benefit, choose a teacher who will also teach your child to read music. Some methods use memorization initially, which is fine. But, your student should learn to read music at some point

One of the benefits of being a homeschooler is that you have greater flexibility in setting lesson times. Children who attend public or private schools must get lessons after or before school. You can take advantage of your flexibility and get lessons scheduled during school hours in some cases.

You should include regular periods of practice in your lesson plans to help your students learn to be disciplined and consistent.

Exercise, Sports, and Your Homeschool

Because of its physical and mental benefits, exercise is important for everyone, including kids. Although most kids get a fair amount of activity on their own, they will benefit from intentional exercise as well. Developing a habit of regular exercise from early in life will make it more likely that your children will continue throughout their lives. In addition to the exercise, sports offer other benefits for your children including learning discipline of mind and body. In sports, they will also have lots of opportunity for interaction with other children and can get valuable experience in being coached and participating on a team.

note

Upon the subject of education, not presuming to dictate any plan or system respecting it, I can only say that I view it as the most important subject that we as a people may be engaged in. That everyone may receive at least a moderate education appears to be an objective of vital importance.
—Abraham Lincoln

Making Exercise Part of Your School Days

If you remember the example lesson plans and schedules in previous chapters, you might recall that they included specific exercise periods. I believe that you should include exercise as a regular part of your homeschool activities. There are many options for exercise for children. Some are more regimented, such as aerobic training regimens, while others are more "play" oriented, such as outdoor games.

For best results, your homeschool plans should include both types of exercise for your kids. You should also try to include a variety of activities. Studies show that varied exercise programs provide the most health benefit; they also are easier to keep regular because your kids won't get as bored as

note

There are lots of good exercise programs that are appropriate for kids that are delivered via videotape or DVD, especially for younger children. One of the benefits of this medium is that you don't have to lead the activity yourself.

they might by doing the same activity all the time.

Some possible indoor exercise programs including the following:

- Aerobics (there are lots of programs available on videotape, DVD, or on television)

- Basic calisthenics (sit-ups, push-ups, deep-knee bends, jumping jacks, and so on)

- Treadmills, elliptical machines, or other exercise equipment you might have in your home

Outdoor activities that are good exercise abound:

- Biking
- Rollerblading or roller-skating
- Walking
- Running
- Jumping rope
- Jumping on a trampoline
- Swimming

tip

If you want to kill two birds with one stone, consider joining your kids during their workout. You can get in your own exercise while enjoying some bonding time with your kids.

Biking, jumping rope, jumping on a trampoline, and swimming are especially good choices because most kids will do these activities just because they enjoy them so much.

The most important factors in choosing exercise activities for your kids are the amount/intensity of the exercise they get and how consistent they will be in doing those activities. Obviously, in order to be of any value, the activity has to be one that your children will do regularly. Although it is important that kids exercise in a way that causes physical improvement (determined by intensity and duration), it is more important that they at least do something regularly.

When you create your homeschool schedules, be sure to include blocks of time for these activities and treat them as being as important as the academic work you will do.

Finding Sports Activities for Your Students

One disadvantage that homeschoolers have when compared to their counterparts in traditional schools is the availability of sports programs. Most schools offer lots of opportunities for students to participate in sports. As a homeschooler, you won't have the same amount of sports activities that are sponsored by schools.

Fortunately, there are many, many sports programs that are not affiliated with schools and your homeschooled kids have the same access to these programs that kids in traditional schools do. There are local sports programs for just about any sport you can imagine. Your means to locate and participate in such programs are the same as for any other family.

Even better, there are many sports programs that are designed specifically for homeschoolers. These include team sports, such as basketball, volleyball, and baseball. Although the number of these programs is somewhat limited, as homeschool continues to increase in popularity, these programs become more prevalent.

One valuable resource in your search for homeschool sports is the Home School Sports Network. This Web site, located at www.hspn.net, provides information about and access to homeschool sports programs across the United States (see Figure 14.3).

tip

Although many school systems won't allow homeschooled children to participate in their sports programs, some do allow this. To see if your children are able to participate in some of your local school's sports programs, contact school officials. Of course, before your child actually participates, you should check out the programs in which you are interested. The sports programs at some school suffer from many of the same problems that the schools themselves do.

FIGURE 14.3

The Home School Sports Network Web site offers resources you can use to locate homeschool sports programs in your area.

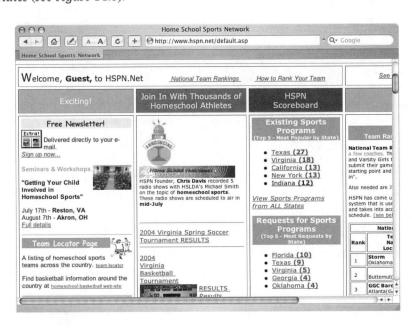

Of course, your best source for information about local sports programs that are friendly to home-schooled kids is your homeschool network. The odds are very great that someone in your network either has kids that participate in sports programs that might interest you or knows someone who does.

Incorporating Sports into Your Homeschool

The primary impact of your kids participating in a sports program (no matter what the source of that program is) is on your schedule. You will need to adapt your homeschool schedule to whatever commitments are required by the sports in which your kids participate. This includes making time for practice and competitions. Additionally, you will have to allow for the time and effort it takes for you to transport your children to and from sports activities.

note

Competitive home-school sports programs often compete against other homeschool teams as well as teams from public and private schools.

Education is like a double-edged sword. It may be turned to dangerous uses if it is not properly handled.—Wu Ting-Fang

SPORTS AND PERSONALITY TYPES

Like so many other aspects of life, the sports in which your children will participate and excel in depend on their personality types. All kids can find sports they like, but some will have a harder time than others.

Perhaps the biggest influence personality type has on the selection of a sport is the preference toward individual or team sports. Extroverts, especially those who also have sensing and judging preferences, will be drawn to team sports (such as baseball and football) where the opportunity to interact with others according to set rules abound. People with introversion and intuitive tendencies tend to prefer individual sports (such as tennis, racquetball, biking, and track) because they have the chance to excel on their own merits and don't have to interact with teammates to the same degree.

Team sports and individual sports both offer many benefits so it shouldn't be too terribly important to you which type your child prefers. As with exercise, it is more important that your child participate in some form of sports rather than being too concerned about the specific sport in which they participate.

Service/Volunteer Work and Your Homeschool

Another opportunity for learning and maturation for your students is service/volunteer work. Service work provides your kids with a broader view of the world around them and helps them grow out of the self-centered perspective that we are all born with. Service work also provides your children with the chance to work for and with other people. And, it is always good to be doing good things for other people. Service and volunteer work is a great way to round out your child's education and maturation.

Finding Service/Volunteer Opportunities

There are bound to be numerous volunteer and service opportunities in your area. These can include the following:

■ Missions, food pantries, and other organizations that serve the homeless and poor (see Figure 14.4)

FIGURE 14.4
Organizations that serve the needy, such as Wheeler Mission Ministries, are often good places to look for service opportunities.

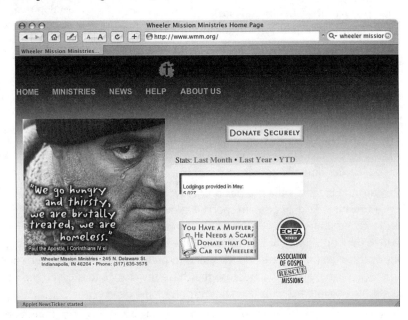

■ Nursing homes

■ Hospitals

■ Social aid groups

■ Neighborhood reclamation projects

■ Home-building programs such as Habitat for Humanity (see Figure 14.5)

FIGURE 14.5

Habitat for Humanity builds housing for low-income families; there are probably projects in your community that your family can get involved in.

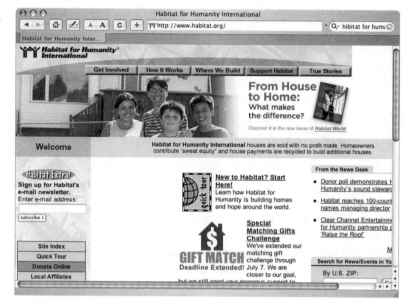

- Refugee and immigrant relocation organizations
- Service projects through your church

The specific opportunities that you might want your child to participate in depend on the child's interests, personality, and age. No matter who your child is, however, you will likely have to push them into this type of work initially just because it doesn't come naturally to most children. However, after they become involved, you probably won't have to push them any more.

tip

When you are looking for service and volunteer opportunities, don't forget to use your homeschool network. Other homeschoolers might already be involved in activities that will be of interest to you.

The best way to get started with service and volunteer work is to get the whole family involved, especially when your children are young. Look for an opportunity in which everyone in your family can participate. This will help your kids see such work as a "normal" part of life and will build good habits in a number of ways.

As your children age, you will be able to start finding opportunities for them to participate by themselves. This helps children start making the transition toward independence.

Service and volunteer work is another area in which your home-school schedule's flexibility is a bonus. You can often take advantage of opportunities during the day at which times volunteers are sometimes scarce.

Incorporating Service/Volunteer Work into Your Homeschool

Some service work will directly lend itself to topics that you have planned in your lesson plans. Suppose you are studying the history of Asia. Volunteering with an organization that assists Asian refugees moving to the United States can be a great way to gain insight into Asian culture while helping individuals at the same time. Projects, such as the construction of a home, provide opportunities for your kids to see how some of the topics that they learn about, such as math and science, have an impact in the real world.

In other cases, you might not be able to tie service work directly to your lesson plans. If the opportunity can provide maturation and character formation for your child, it still can be a very worthwhile addition to your homeschool schedule.

You should decide on a level of participation and then allow for that amount of time in your homeschool's schedule.

Service can be done periodically as well. During certain periods you might have more service work in your schedule than you do during other periods of time.

caution

Before involving your children in any service opportunity, you should thoroughly investigate the organization you are considering. Some organizations, even though they also perform worthwhile activities, have political and social agendas to which you might not want your child exposed; sometimes these agendas aren't clear from a casual examination.

note

Education has for its object the formation of character.—Herbert Spencer

Other Activities to Include in Your Homeschool

Almost every activity has something to offer to your children's growth and development. There are many activities through which you can add variety and experience to your homeschooler's education.

Using Jobs or Home Businesses in Your Homeschool

Participation in a business of some type is a great way for children to learn how their education can be practically used in life. This kind of experience can also teach them valuable lessons about working for other people and how to serve other people (customers) properly.

There are two basic ways to involve your kids in work during their homeschool years. One is to have them get a job in someone else's business. The other is to have them participate in a home-based business that you run.

note

Another benefit of including participation in a business during your child's education is that they can build an impressive amount of work experience for their resume. This will impress people who will be evaluating them later in life for other work or educational opportunities. (And, who knows, they might actually be able to save a little money for their college education or vocational training.)

MANAGING MONEY

One area that is vitally important for your child's future well being, which is often neglected, is the education in the management of personal finances. This is something that is critical to your child's ability to prosper later in life; you should start educating your child in basic principles of managing money from an early age.

When your child is young, you can provide an allowance or even better, pay your child small amounts for simple jobs around the home. Help your child understand how to save money and also how to spend it wisely.

As your child grows and starts to earn an income in various ways, help them establish and use a bank account. You can start with a savings account and eventually move toward a checking account or other options. You can even help your child learn about the economy by having them invest money in various ways.

Helping your child learn how to manage finances is one of the most important ways you can educate them, and everyone needs to have at least a basic understanding of how the financial system works.

Including an Outside Job in Your Child's Education

Part-time jobs are great ways to help children develop responsibility and good character. They also provide the opportunity to learn about cooperating with others on the job and how to work for someone other than a parent. They also provide an income for your child that you can use to help them learn to manage their own finances.

There are lots of opportunities for children to be employed in part-time work. Common examples are newspaper delivery, various jobs at retail sites, and, of course, good old manual labor such as carrying supplies at a work site.

Of course, you will need to account for your child's job in your homeschool schedule. Again, your flexibility as a homeschooler comes in quite handy.

Including a Home-Based Business in Your Child's Education

There are lots of ways to help your child gain work experience without having a formal job outside the home. This is especially useful for younger children who aren't really old enough to get a job in an established business.

In my opinion, it is unfortunate that jobs for kids are no longer part of many children's lives. Although work used to be part of most kids' lives, it seems unusual these days for a child to work before they become a teenager.

There are many ways to include this kind of work experience in your child's homeschool education. The following are just a few examples to get your started:

- **Babysitting**. Babysitting is a service that every family with children needs. It is also a task that kids can perform from relatively young ages. And you can easily control the amount of work a child does.

- **Yard work**. Kids of almost any age can help with yard maintenance, such as lawn mowing, weeding, and so on.

- **Pet care**. Many people have pets; they often need help caring for these pets on both a regular basis and during specific times (such as vacations). Taking care of pets is a great way for kids to experience work.

- **House sitting**. Your kids could watch over a neighbor's house while those neighbors are away on vacation. Their duties could include collecting the mail and newspaper, watering plants, and so on.

- **Home improvement projects**. Painting, cleaning, and remodeling are all examples of projects people do around their home and with which your kids can help.

- **Car washing and waxing**. Almost every family in the United States has at least one car. Washing and waxing those cars is a great way for kids to earn an income.

Including activities like these in your homeschool education provides many learning opportunities for your children. In addition to learning and developing a responsible character, they can also put other parts of their education to work to advertise their services, interact with their customers, manage the money they earn, and so on.

Adding Hobbies and Other Interests to Your Homeschool

There are also many ways to include your child's hobbies and interests in your homeschool to increase their interest and to make learning more effective and enjoyable.

Hobbies are a great way to combine education and fun. Suppose you have a child who is interested in building or flying model airplanes or rockets. This provides great opportunities for learning fundamental scientific principles including aerodynamics, physics, and more. If your child is interested in animals, you can further inspire that child by including biology and animal studies in his education. If your child is interested in fashions, include art and sewing on her educational agenda.

Education is a progressive discovery of our own ignorance.—Will Durant

Homeschool can help you take advantage of almost any interest your child might have to help them learn. The best part is that their natural interests make the learning fun and interesting so that they don't even realize how much they are learning.

THE ABSOLUTE MINIMUM

Homeschool, just like life itself, is about a lot more than academics. There are a number of activities that should be part of every student's educational experience to make him or her a well-rounded person.

- Music is one of the joys of life. You can help your kids enjoy music throughout their lives by including music education in your homeschool. Consider basic music appreciation at the least. Most kids will also benefit from learning to play an instrument, too.

- Exercise is very important to keep the body healthy; it also provides mental benefits. You should include regular exercise as part of your homeschool days. You can also bring health and other benefits of sports to your kids through homeschool and other sports programs.

continues

- Service and volunteer work is a great way to expand your children's horizons and give them a broader perspective of life. Consider including service work as part of your overall homeschool program.

- Formal or informal jobs are a great way to help your kids develop character and to learn essential life skills such as the ability to manage money and to work with and for other people. Your children can also practice and improve their knowledge of the subjects they learn in school.

- Hobbies and other interests can be springboards to learning in many areas. Using a child's hobby to provide real world examples of concepts they learn in school will make those concepts real to the child.

IN THIS CHAPTER

- Identify home projects for your homeschoolers
- Include home projects in your lesson plans
- Work on home projects as part of school
- Document your home projects for school purposes

15

INCORPORATING HOME PROJECTS INTO YOUR HOMESCHOOL

Home projects are a great way to show your kids how the academic subjects that you are teaching them can be used in real life. Plus, home projects also provide the opportunity for your kids to learn valuable skills, such as the ability to plan, organize, and manage a project. If you work on these projects as a family, your children will also learn how to work with others and you will get to enjoy bonding with your kids. As an added benefit, doing home projects as a family can be fun for everyone.

Identifying a Home Project

The home projects you include in your homeschool can include any sort of project on which you want to work. Examples include the following:

- **Relandscaping part of your yard**. This type of project provides great opportunities to learn. First, your kids can help you design the new part of the yard. Second, you can determine the materials you need. Choosing new plants can be a lesson in botany and how the environment influences the growth of plants. Next, you and your children can plan the project by laying out the steps, a budget, and a schedule from start to finish. A trip to your local home improvement stores can help your students learn about the economics of a project. When it comes time to do the work, a little exercise and work discipline will be an inevitable result. Finally, the resulting new flora will require maintenance—more opportunities for your kids to be involved.

- **Remodeling an area of your home**. Designing a room in your home offers many chances to learn. The learning starts from the redesign of the space, which exercises math and drawing skills along with creativity, research, and design capabilities (see Figure 15.1). As you move into the planning phase, kids can help you develop the list of materials you need and scope out the project's budget and schedule. Trips to hardware and home improvement stores help kids understand how to manage the finances associated with a project and how to do comparative shopping. Working on the project gains valuable work experience for your students and will likely build some character in them as well. Being able to enjoy the results of the project will make the link between hard work and good results clear.

- **Organizing family photos and video**. If you have a pile of photos lying around, a project to organize them can be a fun and educational experience. Gather all the items you want to include in your new family archive together. Have your kids come up with ways to organize and present them. Photo albums and scrapbooks are good places to start. If you have a computer capable of creating DVDs consider having your kids create DVDs for your photos and pictures. In addition to gaining and practicing computer skills, your kids' creativity will get a workout, too.

FIGURE 15.1

A Web site such as homeand-familynetwork.com can be useful when helping to teach your students how to do research needed for a home remodeling project.

- **Perform car maintenance**. A fact of owning a car is the need to maintain it. Teaching your kids how to maintain a car provides you with the chance to also teach them about how internal combustion engines and other mechanical devices work (which includes chemistry, physics, and many other science topics). You can also use a car to talk about the application of electricity to systems. Teaching your child about basic car maintenance also prepares them for the day when they start driving (see Figure 15.2).

FIGURE 15.2

Even if you aren't a skilled mechanic yourself, teaching your kids about car maintenance provides an entry into many other topics.

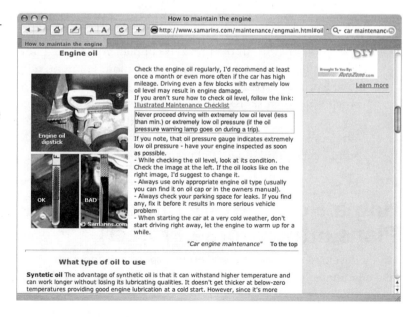

■ **Prepare a feast**. Have your children help you prepare a feast for the family. Start with menu planning; take the opportunity to learn about the various properties of food that are important to the body, such as calories, vitamins, carbohydrates, and so on (great discussions about the study of anatomy and chemistry). Have your kids develop a menu to meet specific goals; take advantage of Web resources to help them learn how to conduct research (see Figure 15.3). Then have them search for or create recipes and build shopping lists.

FIGURE 15.3

Your students can use the Food Finder Web site (located at www.olen.com/food/) to design a menu to meet specific goals.

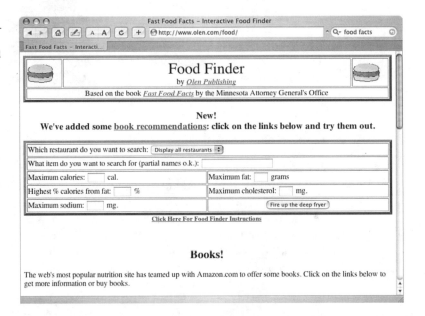

■ **Plan a vacation**. In the previous chapter, you learned how valuable a family vacation can be for your child's education. Planning a vacation can be a good learning experience for your child. They can explore geography and practice research skills as they search for destinations. Developing an itinerary practices math and organization skills. Budgeting for the trip can help kids learn about economics. Deciding what items to take along can help build logical thinking and planning skills.

Integrating a Home Project into Lesson Plans (or Lesson Plans into a Home Project)

As you develop lesson plans, you can incorporate a home project into those plans to take advantage of the education the home project can provide. For example, rather than having standard math lessons for a few days, perhaps you can have your students calculate the amount of material needed for a project. In addition to basic math skills, such as addition, subtraction, multiplication, and division, your students can exercise geometry by making and reading drawings. Or, when you are planning a vacation, focus your history lesson plans on the part of the world you will be visiting.

The basic point here is that you can adapt your lesson plans to take advantage of the learning experiences that home projects provide. Or, you can plan your home projects to take advantage of the lessons you want to teach, depending on your point of view.

note

The very spring and root of honesty and virtue lie in good education.—Plutarch

Working on a Home Project During School (or Doing School While Working on a Home Project)

While working on a home project isn't what you might picture when you think of a school day, time spent planning for and performing a home project can be just as valuable or more valuable than days spent in the classroom. One of the best ways to learn is by doing; a home project provides the opportunity for your students to do just that.

One thing you do need to do is to make sure that your lesson plans and schedules reflect the work your students do on a home project. This will ensure that the home project is a deliberate part of your homeschool. You need to do this for a couple of reasons. One is to ensure you are making appropriate progress toward your educational goals. The other is to be sure that you are meeting any requirements for your homeschool, such as hours of instruction.

Documenting a Home Project for Homeschool Purposes

Just like other aspects of your homeschool, you should document your home projects when they are part of your homeschool plans. Here are some ways you can easily document the projects on which you work:

■ Use a still camera or video camera to capture your work on the project at various stages. For example, take before, during, and after pictures. Include some video of students actually working on the project.

■ Save plans that your kids create as part of project planning. These plans can include floor plans, yard designs, menus, and so on.

■ Have your kids keep and maintain and schedules for the project. In addition to documenting what has been accomplished, this helps students learn about scheduling, which is a valuable skill for most areas of life.

■ Document research your students do for the project by having them keep records of Web sites they visit or books they use.

■ Have students create and keep a project journal in which they describe the project from start to finish. Encourage them to use this journal to capture their thoughts about the project along with facts about it.

When you finish a major project, consider creating a scrapbook or portfolio that includes the materials shown in the previous list. Describe the types of work done by each student and how they contributed to the overall result. This material can be excellent additions to the student's overall homeschool portfolio.

Innately, children seem to have little true realistic anxiety. They will run along the brink of water, climb on the window sill, play with sharp objects and with fire, in short, do everything that is bound to damage them and to worry those in charge of them, that is wholly the result of education; for they cannot be allowed to make the instructive experiences themselves.—Sigmund Freud

THE ABSOLUTE MINIMUM

Home projects are a great way to put a practical face on your kid's education. In addition to reinforcing many of the topics you will be teaching them, home projects provide opportunities for your kids to acquire skills and experience that will benefit them throughout their lives.

■ There are many kinds of home projects that tie in nicely with homeschool. These range from major projects such as remodeling a part of your home to simpler ones such as preparing a family feast.

continues

- You should build lesson plans to account for the home projects that you consider to be part of your homeschool program. This is to both relate the projects to the subjects you are teaching and to document that you have done so.

- While working on a home project might not seem like "school," the lessons your kids can learn can be just as meaningful and useful to them as the academic subjects you will teach them.

- Work on projects that are done as part of your homeschool should be documented just like other aspects of your homeschool.

16

Homeschooling with Tutors, Outside Classes, and Online Courses

Although as a homeschool parent you are primarily responsible for your child's education, this in no way means that you must be the one that teaches every topic to your students. There is no reason you have to "go it alone." In fact, there are many reasons that you shouldn't go it alone. For best results, especially as your child reaches the later grades, you should include "outside" instruction in your homeschool program, which by no coincidence, is the topic of this chapter.

Understanding Why Tutors, Outside Classes, and Online Classes Are Beneficial

There are two sources of outside instruction that you are likely to want to include in your homeschool program. I'll call one of these sources *tutors* and the other *outside classes*. Tutors teach your children on an individual basis. Outside classes are any classes that someone other than you teaches. Although these sources are fairly different in concept and approach, the benefits they offer to you are similar and include the following:

- **Takes some of the teaching effort off you**. Homeschooling is hard work. Including outside sources of instruction is good for you because you can share some of the work with others.

- **Addresses topics that you aren't qualified to teach**. Tutors and outside classes are a great way for you to address topics in which you might be weak or feel that you aren't really capable of teaching. Although there probably won't be many of these subjects early in your children's education, as they approach high school and even go into homeschool high school, you might find them needing topics that you simply don't feel qualified to teach. Using tutors and outside classes are great ways to make sure your children are educated properly in these subjects.

- **Gives your children experience in learning from others**. It is good experience for your children to learn from people who have different techniques, experiences, and perspectives than you do. This broadens the scope and depth of their learning experiences. Plus, if your children go onto a public or private high school, college, or vocational school, they will be learning from all sorts of people. Providing this experience during homeschool better prepares them for a transition to one of these types of schools.

- **Prepares your child for future traditional education**. At some point, your child is likely to make a transition from homeschool to a more traditional school, whether that is high school, college or university, or a vocational school. Including outside classes in your homeschool program prepares your students for such transitions because it gives them some experience operating in a more traditional learning situation before they make the transition.

- **Enables students to socialize**. Both of these sources of outside learning offer additional opportunities for your children to socialize with other kids and with the adults who teach them.

As you read earlier, the basic purpose of tutors and outside classes is the same—that is, to teach your children specific topics or skills. The difference between these sources is how your children will be taught.

A tutor will teach your child on an individual basis. In most cases, a tutor will be teaching only your child during the tutoring session. In most cases, a tutoring situation will be relatively informal.

An outside class, on the other hand, is just what you probably think it is. These are formal classes in a specific topic that are usually taught in a classroom setting similar to how classes are taught in traditional schools. Students are taught *en mass* (in this case, that means two or more students) in some sort of classroom. These types of classes usually involve some form of lecture, and include homework, tests, and the other accoutrements of "regular" school.

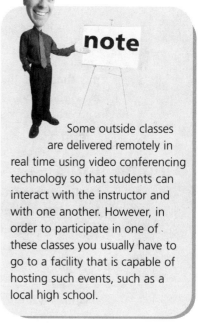

There is a third source of outside instruction that might also come in handy from time to time. This source is the many online classes that are available. Your students participate in these classes via the Internet, more specifically, the Web. Online classes don't offer as many benefits of the other types of outside instruction because your students will really just be working independently, as if they were using a textbook except that the instruction can include lectures by various people delivered over the Web. Even so, online courses can be a good way to have your children learn topics that you might not want to teach them yourself.

Some outside classes are delivered remotely in real time using video conferencing technology so that students can interact with the instructor and with one another. However, in order to participate in one of these classes you usually have to go to a facility that is capable of hosting such events, such as a local high school.

Using Tutors in Your Homeschool

Tutoring has probably existed as long as humans have taught one another. Until relatively recently (in historical terms), most education was provided via tutors rather than the schools we naturally think of today. Instruction by tutoring is simply one person teaching one student in a specific topic or skill. Tutoring in an extremely good way to educate children because it offers focused, one-on-one instruction which is as good as education gets. A tutor can tailor the instruction to fit the student's strengths and weaknesses, which makes it about the most effective type of instruction there is. Of course, for this reason, tutoring is resource intensive because it requires someone dedicated to teaching one person at a time.

Earlier in the chapter, you learned some of the benefits that tutoring can offer your child. However, there are two primary obstacles to using tutoring in your homeschool program. The first is finding a tutor for a subject in which your child needs to be instructed. (You'll get some help with this task in the next section.) The second issue is the cost of the instruction; because a tutor is involved with only one student at a time, the costs associated with this type of instruction tend to be higher than those associated with other types.

Because of the cost implications, you probably won't use tutors as much as the other types of outside instruction you are learning about in this chapter. Still, in certain situations, tutoring might be very useful to you and so you should understand how to include tutoring in your homeschool.

> **tip**
>
> When exploring a tutor for your children, consider bartering with the tutor for his or her services. If you can offer a service in return, you might be able to lower the cost of tutoring.

Finding Tutors

Finding a tutor for a specific topic can be a bit of a challenge. In this section, you'll learn some techniques that can help you find the right tutors for your homeschool.

One great place to find tutors is your homeschool network. Ask others in your network if they know of any tutors or if they know of anyone who uses a tutor. This will likely get you several leads that you can follow to find the tutors you need.

Schools, colleges, and universities in your area can also be a good source of tutors. You can ask about teachers in specific topics who might be interested in tutoring your child. However, don't limit yourself to teachers. Sometimes, especially in colleges and universities, students can make great tutors. They are close to the topic because they have recently taken or are taking advanced classes in that topic and they usually need money and will tutor for a relatively inexpensive amount (see Figure 16.1). Students in certain

> **tip**
>
> When looking for a tutor, don't limit yourself to people who are formal tutors or teachers. Many people can tutor very well even if they don't have formal teaching experience. For example, someone who works in science might be a great tutor for a science subject. Likewise, an engineer might be a great tutor for math or science topics.

disciplines can also get college credits for tutoring children. Some college tutoring programs are funded through federal and other types of grants that make the cost of tutors less expensive.

FIGURE 16.1

Many universities and colleges, such as Indiana University, offer tutor programs that you can take advantage of to find tutors for your children.

There are companies whose function is to provide tutors in specific topics for children. You can contact such companies to locate the tutor you need (see Figure 16.2). These companies can offer additional services such as specialized assessments of your child's strengths and weaknesses. They will then develop a tutoring program to help your child learn. Most of these companies are geared toward children being educated in traditional settings, but their services can be equally valuable for homeschoolers.

Another source of tutors is the group of people you know. Some of these people will be associated with a job or profession that is related to the subject you are looking for a tutor. Ask these people if they would be interested in tutoring your child in the subject. In many cases, people who have some relationship to your child will be happy to help in this way. There are a couple of things to be careful of when finding a tutor in this way. One is that just

If your child is involved in activities, it is likely that you already have them in a tutor situation. For example, music instructors who teach a single student at a time are really tutors.

because someone works in a field, that doesn't mean that person will make a good tutor. Second, because the tutoring would most likely be done on a personal basis, there can be difficulties in the tutor relationship if you already have a friendship with the person you are asking to be a tutor for you.

FIGURE 16.2

The Sylvan Learning Center (located at www.educate. com) can provide tutors for your children along with specialized assessments.

Working with Tutors

Before agreeing to work with a tutor that you find through any source, make sure you evaluate them by doing the following tasks:

- **Get information on the tutor's educational background**. It should go without saying that a tutor should be educated in the topic you are asking them to tutor—but you should ask anyway.

- **Find out how much tutoring experience the person has in the topic**. More experience is generally better, but it also can be more expensive. Someone who doesn't have a lot of tutoring experience isn't automatically a bad choice (everyone has to start somewhere!), but a tutor with less experience will require that you need to keep a closer eye on the tutoring process.

- **Schedule a trial tutoring session or two and sit in on those sessions**. If you are hiring a tutor, that tutor should be willing to commit to at least one trial session (which you should expect to pay for). You should sit in on this session (while not interfering with it, of course) to observe how the tutor conducts himself.

■ **Follow up on references**. If a tutor has experience, get references from that tutor and follow up with the references the tutor provides.

After you have identified the tutor with whom you want to work, you need to set some basic ground rules or conditions for the tutoring relationship.

Explain your goals and expectations for the tutoring services that will be provided to the tutor. For example, do you want the tutor to work with your child to improve a specific skill? Or do you want the tutor to teach your student an entire subject, such as a certain grade level or topic in math? Explain how long you expect the tutoring to continue. Be as clear as possible about what you want and expect the tutor to do. If possible, write your requirements down and have the tutor agree to them (or suggest alternatives) before getting started. A clear, written agreement will go a long way toward making sure you accomplish your goals through the tutor.

With the tutor, define how you will measure success. This will help you know if the tutoring process is achieving your goals or not. If you are hiring the tutor for a specific purpose, such as to teach your child a specific skill or to help your child catch up in a certain topic, define how you will know those goals have been achieved. Suppose you hire a tutor to help your child master a mathematic topic, such as algebra. You could choose a specific test that measures that skill and agree with the tutor what level of performance you will consider to be a success.

After you have fully defined your goals and expectations to the tutor, have the tutor explain her expectations to you. For example, ask about the

Education is not the filling of a pail, but the lighting of a fire. Of such is wisdom.—W. B. Yeats

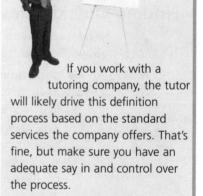

If you work with a tutoring company, the tutor will likely drive this definition process based on the standard services the company offers. That's fine, but make sure you have an adequate say in and control over the process.

One of the benefits of a tutoring company is that it will have access to lots of performance assessment tools that you can use to define and measure successful outcomes for tutoring.

amount of outside work that will be required from your child. Find out how you can support the tutor and make it clear that you want and expect the tutor to let you know if any situations arise that might keep the tutor from meeting your goals.

Then, define the logistics of how the tutoring will take place, such as times, locations, and so on.

After the tutoring begins, you should sit in on some tutoring sessions to make sure the tutor and your child are relating in a positive and constructive way. As the process continues, make sure your child is meeting the tutor's expectations. Periodically assess your child's progress through tests and other means.

Adding Outside Classes to Your Homeschool

Outside classes offer the chance for you to share the teaching load with someone else and to give your child experience in learning in more traditional settings, such as those they will experience in high school or college.

There are a couple of downsides to outside classes. One is their expense. Outside classes can be quite expensive depending on the topic and number of hours spent in class. The other is that you will have to conform to the class schedule and so will lose a bit of the flexibility that you enjoy as a homeschool family.

Finding Outside Classes

There are several sources for information about outside classes, including:

- **Your homeschool network** (You would have been surprised not to have found your network on this list, wouldn't you?). It is very likely that people in your homeschool network are either currently involved in outside classes or know someone who is. These people can put you in touch with the source of those classes along with recommendations about their experiences with them.

note

There are some people who generate or augment their incomes by teaching classes "on the side." These people often cater to homeschoolers.

- **Web sites that provide references to outside class opportunities in specific areas** (see Figure 16.3). To find sites like this, use a Web search engine (such as www.google.com) and search for homeschool classes *yourarea* where *yourarea* is the name of your city or state.

- **Formal organizations that provide classes for homeschoolers as a means of generating income** (see Figure 16.4). This type of class can be relatively expensive, so you need to be thoughtful about how you can use these in your homeschool.

FIGURE 16.3

There are many organizations that provide classes in specific topics that your children can take; this Web page shows a number of possibilities in the San Francisco area.

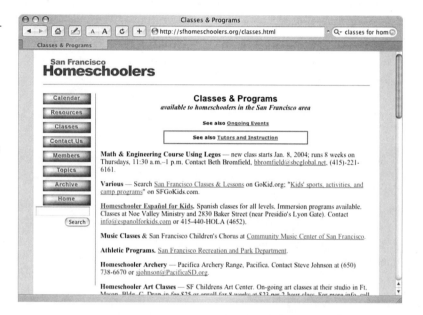

FIGURE 16.4

This is an example of classes that are offered for homeschoolers in a number of topics.

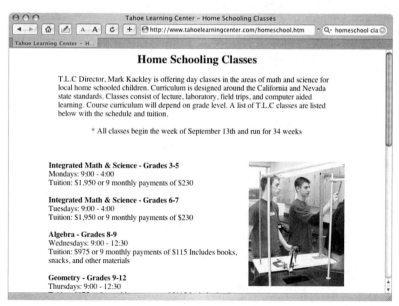

■ **Local schools**. Some public and private schools, including high schools, colleges, and universities, will allow your children to attend classes without being a registered student at that school (usually referred to as *auditing*). Check with the schools in your area that offer subjects in which you might be interested to see if they offer classes to people who don't attend that school.

Working with Outside Classes

After you have located an outside course in which you would like your child to participate, you will have to follow whatever processes are in place to register your child for that class. If an independent individual teaches the class, this process will likely be relatively simple. You usually just have to sign up for the class and pay any required fees. In more formal circumstances (such as with a public school), you might have to go through a formal application process along with paying any required fees.

Before your child starts a class, you should interact with its teacher to ensure that you understand the goals of the class and the expectations for your child, such as the amount of homework required, books and other supplies that will be needed, and so on. It is a good idea to explain to the teacher that you are eager to see your child make good progress in the class and that the teacher should feel free to contact you at any time.

You should also review the syllabus/curriculum for the class, including any textbooks or other material that will be used to teach the course.

When the class is underway, you won't have a lot of opportunity to determine how it proceeds (that is part and parcel with someone else taking on the teaching role for you). However, you should closely monitor your child's progress, keeping track of how your student is doing with homework, on tests, and so on. You will likely receive progress reports for your student, including grades.

tip

If possible, you and your student should try to "shadow" any outside class before you sign up for it. This means that you sit in on the class as an observer. This experience will provide you with a good feeling about how the class is conducted before you commit. Not all instructors will permit this, but many will.

note

The fate of empires depends on the education of youth.—Aristotle

Adding Online Classes to Your Homeschool

There are lots of sources of outside classes that don't require that your student actually go anywhere. These are online classes that are delivered over the Internet via the Web. These classes can be useful additions to your homeschool program because they can provide instruction in topics that you might not feel qualified to teach. Also, they typically offer flexibility in the appointed time of instruction, and just how your students will work through the class requirements.

Some online courses are free although others require a fee. Many online courses are offered by traditional educational institutions while others are offered by different types of organizations, such as social groups, interest societies, professional organizations, and so on.

Finding Online Courses

There are a couple of ways to find out about the online courses in which you might be interested.

Your homeschool network, as always, is a good place to start. Ask if anyone is using an online course and find out whether they recommend it or not.

The other source is the same medium you will use to take advantage of online courses—that is, the Internet. Use a Web browser to search for online courses. In addition to course topics, you can also include your area, grade levels, and other factors to limit the scope of your search. It is likely that you will find a number of online courses from which to choose (see Figure 16.5).

note

You will have a much better experience with most online courses if you have a high-speed Internet connection through a cable modem or a DSL connection. Many of these courses use video and other tools to deliver their material, and a high-speed connection will enable you to take advantage of such resources.

Working with Online Courses

You will need to register for the online courses that you want to take. Most of the time, this is done by completing an online registration process that includes the payment of fees if any are required.

How an online course works will vary depending on the specific courses you use. Most courses are organized into a series of lessons that the student works through; some courses include an online lecture while others present text, graphics, and animation to teach the student. After a certain number of lessons, there is typically a test to measure the student's progress.

FIGURE 16.5

A quick search for online math courses found the NetMath program hosted by the University of Illinois at Urbana-Champaign from which your student can take a variety of math courses.

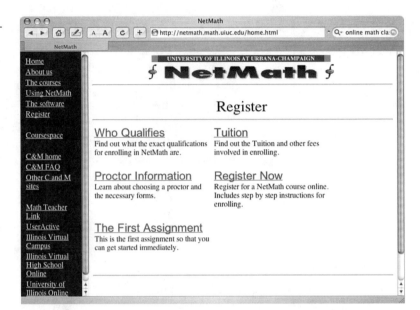

Integrating Tutors, Outside, and Online Classes into Your Homeschool

The amount of flexibility you have with outside sources with respect to your homeschool plans depends on the source of that instruction. Sometimes, as with tutors, you will have a lot of control over the topic, for example choosing the curriculum that is used. In most cases, the curriculum used will be part of your decision-making process. In most cases, you will have to take or leave the curriculum that is being used outside classes.

Similarly, the schedule flexibility you have will depend on the type of resource you are using. The most flexible will be online courses because many of these are independent and so your student can work though them at any time of day (or night). Tutors should be able to offer some degree of flexibility depending on the other obligations the tutor has. The least flexible option will be outside classes; you'll have to adapt your homeschool schedule to the class schedule.

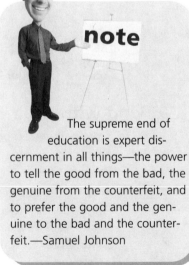

note

The supreme end of education is expert discernment in all things—the power to tell the good from the bad, the genuine from the counterfeit, and to prefer the good and the genuine to the bad and the counterfeit.—Samuel Johnson

Documenting the Results of Tutoring and Outside Classes

Just like the other parts of your homeschool, you need to document any work your student does through outside sources. In the case of classes (online or in the "real world"), your student will usually be tested during the course and her progress will be measure by grades. Successful completion of the course usually involves a final grade and some type of certification that your student completed the course. These should become part of your homeschool documentation along with information about the course itself, such as the syllabus or curriculum used.

Documenting the results of tutoring can be a bit more difficult. However, if you established goals and a measure of success for the tutoring process, you can use these to document the results. For example, if the goal of tutoring is for your child to achieve a specific score on a certain test, the before and after results for that test can serve as documentation of the results. You can also keep a log of tutoring time and ask the tutor for an evaluation of your student when the tutoring is complete. This evaluation should include a description of the work done, achievements of the student, and recommendations for the future.

note

Education is the best provision for the journey to old age.—Aristotle

THE ABSOLUTE MINIMUM

Adding resources outside your home is a great way to improve the effectiveness of your homeschool program. These sources include tutors, outside classes, and online classes. Each of these sources offers benefits to you, including a lower workload and coverage of topics you might not feel qualified to teach.

- Tutors are a great way to get one-on-one instruction for your students in topics in which they might be struggling or for topics that you don't feel qualified to teach. Tutoring is an excellent way to address specific problem areas a student might have.

- Outside classes give your students experience in more traditional settings, such as those they will experience in high school or college. There are many sources of outside classes you can participate in, including individuals who

continues

teach specific classes to schools that allow homeschoolers to take courses they offer.

■ Online courses can be a convenient way to expose your students to topics that you don't want to teach yourself.

■ Any outside source of instruction you use needs to be integrated into your overall homeschool program.

■ Any work your students do, including that work that is part of an outside class, tutor, or online course, should be documented along with the work they do within your homeschool.

IN THIS CHAPTER

- Understand how you can evaluate the progress of your students

- Test your students with curriculum-based tests

- Test your students with reports and projects

- Test your students with standardized tests

- Give your students grades, or not

- Promote your students to the next grade level

- Make changes to your homeschool based on your evaluations

17

EVALUATING THE PROGRESS OF YOUR STUDENTS

As your students learn, you need to evaluate or measure their progress. There are several reasons for this. The first, and the most important, reason is that you need to make sure that they are learning the material you are trying to teach them. In areas where you find that they are not making the progress you expect, you need to adjust your plans to make changes that are needed to get the student back on track, to shore up areas in which the student is weak, and so on. Second, when you find areas in which your student is not making the expected progress, you might need to reconsider your teaching methods, curriculum choices, and other aspects of your homeschool program to better suit the student. Third, you need to demonstrate that your students are performing at specific grade levels, either to meet state requirements or to qualify your students for transitions to traditional schools, scholarships, and for other reasons.

Understanding the Evaluation Methods You Can Use

There are several evaluation methods you should use in your homeschool. These include

- **Curriculum-based testing**. Any curriculum your child works through should include tests. Your child's ability to take and score well on these tests indicates that she is making good progress through the curriculum. Conversely, if he is having a hard time with the tests, you probably need to make some changes in the way you are teaching that topic to the child.

- **Reports and other projects**. You can assess your child's progress by having the child write reports or complete other projects related to the topics you are teaching. Having a child use the information you are attempting to teach through reports or other projects will help you assess their comprehension and retention of that material.

- **Standardized tests**. Standardized tests measure your child's education level in various subjects and evaluate your child by comparing him to national averages or standards for grade levels. Standardized tests are required for all public school children and most private schools use some form of standardized testing as well.

The results of any evaluation that you do should tell you one of two things: whether your child is on track and is achieving the expected levels of learning or your child is not on track and is not learning as expected. In the former case, you should feel good about your homeschool and continue in the same vein. When your testing and evaluation reveal problem areas, you need to make changes to what you are doing in order to help your child learn more effectively.

As you evaluate your child, she will achieve certain levels of performance and progress. You can recognize your child's accomplishments by assigning grades and by promoting your child to higher grade levels.

note

He who asks a question may be a fool for five minutes. But he who never asks a question remains a fool forever.
—Tom J. Connelly

Testing Your Students Using Curriculum-Based Tests

Almost all formal curricula that you purchase for use in your homeschool will include some sort of testing (see Figure 17.1). As your student works through the curriculum, she will take these tests. Some curricula test frequently, such as at the completion of each lesson, while others test after a certain number of lessons have been completed.

After your child completes a test, you will "grade" it to see how your child performed. If the child was able to complete the test with reasonable success, the child has demonstrated progress in learning the material. Of course, what reasonable success *is* depends on the standards you want to maintain.

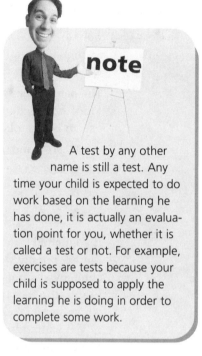

note

A test by any other name is still a test. Any time your child is expected to do work based on the learning he has done, it is actually an evaluation point for you, whether it is called a test or not. For example, exercises are tests because your child is supposed to apply the learning he is doing in order to complete some work.

FIGURE 17.1

This Saxon Math 8/7 curriculum is an example of curricula that include several types of tests that you administer to measure the progress of your child through the curriculum.

In most cases, you should develop and keep some standard means of grading test results. Typically, you will calculate a percentage score by dividing the number of right answers by the total number of problems on the test to generate a percent. For example, if a test has 10 problems and your child completes 8 of them correctly, he would receive a score of 80%.

The percentage score that you consider to be successful is largely a judgment call. Many homeschoolers adopt a philosophy that is similar to what traditional schools use, as in the following example:

- 90% and above: Excellent
- 80%-90%: Good
- 70%-80%: Adequate
- 70% or less: Not adequate

If your child is achieving scores of 80% or better regularly, she is likely learning the material pretty well. If your child frequently achieves scores in the 70%, you should carefully evaluate your child in that area. While many schools consider 70% passing, realize that this means your child is missing almost one-third of the material, which should cause you some concern. Any scores less than 70% should really result in you examining the child's learning in the area in which you are testing because something has gone amiss.

You can choose to attach a letter grade to test results if you want to (for example, 90% and above is an "A"). In reality, the percentage score is really what is important because it tells you how well your student is performing. A letter grade only becomes meaningful when a level of performance (a percentage score) is associated with it.

As you grade or assess your student, realize that the main purpose in doing so is not to provide the grade per se. What you are really looking for is the information that the grade communicates to you—that is, the progress your student is making in learning the material. A "good" grade indicates that appropriate progress is being made. A "bad" grade indicates that there are areas where improvement is needed, and you need to take action to help the student achieve more acceptable learning progress. (In the last section in this chapter, you'll learn about some of the corrective actions you can take in these cases.)

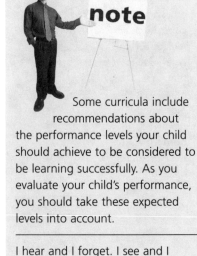

note

Some curricula include recommendations about the performance levels your child should achieve to be considered to be learning successfully. As you evaluate your child's performance, you should take these expected levels into account.

I hear and I forget. I see and I remember. I do and I understand.—Confucius

TIME LIMITS

Most tests include a recommended time limit for your student to take the test. It is very important that you use these time limits when you administer tests to your students. Placing a limit on the amount of time a student has to complete a test increases the effectiveness of the test because it encourages the student to work through the material to the best of his or her ability.

Time limits also prepare the student better for the real world. It is rare in life that people have unlimited time to complete tasks assigned to them. While we are usually allowed more time for the significant tasks we do than are typical for tests, time pressure is simply a fact of life. Placing time limits on the tests you administer helps your student understand and cope with this fact.

You should consider placing time limits on most homeschool activities that your student does. For example, when you assign reading, reports, or other schoolwork, also provide your student with a specific period of time in which to do them.

Testing Your Students Using Reports and Other Projects

Curricula-based tests are only one way you will evaluate a child's learning progress. They are also among the most straightforward ways because the results are usually indicated by a straight percentage-based score. However, there are many other ways that you should evaluate your students' progress as they work through the curricula you have designed. Some of these are formal and can also be graded in a quantitative way. Many, on the other hand, are not so formal or have to be graded in a qualitative way, which can be a bit trickier for you to assess.

Non-test means of evaluation can include any and all of the following:

- **Exercises**. All curricula will include some sort of exercises that your child will need to complete as part of the learning process. Although these aren't called "tests," they serve the same purpose in many ways. You typically will score or grade exercises (or the students will do so themselves). Low scores on an exercise indicate that a student did not understood or can't apply the material. This should cause you to take some type of corrective action.

- **Other homework assignments**. Other kinds of work are part of many curricula. This work can include reading assignments, various writing assignments (essays, stories, and so on), experiments, and other forms of work.

- **Reports**. Reports are a good way to help a child learn a topic and to asses his learning at the same time. Having children write a report to summarize a topic that they are learning is a great way to "test" them on that topic. You can also use reports to help you evaluate non-academic activities, such as field trips. Reports are also beneficial because your child exercises other skills as the same time, such as organization, spelling, grammar, writing, and so on. Reports also enable your child to exercise her creativity.

■ **Projects**. Projects are an excellent way to help your child apply their knowledge of a topic in a real and visible way. In many ways, projects are among the best ways to evaluate a child's learning because they demonstrate the child's ability to practically apply what they have learned. They also allow a child to exercise and demonstrate multiple skills at the same time.

The bottom line is that you should use everything your student does as an opportunity to assess how well they are learning the material they are supposed to be learning. Even if you don't formally grade an activity as you do as test, you should keep close tabs on what your child is doing and make some type of assessment of how well they are doing it.

Many of these evaluation tools require that you assess a student's performance in a qualitative way rather than a quantitative way. This requires that you exercise more judgment because unlike quantitative measures, such as tests for which you can easily calculate a percentage score, you have to make a qualitative judgment about how your child has performed. For example, suppose you have your child write a report to summarize his learning in a specific area; when you evaluate that report, you can't easily score it by comparing the number of correct answers to the number of incorrect ones. Instead, you must judge how well the child did on the report by considering how well they communicated his understanding, how well it was organized and written. These judgments, while being more difficult to make than grading a test, are just as important as the quantitative evaluations you will make.

When you use a tool for which you can't really calculate a percent score, you can apply a letter grading system to indicate your child's relative performance. Just like quantitative grades, when your child doesn't perform up to the levels you expect, that should be a sign to you that you need to take some corrective action to help your child learn the specific topic more effectively.

Testing Your Students Using Standardized Tests

Standardized tests measure your child's education levels by comparing them to specific standards (which is why they are called standardized). These standards usually relate to the average scores of groups of students based on some attribute, which is grade level in most cases. The most typical standards are the national averages cal-culated from the performance of students in the same grade level throughout the nation. (If you were ever involved in any form of traditional education, you are familiar with standardized tests because they are a part of all public and most pri-vate schools. You probably remember filling in dots on an answer sheet yourself—using number 2 pencils only!)

Standardized testing is valuable for several reasons.

The most important reason is that standardized tests provide an objective measure of your students' education level compared to "accepted" levels (also called *norms*). By comparing your students to these norms, you can get a good idea about how well your students are being edu-cated compared to the education provided by pub-lic and other traditional schools (the standards are mostly determined by the children being educated in these arenas). This is very useful as a measure of how well your homeschool is achieving results com-pared to these traditional sources of education. Where your student performs at or better than the standard levels, you can be confident that your homeschool is working at least as well or better than a traditional school would. Where your stu-dent performs below the standards for her grade level, you know you have some additional work to do. In other words, the standards established by these tests give you an objective target by which to measure the results you are achieving through your homeschool.

note

Don't be surprised if your homeschool students regularly achieve better than aver-age performance on the standard-ized tests that they take. Statistics reveal that homeschoolers per-form significantly better on these tests than do children being edu-cated in public and other tradi-tional schools.

Another reason to use standardized tests is to provide "proof" of how well your homeschool is working. This is the reason that some states require that you adminis-ter such tests and provide the results to the government body with oversight over the students in your area, such as a local school superintendent. Because traditional school systems use these tests to measure the effectiveness of their own systems, they also recognize them as a means to judge the results of your education system (your homeschool).

A third reason to administer standardized tests is to qualify your students for some-thing, such as the SAT to qualify a student for entrance into a college, or to judge a student as part of a competition for a scholarship.

ASSESSMENT OR PLACEMENT STANDARDIZED TESTS

There are many kinds of standardized tests that are used to assess a person's appropriateness for entry into college, specific careers, and in other avenues. Although these tests are somewhat different than the standardized tests you will use to assess your child's educational achievements, the mechanics of taking and scoring these tests are nearly identical. (This is a fourth reason that including standardized tests should be part of your homeschool—they provide experience to prepare your child to take other standardized tests later in life.) Here are some of the more well known standardized entrance exams that are used for various levels of college:

- **SAT.** The Scholastic Assessment Test (SAT) is the most widely used standardized test for entry into colleges and universities. It is usually administered to high school juniors or seniors. Good SAT results can be a great help to gain entry into college for any student. Because homeschoolers don't have some of the documentation generated by publicly schooled kids, such as transcripts from a traditional school, the SAT is especially important. There are many ways to prepare for the SAT, such as specialized courses, books, and more. SAT scores are provided as an overall score, a math score, and an English score. Changes are being made in the SAT and students who will be high school seniors in 2006 will be the first to use the revised test (see Figure 17.2).

FIGURE 17.2

The SAT has been changed for 2006; whether it has been improved or not is a matter of some controversy.

- **ACT**. The American College Testing Program (ACT) is another standardized exam that is widely used as part of the acceptance process for colleges and universities. It is used for similar purposes as the SAT, but the results are reported somewhat differently. The ACT measures a student in English, math, reading, and science (see Figure 17.3).

FIGURE 17.3

The ACT is also widely used as part of the college entrance process.

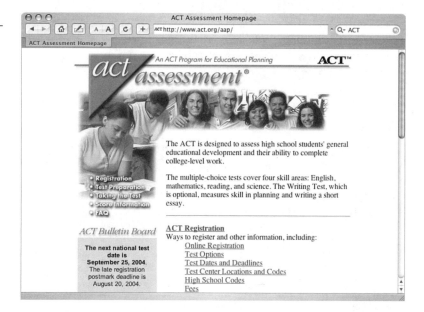

- ■ **GMAT**. The Graduate Management Admission Test (GMAT) is similar to the SAT and ACT except that it is used for entrance into graduate school.

- ■ **GRE**. The Graduate Record Examination (GRE) is another test used to assess students for entry into graduate schools in fields other than business, law, and medicine.

Choosing and Obtaining Standardized Tests

In a somewhat ironic turn of events, there is more than one standard for standardized tests. The following is a list of some of the most common standardized tests that homeschoolers use today:

- ■ **Iowa Test of Basic Skills**. This is one of the most widely used tests and it has a reputation of being among the most difficult to take, but it also takes less time than some of the other tests. This test is widely used in public school systems as well. You can use this test for children in grades K-12. One of its benefits is that you test students in grade 3-8 at the same time, which isn't true of all tests. In order to be able to administer this test, you must have a 4-year baccalaureate degree.

- **Stanford Achievement Test**. This is also a widely used test that measures a student's overall education level. The test can be used for children in grades K-12. To administer this test, you must also have a baccalaureate degree. The publisher also has additional requirements about administering the test to family members that you need to be aware of.

- **California Achievement Test**. This test, which can be used for students in grades 2-12, is popular among homeschoolers. Its topics include reading, language, math, study skills, science, and social studies. One of its benefits is that it has less stringent requirements about administering the test than do some of the other options.

- **Comprehensive Test of Basic Skills**. This test can be used for grades 1-12 and covers reading, language skills, spelling, math, science, social studies, and reference skills.

This list is by no means comprehensive. There are many other standardized tests available to you. Some of these go beyond educational testing and delve into personality and other personal characteristics.

Which test you use is a largely a matter of personal preference because they all offer benefits and typically provide similar types of results, those being a comparison of your child's performance with standard levels of performance based on grade level. It is more important that you use some sort of test than which specific test you use.

If you will be administering the test yourself, which you probably will be as a homeschooler, you need to pay attention to the administration requirements. The Iowa and Stanford tests require that you have a baccalaureate degree to administer the test; you'll have to sign a form on which you promise you have the required degree. If you don't have such a degree, you will need to either find someone else to administer the test for you or choose a different test, such as the California test.

I recommend that you check with people in your homeschool network to see which tests they use. It can be helpful to use the same test as others in your network so you can get advice and help in understanding the test process and recommendations about the specific tests people you trust suggest.

note

Earlier in this book, you learned about the Myers-Briggs personality types. There are several tests you can administer to your children to determine their personality preferences. These are another form of standardized test.

In case you are wondering, my family uses the Iowa test. It is quite comprehensive and the results you receive are very detailed.

Whatever test you choose, you should plan on using the same test throughout your child's education. This will help your comparisons from year to year be more consistent because you will be measuring progress against the same set of standards. (If you use different tests, you will be comparing your child against different sets of standards.)

You don't have to use just one test; you could choose a combination such as the Iowa and Stanford tests.

Be aware that administering a standardized test takes a significant amount of time; for example, the Iowa test is designed to be delivered over several days. Many homeschoolers devote one week per school year to standardized tests. If you use more than one test, the time required will be even greater.

To use a standardized test, you must purchase it. The price of the test will include all testing materials, such as instructions, test booklets, answer sheets, along with scoring and reporting of the results back to you. There are a number of sources of standardized tests from which you can choose (see Figure 17.4). Again, check with people in your homeschool network to see if they recommend specific sources of testing material for you.

FIGURE 17.4

One testing source I have used and recommend is Bob Jones University press (www.bjup.com).

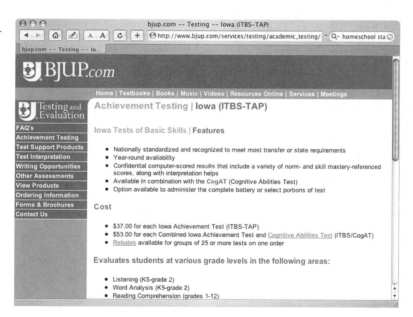

After you have selected a source, you can choose the test you want to purchase for the grade levels you need to test. You will need to purchase a version of the test for each child by grade level. If the test requires that you have some qualifications to be able to administer the test, you will need to complete some type of verification process before you can order the test materials.

You need to allow plenty of lead time when ordering tests. The order process can take a while, especially if you need to verify that you meet the requirements to administer the test. Typically, you should allow 30-60 days between the time you place an order and when you want to administer the test.

Also, most tests require that you administer the tests and return the tests within a specific amount of time after you receive them. For example, you might have to administer the test and return the results within 50 days after you have received the test materials. It can take another 4-8 weeks to get the results.

The test package you receive will usually include the following items:

- **Administration instructions**. These will explain the process you need to follow to administer the tests.

- **Test booklets**. These booklets contain the questions your children will answer when they take the test.

- **Answer sheets**. Most tests use a computer-scored form as an answer sheet. (You know the type—fill in the circles with a number 2 pencil.)

- **Return instructions and shipping materials**. You will use these items to return the test materials and to submit the score sheets for grading.

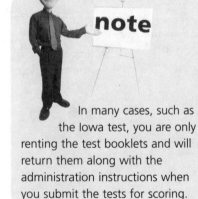

tip

Most tests offer practice versions. You can use these to help your children practice taking the standardized test you have selected. You will grade the practice tests yourself. These are especially useful if your child has never taken a standardized test or if it has been a long time since she has done so.

note

In many cases, such as the Iowa test, you are only renting the test booklets and will return them along with the administration instructions when you submit the tests for scoring.

Administering Standardized Tests

Determining when to administer standardized tests can be a bit of a dilemma. There are two general schools of thought on this. One is that you should test your child based on his completion of a grade level. In other words, test a child who is completing the fifth grade at the fifth grade level at the end of the school year. The benefit of this approach is that your child's learning is fresh and the test provides a good measure of your child's performance based on completion of that grade. Most homeschoolers adopt this approach.

You also could test your child before the school year starts at the grade level they will be taking during the upcoming year. This "prequalifies" them for the grade level and provides a guide for you as to the areas in which you really need to focus for the upcoming year. The benefit is that you can use the test results a bit more proactively. Of course, you also will be testing your child in some topics in which he might not have been exposed yet if a topic is not covered until the upcoming grade level.

You also should consider how often you should administer the standardized test. Many people test their students every year while others feel that every other or every third year is often enough. How often you test will depend on how useful you find the results. Typically, testing becomes more important as a child moves into higher grades, but you can test as often as you feel the need. At the least, you will feel more confident about how effective your homeschool is if you test more frequently.

Decide which approach you will use and then stick with it for your entire homeschool career. You should try to standardize your approach to standardized tests (pun intended).

When it comes time to administer standardized tests to your students, follow the instructions that come with the test. You will have your students use the test booklets to guide them through the test. Assessment tests are divided into modules based on specific skills

tip

If you don't meet the administration requirements for a test, that doesn't mean you can't use that test. You might be able to find someone to administer the test for you. For example, someone in your homeschool network might be administering the test to her own students. Your kids might be able to take the test at the same time.

note

Many states require that you test your children periodically such as once per year. If you live in such a state, you need to make sure that you comply with the time requirement and with any specific tests that are required to be used.

within a general topic, such as reading comprehension in the language arts section. As I mentioned before, you need to allow several days for the testing process.

When the tests are complete, you will return the test materials and completed answer sheets to the source from which you purchased them. The answer sheets will be scored.

Obtaining and Using the Results of Standardized Tests

Eventually, you will receive the test results (see Figure 17.5). Remember that all scoring is based on a relative comparison of your child's performance to that of students taking the same test at the same grade level.

note

Most administration instructions include text that you actually read to the students to lead them through the test process. I don't really know why a college degree is required to administer such tests. Doing so is mostly a matter of reading and following instructions.

FIGURE 17.5

Here is a results sheet from an Iowa test; in the upper right corner, you see a comparison of this child's scores with the national percentiles.

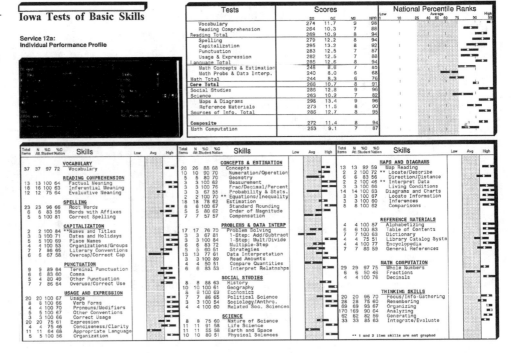

The results will include the actual performance of your student on the test, usually measured as the number of right answers for each test section based on the specific skills being tested. Your child's performance is then compared to the specific standard used in the test. A percentile is calculated to show how your child compares to these standards. For example, you child might be scored at the 90th percentile, which means that your child's performance was better than 90% of the children whose scores make up the standard (and that 10% scored as well or better in that same group). Likewise, if your child was scored at the 50th percentile, he performed at a level above about 50% and below about 50% of the children whose scores make up the standard. This would indicate your child performed at an average level.

You might also see an estimated grade-level performance, comparisons to different national averages, and other performance measures. (The specific measures you see will depend on the test you are using.)

Some tests will also include a more detailed analysis of the results your children achieved.

When you receive the results, you should carefully study them. Especially important are those topics in which your child is doing exceptionally well or those in which your child is not doing as well. Both situations provide information that you can use in your future homeschool planning activities. In the topics in which your child performs at a good level (usually somewhere above the average), you can rest assured that your homeschool program is educating your child effectively.

In the topics in which your child performed exceptionally well, you might want to consider raising the level of education in that topic for the next school period. For example, suppose you have a fifth grade student that performs at the 90th percentile in most math topics. You might need to have that student work through sixth

note

Because you spend so much time in close relationship with your children while you are educating them, the results of a standardized test probably won't surprise you very much as you most likely already have a very good idea of where your students are strong and where they are not.

caution

If your child does perform exceptionally well in an area, you might be tempted to skip over the next grade level entirely. That is usually not a good idea. Concepts are introduced at specific grade levels. If you skip a grade level, you might also skip over topics, too. It is better to accelerate your child's progress through a grade level rather than skipping it entirely.

grade math topics at an accelerated pace or choose additional advanced math topics for that child. For areas of exceptional performance, you should adjust your curricula choices and lesson plans to make sure that you are helping your child fulfill her potential in that area.

For any areas in which your child doesn't perform as well as you would like, don't panic. Knowing this is a good thing. This information should help you better teach specific areas in which your child isn't performing as well as you'd like. If your child is performing below average in a topic, this indicates that you need to take some corrective action in that area, which means taking more time and working harder in that area than you might have planned for the upcoming year. It also might mean that the way in which you are teaching that topic to that child is not working very well. You might need to use a different curriculum. Or, perhaps you aren't accounting for the child's learning style in that area.

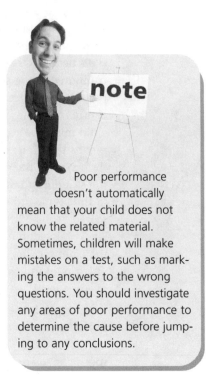

Poor performance doesn't automatically mean that your child does not know the related material. Sometimes, children will make mistakes on a test, such as marking the answers to the wrong questions. You should investigate any areas of poor performance to determine the cause before jumping to any conclusions.

Giving Your Students Grades

In traditional schools, students are awarded letter grades to indicate their performance on tests and for subjects over a period of time (the dreaded report card). In a homeschool, you don't really need to provide letter grades for your students; after all, in traditional schools the primary purpose of grades is to communicate a child's performance to the parent. Because you are the parent, you already know your child's performance.

However, some homeschoolers enjoy providing their children with letter grades and report cards at the end of the school year. This can be a good way to "close" out a school year and to let your child know how well they did over the year.

When you send your child to outside classes, you should receive a grade and other evaluations for that child for the class.

If you choose to continue homeschool through high school, you should provide grades for topics you teach at the high school levels. You can combine these grades with those received from outside classes to develop transcripts for the student. These transcripts might be required when the student applies to certain colleges or universities (though many rely only on test scores to measure academic performance, such as the SAT).

Promoting Your Students to the Next Grade Level

The primary purpose of grade levels in the context of homeschool is to help you choose curricula elements that are appropriate to your child's education level. Because you can tailor your curricula to your child's status, you might mix grade levels (such as using eighth grade math and seventh grade English for a student who has strong math skills), which further devalues grade levels in the context of homeschool.

However, it can help your child understand the progress they are making if you promote your child at the successful conclusion of each school year. While I wouldn't go as far as having graduation ceremonies, it can be fun to recognize each child's promotion from one grade to the next.

note

I have learnt silence from the talkative, toleration from the intolerant, and kindness from the unkind; yet strangely, I am ungrateful to these teachers.—Kahlil Gibran

There are three principal means of acquiring knowledge…observation of nature, reflection, and experimentation. Observation collects facts; reflection combines them; experimentation verifies the result of that combination.
—Denis Diderot

Making Changes Based on Your Evaluations

The primary purpose of all the evaluations you do for your child, including tests, standardized tests, grades for projects, and so on, should be to help you know where you need to make changes to your homeschool curricula and lesson plans.

When your child is not learning effectively, this should be indicated by low evaluations, such as poor test scores. This should cause you to make changes to how you are teaching that topic to the child. This might be as simple as having the child go over material again. Or, it might be as complex as changing the curriculum you are using for that topic.

When your child is performing "too well," that should be evident as well. For example, if a child is "ace-ing" tests regularly, you probably aren't pushing that child enough to maximize his potential. You should consider accelerating that child's progress through the topic or choosing a more advanced curriculum.

Just remember that evaluating a child should be all about evaluating how well the child is learning, which actually means how well the child is being taught. Use the results of your evaluations to help you know how to teach the child more effectively.

The Absolute Minimum

An extremely important part of homeschooling is the evaluation of the progress your students are making. There are many ways to measure progress and you should use all of them to help you make needed changes to your homeschool program. Evaluation methods you use should include the following:

- Curriculum-based tests help you evaluate the progress your child is making through a specific curriculum. These tests are usually part of the teaching materials you use for that curriculum.

- Having a student write reports or do projects is another way to assess whether they are learning material you are trying to teach. These tools sometimes reveal whether your child is actually assimilating material.

- Standardized tests are a great way to objectively measure your children's education level because their performances are measured against quantifiable standards, such as national scores on the same tests.

The end result of all your evaluations should be that your child is performing as expected, meaning you don't need to make changes to your program; your child is performing better than expected, meaning you should consider accelerating her education; or your child is not performing as well as expected, meaning you need to make changes to help that child learn more effectively.

18

DECIDING IF AND WHEN TO TRANSITION STUDENTS TO PUBLIC OR PRIVATE SCHOOL

As you move through the homeschool years, you might start wondering if it would be good for your children to move from homeschool into a traditional, institutional education setting at some point in time. Frankly, unless you have a life circumstance that prevents you from being able to continue homeschooling, there really isn't a reason you can't continue to successfully homeschool your children through high school. However, in some cases, you might decide that it is better for your family to move a child into a public or private school. The purpose of this chapter is to describe some circumstances in which you might want to consider making such a change. If you do make this decision, the remainder of the chapter identifies some things you need to be aware of to help your child make the transition smoothly.

Knowing If and When to Move a Student Back to "Regular" School

In most cases, you will be able to educate your children via homeschool quite successfully, so not being able to educate them well usually isn't a reason to stop homeschooling. (If you follow the evaluation practices described in the previous chapter, you are well aware of how well your homeschool is doing.)

However, there are a number of circumstances that might cause you to consider transitioning children from homeschool to an institutional school. These might include the following:

- **Life changes that prevent you from being able to homeschool**. There are situations that can occur in your family, such as a long-term illness or injury or change in your family's financial status, which can preclude you from being able to continue homeschooling. In such circumstances, you might have no choice but to transition your child to a public or private school.

- **Extreme personal conflicts**. In rare situations, a parent who homeschools can have major and continuing conflicts with a student. The conflicts can become so great that effective learning at home just isn't possible. Sometimes, transitioning such a student to a public or private school is the best for everyone involved.

- **Extreme personality type**. Some children with certain extreme personality types (for example, one who is extremely extroverted and has strong sensing preferences) just might not be a good fit for the homeschool environment, especially as they approach their high school years. Children of this type might actually do better in an institutional setting because they can get more external stimulation without disrupting the entire homeschool process. This is also a relatively rare situation.

> **caution**
>
> Before giving up on homeschooling because of personality conflicts with a student, make sure you allow lots of time to pass. The kind of conflicts I am referring to are severe and can last over a long period of time. Hopefully, you won't ever experience these kinds of conflicts with your children.

Outside of these life circumstances, there are some who believe that it can be beneficial to transition students to an institutional school setting at specific points in time.

A common time for this kind of "pre-planned" transition is when a student becomes ready for high school. The idea is that institutional high school provides a good transition between the closely supervised environment of a homeschool and the totally unsupervised environment of living away from home while attending college. Plus, high schools make participation in sports and other activities easier. And, although it isn't true, people in this camp sometimes assume that homeschooled students will have a hard time getting into a good college or university.

You can actually achieve many of the "benefits" of an institutional high school by including outside classes, tutors, and other activities in your homeschool as described earlier in this part of the book. You can also continue to avoid many of the negatives of an institutional school environment, many of which become more extreme at the high school level. Personally, I don't believe that there is a lot to be gained from transitioning a student to an institutional high school "just because," as long as you develop a good plan for completing the high school years in a homeschool. Still, this idea does have some merit and I wouldn't totally discount it as a viable strategy.

note

Humans hardly ever learn from the experience of others. They learn—when they do, which isn't often—on their own, the hard way.
—Robert Heinlein

Preparing a Homeschooled Student to Move to Public or Private School

If you have decided to transition a student to an institutional setting, you need to prepare the student for some dramatic changes in his life. These include

- Loss of freedom and flexibility because of a more rigid schedule.

- Exposure to more people; most of that exposure will be out of the student's control.

- Negative behaviors of children who are mostly driven by peer social pressure (such as teasing, taunting, bullying, and so on).

- More opportunity for self-destructive, dangerous, or immoral behavior.

- Longer school days.

- Less interaction with family members.

- Lots of busywork.

note

Of course, not everything about an institutional school environment is negative. However, you can re-create almost all the positive aspects in your homeschool program.

- Fewer work assignments that are significant to him.
- More homework (sometimes depending on the school).
- Lots of administrative and other ineffective time.

If the student has never been in an institutional education setting before, you should have extensive discussions with the student about these changes. The student will likely have some anxiety about the change and you will need to help the student work through this.

Some schools allow perspective students to "ghost," which means they can participate in a school day without actually being a student there. Having a child ghost at the school to which you will be sending him can help ease the transition.

In addition to the changes experienced directly by the student, your entire family will experience some degree of change. The most significant is that you will have to adhere to the institution's schedule. You will have to make sure that your student is in school when required. This will eliminate much of the schedule flexibility that homeschooling families enjoy. You will also have to participate in the school's activities to some extent, such as interacting with teachers and administrators, attending school functions, and so on. These activities take up time in your family's schedule, not to mention the time and expense they require.

note

He helps others most, who shows them how to help themselves.—A. P. Gouthe

Managing the Education of a Child Who Has Been Homeschooled in Public or Private School

When you transition a student to an institutional school, you transfer the bulk of the day-to-day responsibility for that student's education to the school. However, I'm sure that you realize that as the child's parent, you still have the ultimate responsibility to make sure that your child is properly educated.

Fulfilling this obligation starts by you ensuring that the institution to which you transition your child is worthy of your trust. Don't just assume all schools are equally capable of providing the education you child needs. Do your homework on the schools that are available to you. You should have the option for at least one public school in your area; hopefully, you will have private schools from which to choose as well. Make the most informed choice that you can.

After your student starts attending the school, you will need to spend time and effort to keep tabs on her experience there. This involves talking to your student about daily happenings, examining progress reports provided to you, interacting with teachers as much as possible, and so on. You should also keep tabs on the "political" happenings at the school such as actions of the school board that might have an impact on how your child is being educated.

You can continue to help your child learn by being involved with the outside work that he is expected to do. In addition to helping with specific problems, you can discuss materials he brings home and ask him about specific topics to see what kind of progress he is making.

A fact of life is that you will still need to spend a considerable amount of time and energy managing your child's education. You just won't have as much involvement in or control over the details.

tip

Some public school districts allow students from outside that school's district to attend school within the district. Typically, you will have to pay additional fees for this because (theoretically) your tax dollars are supporting the institution as much as the taxes paid by people who live in the district are. Still, if you know of a good public school relatively near you, it might be worth exploring this as a potential option.

Preparing a Homeschooled Student for College

In many cases, your homeschooled students will want to attend a college or university. This is definitely a good thing. As a homeschool manager, you can prepare your students for college in a number of ways. You will do this primarily through the high school program that you design and implement. Covering the details involved in doing high school work at home are beyond the scope of this book (this topic is worthy of a book in its own right), but you'll get some general ideas in this section.

note

Education is a companion which no future can depress, no crime can destroy, no enemy can alienate it and no nepotism can enslave.
—Ropo Oguntimehin

To be considered a legitimate high school, most states require that students complete a specific amount of education in specified topics. These requirements are usually expressed as units, as in four units of foreign language studies. When you plan your high school curricula, you should account for such requirements if you state has them. This will ensure that your students have exposure to at least as many topics as their institutionally educated peers.

You should do much of your activity during the high school years with an eye toward college admission procedures, scholarships, and other parts of the college entrance process. You can focus toward this end in several ways.

First, maximize the variety of activities in which your student is involved. In addition to sporting activities, consider volunteer/service work, part-time jobs, and other non-academic activity. These activities are considered during most college's admission's processes. As a homeschooler, your child will occasionally suffer from the misperception that homeschoolers aren't involved outside the home. Maximizing these kinds of activities will be good for your student and will help when it comes time to apply to a college or university.

Second, if you haven't kept formal grades during the years before high school, do so now. You will need to create a transcript for your child's high school years because this is sometimes required by admissions procedures. Grades make the transcript more meaningful because they provide some measure of accomplishment (albeit a subjective one). A transcript doesn't have to be terribly complicated and can be as simple as the example shown in Table 18.1.

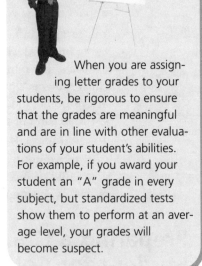

note

When you are assigning letter grades to your students, be rigorous to ensure that the grades are meaningful and are in line with other evaluations of your student's abilities. For example, if you award your student an "A" grade in every subject, but standardized tests show them to perform at an average level, your grades will become suspect.

Table 18.1 A High School Transcript Helps with College Admissions Processes

Grade Level	Course	Description	Hours of Instruction	Course Grade
9th	Algebra I	Fundamentals of algebra	5/wk	B
	English Literature	Study of literature during 1700-2000	5/wk	A
	PE	Aerobics, homeschool basketball	6/wk	A
...				

Third, create and maintain a portfolio of your child's high school years. A good portfolio will be very useful in applying for colleges and scholarships. Include lots of documentation of both the quality and quantity of your child's high school education. (More information about documentation and portfolios is provided in Chapter 12, "Documenting Your Homeschool.")

Fourth, make sure your child has taken standardized tests and that you include the results in the child's portfolio. Particularly important are the SAT, ACT, and other such exams that are relied on by colleges and universities to assess applicants. Somewhere in your child's sophomore or junior year, you should include preparation specifically for these tests. Have your child take these tests in both the junior and senior years (a child can take most of these exams more than once). A well-documented history of excellent performance on standardized tests is a powerful tool when your student is applying to colleges.

Start planning for college early in your child's high school career so that when it is time to apply, your child has a leg up on her competition. One of the advantages of a homeschool is that you can allow for additional time during the high school years for research and college entrance preparation than is allowed to students in institutional schools.

Education is not the filling of a pail, but the lighting of a fire. Of such is wisdom—W. B. Yeats

THE ABSOLUTE MINIMUM

At some point, you might need to transition one or more of your students from homeschool to a public or private school. For many homeschoolers, this transition doesn't happen until the student reaches college, but there are situations that can force this transition to happen earlier.

- Some life changes will require that you move a student from homeschool to a public or private school. Examples include long-term illness, financial difficulties, or other events that impact your ability to spend the time and effort that homeschool requires.

- Some people think making this transition at the high school level makes sense as preparation for college. However, you can prepare your child just as well or better in high school at home.

continues

- When you move a child from homeschool to an institutional school, he will experience significant changes in his daily life. You need to prepare your child for these changes.

- Even if a student moves into a public or private school, you need to remain involved with that child's education. This means you have to be proactive in dealing with the child's school.

- With some foresight and a bit of work, you can prepare your child for college as well or better than students being educated in public or private high schools.

PART V

Homeschool Resources

A

HOMESCHOOL ASSOCIATIONS AND CONVENTIONS BY STATE

As you have learned throughout this book, participating in homeschool associations and conventions is extremely useful when building your homeschool network, making important connections, researching teaching materials and curricula, and much more.

Table A.1 presents information about homeschool associations and conventions for each state in the United States. Contact information and a Web address is provided for many of these organizations so that you can check them out for yourself.

Table A.1 Homeschool Associations and Conventions by State

State	Association Name	Address
Phone Number	**Association Web Site**	**Convention Information (Web site or Email address)**
Alabama	Christian Home Educators Fellowship of Alabama, Inc. (CHEF of Alabama)	P.O. Box 20208 Montgomery, AL 36120
(334) 288-7229	http://www.chefofalabama.org/	http://www.chefofalabama.org/state_conv.htm
Alaska	Alaska Private and Home Educators Association (APHEA) http://www.aphea.org/	P.O. Box 141764 Anchorage, AK 99514 convention@aphea.org
Arizona	Arizona Families for Home Education (AFHE)	P.O. Box 2035 Chandler, AZ 85244-2035
(602) 235-2673	http://www.afhe.org/	http://www.afhe.org/index.cfm?fuseaction=view_template&id=2
Arkansas	Family Council	414 S. Pulaski, Suite 2 Little Rock, AR 72201-2930
(501) 375-7000	http://www.familycouncil.org/eahms.htm	http://www.familycouncil.org/eahms01conv.html
California	Christian Home Educators Association of California (CHEA)	P.O. Box 2009 Norwalk, California 90651-2009
(800) 564-CHEA	http://www.cheaofca.org/	http://www.cheaofca.org/AC/index.htm
Colorado	Christian Home Educators of Colorado (CHEC)	10431 S. Parker Rd. Parker, CO 80134
(720) 842-4852	http://www.chec.org/	http://www.chec.org/Events/StateConference/
	Concerned Parents of Colorado (CPC)	P.O. Box 547 Colorado Springs, CO 80901-0547
(719) 748-8360	http://www.cpco.info/	
Connecticut	The Education Association of Christian Home-schoolers (TEACH of CT)	10 Moosehorn Rd. West Granby, CT 06090
(860) 793-9968	http://www.teachct.org/	http://www.teachct.org/convention2004.htm

State	Association Name	Address
Phone Number	Association Web Site	Convention Information (Web site or Email address)
District of Columbia	Bolling Area Home Educators (BAHE)	P.O. Box 8401 Bolling AFB, Washington, DC 20032
(202) 562-1141	http://www.bahedc.org/	
	Christian Home Educators of DC, Inc. (CHEDC)	PO Box 29577 Washington, DC 20017
(202) 526-4108		
Delaware	Delaware Home Education Association (DHEA)	P.O. Box 268 Hartly, DE 19953
	http://www.dheaonline.org/	
Florida	Christian Home Educators of Florida (CHEF)	P.O. Box 5393 Clearwater, FL 33758-5393
	http://www.christianhomeeducatorsofflorida.com/	http://www.christianhomeeducatorsofflorida.com/events.htm
	Florida Parent-Educators Association Inc. (FPEA)	9951 Atlantic Blvd. Ste. 102 Jacksonville, FL 32225
(904) 338-9857	http://www.fpea.com/	http://www.fpea.com/Convention/main.htm
	Florida Coalition of Christian Private Schools Association (FCCPSA)	P.O. Box 13227 Fort Pierce, FL 34979-3227
(772) 344-2929	http://www.flhomeschooling.com/	
Georgia	Georgia Home Education Association (GHEA)	141 Massengale Rd. Brooks, GA 30205
(770) 461-3657	http://www.ghea.org/	http://www.ghea.org/pages/events/convention.php
	North Georgia Home Education Association	P.O. Box 5545 Fort Oglethorpe, GA 30742
(706) 861-1795		
	Georgians for Freedom in Education	209 Cobb St. Palmetto, GA 30268
(770) 463-1563		
Hawaii	Christian Homeschoolers of Hawaii (CHOH)	91824 Oama St. Ewa Beach, HA 96706
(808) 689-6398	http://www.christianhomeschoolersofhawaii.org/	

Table A.1 (continued)

State	Association Name	Address
Phone Number	Association Web Site	Convention Information (Web site or Email address)
Iowa	Network of Iowa Christian Home Educators (NICHE)	P.O. Box 158 Dexter, IA 50070
(515) 830-1614	http://www.the-niche.org/	http://www.the-niche.org/Pages/2004conference.html
Idaho	Christian Homeschoolers of Idaho State (CHOIS)	P.O. Box 45062 Boise, ID 83711-5062
(208) 424-6685	http://www.chois.org/	http://www.chois.org/convention2005.html
	Idaho Coalition of Home Educators	5415 Kendall St. Boise, ID 83706
	http://www.iche-idaho.org/	
Illinois	Christian Home Educators Coalition of Illinois (CHEC of Illinois)	P.O. Box 47322 Chicago, IL 60647-0322
(773) 278-0673	http://www.chec.cc/	
	Illinois Christian Home Educators (ICHE)	P.O. Box 775 Harvard, IL 60033
(815) 943-7882	http://www.iche.org/	http://www.iche.org/events/index.htm
Indiana	Indiana Association of Home Educators (IAHE)	8106 Madison Ave. Indianapolis, IN 46227
(317) 859-1202	http://www.inhomeeducators.org/	http://www.inhomeeducators.org/events/
Kansas	Christian Home Educators Confederation of Kansas (CHECK)	P.O. Box 1332 Topeka, KS 66601-1332
(785) 272-6655	http://www.kansashomeschool.org/	http://www.kansashomeschool.org/2004/2004_Conferences.htm
	Teaching Parents Association (TPA)	P.O. Box 3968 Wichita, KS 67201
(316) 945-0810	http://www.wichitahomeschool.org/	
Kentucky	Christian Home Educators of Kentucky (CHEK)	691 Howardstown Rd. Hodgenville, KY 42748
(270) 358-9270	http://www.chek.org/	http://www.chek.org/conf04/index.html

State	Association Name	Address
Phone Number	Association Web Site	Convention Information (Web site or Email address)
	Kentucky Home Education Association (KHEA)	P.O. Box 51591 Bowling Green, KY 42102-5891
(270) 779-6574	http://www.khea.info/	
Louisiana	Christian Home Educators Fellowship of Louisiana (CHEF of Louisiana)	P.O. Box 74292 Baton Rouge, LA 70874-4292
	http://www.chefofla.org/	
Massachusetts	Massachusetts Homeschool Organization of Parent Educators (MassHOPE)	46 South Road Holden, MA 01520
(508) 755-4467	http://www.masshope.org/	http://www.masshope.org/ fr_convention.html
Maryland	Christian Home Educators Network (CHEN)	1153 Circle Dr. Baltimore, MD 21227
(410) 247-4731	http://www.chenmd.org/	
	Tri-State Home School Network	35 Mary Anita Ct. Elkton, MD 21921
	Maryland Association of Christian Home Educators (MACHE)	P.O. Box 417 Clarksburg, MD 20871-0417
(301) 607-4284	http://www.machemd.org/	
Maine	Homeschoolers of Maine (HOME)	P.O. Box 159 Camden, ME 04843
(207) 763-2880	http://www. homeschoolersofmaine.org/	http://www. homeschoolersofmaine.org/ convention.htm
Michigan	Information Network for Christian Homes (INCH)	4934 Cannonsburg Rd. Belmont, MI 49306
(616) 874-5656	http://www.inch.org/	http://www.inch.org/ index_page0022.htm
Minnesota	Minnesota Association of Christian Home Educators (MACHE)	P.O. Box 32308 Fridley, MN 55432-0308
(763) 717-9070	http://www.mache.org/	http://www.mache.org/ AnnualConf.htm

Table A.1 (continued)

State	Association Name	Address
Phone Number	Association Web Site	Convention Information (Web site or Email address)
Missouri	Missouri Association of Teaching Christian Homes (MATCH)	2203 Rhonda Dr. West Plains, MO 65775-1615
(815) 550-8641	http://www.match-inc.org/	
	Families for Home Education	P.O. Box 261 Grandview, MO 64030-0261
(816) 767-9825	http://www.fhe-mo.org/	
Mississippi	Mississippi Home Educators Association (MHEA)	3646 Henryville Rd. Cedar Bluff, MS 39741
(662) 494-1999	http://www.mhea.net/	
Montana	Montana Coalition of Home Educators	P.O. Box 43 Gallatin Gateway, MT 59730
(406) 587-6163	http://www.mtche.org/	http://www. 2004montanahomeschoolconvention. com/
North Carolina	North Carolinians for Home Education (NCHE)	4326 Bland Rd. Raleigh, NC 27609-6125
(919) 790-1100	http://www.nche.com/	http://nche.com/conference.html
North Dakota	North Dakota Home School Association (NDHSA)	P.O. Box 7400 Bismarck, ND 58507-7400
(701) 223-4080		
Nebraska	Nebraska Christian Home Educators Association (NCHEA)	P.O. Box 57041 Lincoln, NE 68505-7041
(402) 423-4297	http://www.nchea.org/	http://www.nchea.org/ convention.htm
New Hampshire	Christian Home Educators of New Hampshire (CHENH)	P.O. Box 961 Manchester, NH 03105
(603) 878-5001	http://www.mv.com/ipusers/chenh/	
New Jersey	Education Network of Christian Homeschoolers of New Jersey (ENOCH)	P.O. Box 308 Atlantic Highlands, NJ 07716
(732) 291-7800	http://www.enochnj.org/	http://www.enochnj.org/

State	Association Name	Address
Phone Number	Association Web Site	Convention Information (Web site or Email address)
New Mexico	Christian Association of Parent Educators—New Mexico (CAPE—New Mexico)	P.O. Box 25046 Albuquerque, NM 87125
(505) 898-8548	http://www.cape-nm.org/	
Nevada	The Nevada Homeschool Network	2250 E. Tropicana Ste. 19, Box 378 Las Vegas, NV 89119
(888) 842-2602	http://www. nevadahomeschoolnetwork.com/	
	Silver State Education Association	6590 S. McCarran Blvd. B Reno, NV 89509-6122
(775) 851-0772		
	Catholic Home Schoolers of Nevada	1778 Antelope Valley Ave. Henderson, NV 89012-3408
(513) 661-4758		
	Northern Nevada Home Schools	P.O. Box 21323 Reno, NV 89515
(702) 852-6647	http://www.nnhs.org/	
New York	Loving Education at Home (New York State LEAH)	P.O. Box 438 Fayetteville, NY 13066-0438
(315) 637-4525	http://www.leah.org/	http://www.leah.org/ convention/2004/
Ohio	Christian Home Educators of Ohio (CHEO)	117 W. Main St., Ste. 103 Lancaster, OH 43130
(740) 654-3331		
Oklahoma	Christian Home Educators Fellowship of Oklahoma (CHEF of Oklahoma)	P.O. Box 471363 Tulsa, OK 74147-1363
(918) 583-7323	http://www.chefok.org/	http://www.chefok.org/ conference/index.html
	Oklahoma Christian Home Educators Consociation (OCHEC)	3801 NW 63rd St., Bldg. 3, Ste. 236 Oklahoma City, OK 73116
(405) 810-0386	http://www.ochec.com/	http://www.ochec.com/ convention.htm
Oregon	Oregon Christian Home Education Assoc Network (OCEANetwork)	17985 Falls City Rd. Dallas, OR 97338
(503) 288-1285	http://www.oceanetwork.org/	http://www.oceanetwork.org/ calendar/conference/

Table A.1 (continued)

State	Association Name	Address
Phone Number	Association Web Site	Convention Information (Web site or Email address)
Pennsylvania	Catholic Homeschoolers of Pennsylvania	101 S. College St. Myerstown, PA 17067-1212
(717) 866-5425	http://www. catholichomeschoolpa.org/	http://www. catholichomeschoolpa.org/ccf.html
	Christian Home School Association of Pennsylvania (CHAP)	P.O. Box 115 Mount Joy, PA 17552-0115
(717) 665-6707	http://www.chaponline.com/	http://www.chaponline.com/ convention/
Rhode Island	Rhode Island Guild of Home Teachers (RIGHT)	54 Spring St. Pawtucket, RI 02860
(401) 351-5991	http://www.rihomeschool.com/	
South Carolina	South Carolina Association of Independent Home Schoolers (SCAIHS)	930 Knox Abbott Dr. Cayce, SC 29033-3320
(803) 454-0427	http://www.scaihs.org/	
	South Carolina Home Educators Association (SCHEA)	P.O. Box 3231 Columbia, SC 29230-3231
(803) 772-2330	http://www. schomeeducatorsassociation.org/	http://www. schomeeducatorsassociation.org/ convention.htm
South Dakota	South Dakota Christian Home Educators (SDCHE)	P.O. Box 9571 Rapid City, SD 57709-9571
(605) 348-2001	http://www.sdche.org/	http://www.sdche.org/ convention2004.html
Tennessee	Tennessee Home Education Association (THEA)	P.O. Box 681652 Franklin, TN 37068
(615) 834-3529	http://www.tnhea.org/	
Texas	Christian Home Education Association of Central Texas (CHEACT)	P.O. Box 141998 Austin, TX 78714-1998
(512) 450-0070	http://www.cheact.org/	http://www.cheact.org/ newsevents/conferences/summer04/
	Family Educators Alliance of South Texas (FEAST)	25 Burwood San Antonio, TX 78216
(210) 342-4674	http://www.homeschoolfeast.com/	

State	Association Name	Address
Phone Number	Association Web Site	Convention Information (Web site or Email address)
	Home School Texas	P.O. Box 29307 Dallas, TX 75229
(214) 358-5723	http://www.homeschooltexas.com/	
	North Texas Home Educators Network (NTHEN)	801 E. Main St., Ste. G Allen, TX 75002
(214) 495-9600	http://www.nthen.org/	
	SouthEast Texas Home School Association (SETHSA)	PMB 297 4950 FM 1960 W A7 Houston, TX 77069
(281) 370-8787	http://www.sethsa.org/	http://www.sethsa.org/ summerconference/ 2004summerconference.html
	Supporting Home Educators of Lower Texas Educational Region	2424 Holden Rd. Aransas Pass, TX 78336
(512) 758-2777		
Utah	Utah Christian Homeschool Association (UTCH)	P.O. Box 3942 Salt Lake, UT 84110-3942
(801) 296-7198	http://www.utch.org/	http://www.utch.org/ convention04.htm
Virginia	Home Educators Association of Virginia (HEAV)	P.O. Box 6745 Richmond, VA 23230-0745
(804) 288-1608	http://www.heav.org/index1.html	http://www.heav.org/index1.html
Vermont	Christian Home Educators of Vermont (CHEV)	P.O. Box 206 Newfane, VT 05345
(802) 365-4052	http://www.homeschoolvt.org/	
Washington	Washington Association of Teaching Christian Homes	1026 224th Ave N.E. Sammamish, WA 98074
(206) 729-4804	http://www.watchhome.org/	http://www.watchhome.org/ conference/index.htm
	Washington Homeschool Organization (WHO)	6632 S. 191st Pl., Ste. E100 Kent, WA 98032-2117
(425) 251-0439	http://www.washhomeschool.org/	
Wisconsin	Wisconsin Christian Home Educators Association (Wisconsin CHEA)	2307 Carmel Ave. Racine, WI 53405
(262) 637-5127	http://www.wisconsinchea.com/	http://www.wisconsinchea.com/ Conference/conference.html

Table A.1 (continued)

State	Association Name	Address
Phone Number	Association Web Site	Convention Information (Web site or Email address)
West Virginia	Christian Home Educators of West Virginia (CHEWV)	P.O. Box 8770 Charleston, WV 25303-0770
(304) 776-4664	http://www.chewv.org/	
Wyoming	Homeschoolers of Wyoming (HOW)	4859 Palmer Canyon Rd. Wheatland, WY 82201-9020
(307) 322-3539	http://www.homeschoolersofwy.org/	http://www.homeschoolersofwy.org/cal.asp
Guam	Home Schoolers of Guam	P.O. Box 6361 Tamuning, GU 96931
(671) 565-3406	http://www.tumon.com/ghsa/	

Table A.2 provides information about national homeschool associations that you might find useful.

Table A.2 National Homeschool Organizations

Name	Description (from Organization's Web Site)	Web Site
The Academy of Home Education	We offer an academic program that includes educational advising and counseling. We also keep accurate records of your teen's course work so we can award him an official diploma and transcript, making it simpler for you and your teen to fill out college application forms.	http://www.bjup.com/services/ahe/
Advanced Training Institute (ATI)	The Advanced Training Institute International is an educational program developed by the Institute in Basic Life Principles and dedicated to providing support, Biblically based curriculum, and ministry opportunities for home educating families.	http://www.ati.iblp.org/atii/

Name	Description (from Organization's Web Site)	Web Site
Alpha Omega Publications	Alpha Omega Publications has created valuable experience by developing superior educational material that is built on a solid foundation. We understand that each child is one of a kind, and requires curriculum flexibility and choices that can be adapted to each child's distinct needs.	http://new.aop.com/
BJ HomeSat	Imagine having instant access to home education workshops, Christian living seminars, and cultural programs for your family's enrichment. BJ HomeSat makes all of these possible through their advanced satellite network that brings their resources into your home.	https://www.bjup.com/services/bjhomesat/
Christian Liberty Academy School System (CLASS)	The Christian Liberty Academy School System (CLASS) is an independent and non-denominational K–12 homeschool program. CLASS has helped thousands of families to get started—and persevere—in home schooling.	http://www.homeschools.org/
Crosswalk.com support group	Crosswalk.com is a for-profit religious corporation dedicated to building up the Church.	http://www.homeschool.crosswalk.com/
Home Grown Families	Home Grown Families is a ministry established in 1994 to provide resources to encourage families to grow in their parenting skills, marriage relationships, and in home-schooling their children.	http://www.homegrownfamilies.com/

Table A.2 (continued)

Name	Description (from Organization's Web Site)	Web Site
Laurelwood Publications	In an effort to meet the needs of home educators around the world, Laurelwood Publications brings 15 years of personal service to the Internet. As its site expands, you will find listings for new and used textbooks covering all subjects and ages, specialized materials for developing critical thinking skills, books for pleasure and adventure reading, and much more.	http://www.laurelwoodbooks.com/
Lighthouse Christian Academy	Since 1970, Accelerated Christian Education has published individualized curriculum and provided training in its implementation for grades K-12. Students are tested diagnostically upon entering schools or home schools using the program. Students are then placed in the curriculum in each subject at their own performance levels determined by the results of the diagnostic tests.	http://www.aceministries.com/
National Black Home Educators Resource Association (NBHERA)	NBHERA offers services and information on getting started in home education; assisting veteran home educators in the importance of home school; networking with national/local organizations and pairing new home school families with veteran families; providing a quarterly publication with current updates and information on state and national news and events; and teaching materials and curriculum advisement.	http://www.nbhera.org/

Name	Description (from Organization's Web Site)	Web Site
National Challenged Homeschoolers Association Network (NATHHAN)	Matches special needs babies with loving Christian families. No agency fees. CHASK provides resources, information, and encouragement, so parents can raise their disabled child with joy and competence.	http://www.nathhan.com/
National Home Education Research Institute (NHERI)	NHERI conducts and collects research about homeschooling, and publishes the research journal *The Home School Researcher*. The institute has hundreds of research works documented and catalogued on home schooling, many of which were created by NHERI.	http://www.nheri.org/
Our Lady of Victory School	Since 1977, Our Lady of Victory School has been providing curricula and textbooks to parents who school their children at home.	http://www.olvs.org/
Parents Educating At Home (PEAH)	Provides homeschooling families professional homeschool identification as well as the most extensive list of homeschool and home educator discounts on the Web.	http://www.peah.com/
Seton Home Study School		1350 Progress Dr. Front Royal, VA 22630 (540) 636-9990
Sonlight Curriculum	Empowers parents to raise life-long learners, who are fully equipped to follow Christ (Mt. 6:33; Rev. 5:7) and to reach families worldwide with remarkable, internationally focused, literature-based homeschool curriculum.	http://www.sonlight.com/

Table A.2 (continued)

Name	Description (from Organization's Web Site)	Web Site
The Sycamore Tree Inc.	The Sycamore Tree, Inc. provides homeschool educational services to students in grades K-12 all over the world. Supporting the school or anyone needing Christian-based educational materials is a catalog purchasing service that provides a wide range of more than 3000 educational items. You need not be enrolled in the school to order from the catalog.	http://www.sycamoretree.com/
Traditions of Roman Catholic Homes (TORCH)		3307 Bigelow Ct. Burtonsville, MD 20866 (301) 421-9789

HOMESCHOOL CURRICULUM AND TEACHING MATERIAL PUBLISHERS AND RETAILERS

In this appendix, you will find information about various sources of teaching materials—curricula, textbooks, and so on—that are needed to homeschool effectively. This appendix is by no means comprehensive, as there are literally thousands of publishers and retailers that provide products that are useful to homeschool families. However, this list can be a good starting point for you as you begin to develop your own sources of homeschool materials.

Sources of Materials for Your Homeschool

For each source in this appendix, you will find the following information:

- Name
- Address
- Phone Number
- Email Address
- Web Site Address
- Description
- Web Site Screenshot

The Elijah Company

The Elijah Company
1053 Eldridge Loop
Crossville, TN 38571
(888) 235-4524

elijahco@elijahco.com
www.elijahco.com

This company's Web site is designed for new homeschoolers, and it provides resources such as resource guides, teleseminars, and great beginner information on different methods of homeschooling. This site also offers many different types of curricula resources (see Figure B.1).

FIGURE B.1

The Elijah Store is a good place for new home-schoolers.

Apologia Educational Ministries

Apologia Educational Ministries
1106 Meridian Plaza, Suite 220
Anderson, IN 46016
(888) 524-4724

You can use an online form for email.
www.apologia.com

This is a great resource for science materials for all grade levels. It features many textbooks by Dr. Jay Wile; these are excellent materials for many science topics including general science, biology, physics, and so on (see Figure B.2).

FIGURE B.2

You can get excellent science textbooks written by Dr. Jay Wile at Apologia Educational Ministries.

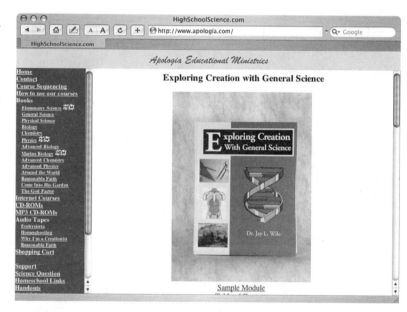

Christian Book Distributors

Christian Book Distributors
P.O. Box 7000
Peabody, MA 01961-7000
(800) 247-4784

You can use an online form for email.
www.christianbook.com

This resource offers many individual and series materials, books, games, and other homeschool materials (see Figure B.3). You can browse materials online or order hard copy catalogs.

FIGURE B.3

Christian Book Distributors provides many types of homeschool materials including books, music, and DVDs.

Alpha Omega Publications

Alpha Omega Publications

300 N. McKemy Ave.

Chandler, AZ 85226

(866) 444-4498

You can use an online form for email.

www.aop.com

Various tools you might find useful in your homeschool, such as curricula, online courses, and so on (see Figure B.4).

Dover Publications

Dover Publications

31 East 2nd Street

Mineola, NY 11501-3852

(516) 742-6953 (Fax)

You can use an online form for email.

store.doverpublications.com

Dover offers thousands of books that you can use in your homeschool (see Figure B.5). This includes many classics that have been reprinted in a very inexpensive format; many of these books can be purchased for as little as $1.

FIGURE B.4

You can access curricula materials and online courses at Alpha Omega Publications.

FIGURE B.5

Dover Publications is a great source of books, including the classics.

God's World Book Club

God's World Book Club
P.O. Box 20003
Asheville, NC 28802-8203
(888) 492-2307

service@gwbc.com
www.gwbc.com

This is a good source of general reading and homeschool books from a Christian
perspective for your family (see Figure B.6).

FIGURE B.6

You can find
books for gen-
eral reading
and for home-
school at God's
World Book
Club.

Amazon.com

Amazon.com
(No mailing address provided)
(No phone number provided)
You can use an online form for email.

www.amazon.com

Although not focused on homeschooling, Amazon.com is a great source for just
about any book ever published, whether it is still in print or not (see Figure B.7). You
can also find videos, music, and almost any other product made here.

FIGURE B.7

Amazon.com's claim to be the biggest bookstore on Earth is just marketing hype.

Barnes & Noble.com

Barnes & Noble.com
(No mailing address provided)
(No phone number provided)
You can use an online form for email.
www.barnesandnoble.com

This Web site is associated with the "brick and mortar" chain of bookstores (see Figure B.8). In addition to books, you can get videos, DVDs, and music that you might find useful in your homeschool.

Heart of Wisdom Publishing

Heart of Wisdom Publishing
13503 Minion St.
Woodbridge, VA 22192
(No phone number provided)

support@heartofwisdom.com
heartofwisdom.com

Heart of Wisdom Publishing offers a variety of materials primarily in history and science topics (see Figure B.9).

FIGURE B.8
Barnes & Noble.com offers more products than most of the physical Barnes & Noble stores.

FIGURE B.9
Heart of Wisdom Publishing offers materials you can purchase, along with other information that you might find useful.

Homeschool Supercenter

Homeschool Supercenter
1182 Market Circle
Port Charlotte, FL 33953
(800) 230-0020

info@homeschoolsupercenter.com
www.homeschoolsupercenter.com

This site provides many different types of curricula and materials that you can use in your homeschool (see Figure B.10).

FIGURE B.10

The Homeschool Supercenter provides materials for a wide variety of topics.

Oak Meadow

Oak Meadow
P.O. Box 1346
Brattleboro, VT 05302
(802) 251-7250

info@oakmeadow.com
www.oakmeadow.com

Oak Meadow is a source of online and printed curricula materials (see Figure B.11).

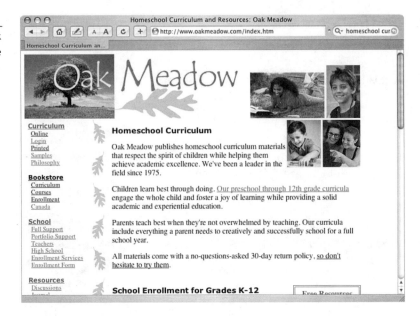

Index

home projects, 227-228
importance of, 176
legal requirements, 45-46
outside class results, 243
portfolios, creating, 185-186
project documentation, 180
test documentation, 179-180
tutor results, 243
weekly record keeping, 179

Dover Publications, 290

drug abuse (public/private school problems), 16

DSL Internet connections, 123

DVDs, obtaining, 101

E

education
effectiveness (homeschool defense), 53-54
legislation, monitoring, 46-47
tailoring (homeschooling benefits), 12

education levels
assessing, 77-78
subjects, choosing, 94-96
teaching options, 165

efficiency (homeschooling benefits), 13

Elijah Company (The), 288

ENOCH (Education Network of Christian Homeschoolers) Web site, 278

establishing homeschooling networks
homeschool associations, 70
finding, 71
joining, 72
homeschool conventions/conferences/seminars, 73
homeschool groups
formal homeschool groups, 66-70
informal homeschool groups, 65, 68
selecting, 67
mentors, finding, 63-64
reasons for, 62-63

evaluating
field trip invitations, 192-194
student progress, 245
changing evaluations, 262
curriculum-based testing, 246-248
grades, 260-261
homework, 249
local legal requirements, 43-45
special projects, 250
standardized tests, 246, 250-260
student promotions, 261
written reports, 246, 250
tutors, 236-237

excellence of education (homeschooling benefits), 11

exercise programs, 212-213

experiential elements (curricula), 97-98

extracurricular activities (homeschool defense), 54-55

extroverted personalities
learning styles, 168-170
versus introverted, 80-81

F

Family Council Web site, 274

family homeschooling requirements, 25-26

family relationships (homeschooling benefits), 13

family vacations as field trips, 202-203

father's homeschooling requirements, 25-26

FCCPSA (Florida Coalition of Christian Private Schools Association) Web site, 275

FEAST (Family Educators Alliance of South Texas) Web site, 280

"feel-goodism" (public/private school problems), 16

feeling personalities versus thinking, 81-82

field trips, 98
assistance, offering, 193
behavioral problems, 194
benefits of, 13-14
business experience, 195-196
conducting, tips for, 200
coordinating, 198-199

G - H

Q - R

X - Y - Z